July 1994

Sean,

bulletproof diva

a young brother
on the rise!

Charge the world
with your fierce
intelligence!!

Lisa Sue

also by lisa jones

Uplift the Race: The Construction of School Days
(with Spike Lee)
Do the Right Thing (with Spike Lee)
Mo' Better Blues (with Spike Lee)

bulletproof diva

tales of race, sex, and hair

Lisa Jones

doubleday new york london toronto sydney auckland

PUBLISHED BY DOUBLEDAY
a division of Bantam Doubleday Dell Publishing Group, Inc.
1540 Broadway, New York, New York 10036

DOUBLEDAY and the portrayal of an anchor with a dolphin
are trademarks of Doubleday, a division of
Bantam Doubleday Dell Publishing Group, Inc.

The majority of the pieces herein originally appeared in *The Village Voice.* "Is Biracial Enough?" "She Came with the Rodeo," and "Looking for Mariah" appear here for the first time.

We gratefully acknowledge permission from the following:

From the book *Three Pieces* by Ntozake Shange. Copyright © 1981 by Ntozake Shange. Reprinted with permission from St. Martin's Press, Inc., New York, NY.

From the poem "Zoom," which appeared in *All the Renegade Ghosts Rise* by Thulani Davis. Reprinted by permission of the author.

From *The Venus Hottentot* by Elizabeth Alexander, the University Press of Virginia, 1990.

Book design by Gretchen Achilles

Library of Congress Cataloging-in-Publication Data

Jones, Lisa.
  Bulletproof diva : tales of race, sex, and hair / Lisa Jones. — 1st ed.
    p.   cm.
    1. Afro-Americans—Drama.   2. Afro-American women.   I. Title.
PS3560.05144B85   1994
814'.54—dc20   93-40749
                                                        CIP

ISBN 0-385-47122-X

Copyright © 1994 by Lisa Jones

All Rights Reserved

Printed in the United States of America

April 1994

10 9 8 7 6 5 4 3 2

for the ladies

Hettie Jones,
Kellie Jones, Cora Coleman, and the gentlewomen Rice,

and in spirit,
Kimako Baraka
and
Anna Lois Russ Jones

contents

five
the hair trade

acknowledgments

Most of the bits and pieces collected here come from a column I began in 1990 at the *Village Voice*. "Skin Trade" (which won out over "Hot Comb," "Booty & Soul," "Reckless Eyeballing," and "Mules & Men") was given a loose mandate: a column on the politics of style. I thank Donald Suggs for suggesting such a beat in the first place, and many others at the *Voice* for their support: editor-in-chief Jonathan Larsen, managing editor Sarah Jewler, and editors Mary Jo Neuberger, Joe Levy, Vince Aletti, and Amy Virshup, though most particularly Thulani Davis and Doug Simmons. My gratitude to columnist-in-crime Leslie Savan for nearly a decade of lipstick tips, and to my research assistant, Mia Mask, and Omoronke Idowu, my intern. Arts editor Lisa Kennedy, prime editrix of "Skin Trade," gets all the thanks in the world. To my colleague Greg Tate, the same.

Shouts to the ancestors (literary and otherwise) and Malaika Adero, the Baraka family, the late Sylvia Ardyn Boone, C & C Computer Tyme, Cesar Cacho Jr., William Calhoun, Gordon Chambers, Nicholas Charles, Faith Childs, Barron Claibourne, Uncle Darryl, Michaela Angela Davis, Peyton Beaumont Farley, Uncle Flat Top, the Glamorous Grandmas of Newark, Cheryll Greene, Kevin Griffith, bell hooks, Sherrilyn Ifil, Jon Jon, Mr. Coyt L. Jones and the Archie family, Stephanie and Suzanne Jones, Katrinia Karkazis, Peter Lau, the late Wyn Loving, the Loving-Cortes family, Slick Mahoney, Manhattan Theatre Club, the late Eduardo Mejia, the New York Joneses, Percidia Alice Norris, One Way Productions, Susan Osorio, the Playwrights' Center, Perez and Associates, Evette Porter, Renée Raymond, Rodeo Caldonia, Alva Rogers, Uncle G. L. Russ, Coreen Simpson, Linda Villarosa, and William Byrd Wilkins.

Big thanks to the Doubleday tribe and to my editor David

Gernert and his assistant Amy Williams. Also to the folks at Lowenstein Associates and to my agent, Ms. Barbara Lowenstein herself.

In her usual way, my lawyer and best friend María Peréz saw this book coming long before I did. Please note, all the hair issues discussed within are hers. I myself have none.

bulletproof
diva

introduction

This is a book of tales.

It may be the ravings of a madwoman who loved having her hands in other people's hair, and who should have gone to beauty culture school and owned a wig shop like her great-aunt, or moonlighted as a barber like her grandfather, but by happenstance became a writer.

Or it's a catalog of American obsessions in the nineties—race, sex, and hair, and the marketing and consumption of race, sex, and hair—that includes close encounters with brown plastic Barbie dolls, corporate boys, polygamists, hair traders, biracial entertainers, skeezers, supermamas, and cowgirls.

Or, more likely, it's a continuous reenactment of my defining moment as experienced in a movie theater in London, England, during a Saturday matinee of *Imitation of Life*, the 1934 version. The year is 1983 and I have just turned twenty-two. I sit in the back of the dark theater thrilled because I am about to see, for the first time, a big-screen version of myself and her name will be Peola. But as the film progresses, I notice that this Peola isn't me at all, she's a remake of Frankenmulatta, that character from *The Octoroon Concubine of Frankenstein*, one of Mary Shelley's lost sequels.

These are funeral rites for the Tragic Mulatto.

Warning: This may also include shameless acts of soapbox politicking toward the cause of politicizing multiracial identity in the nineties. Say that again two more times fast.

This is a passing novel. Guess who's passing? You.

Certainly this is a search for heroines.

Here's a quiz: Why did African-American girls who came of age in the seventies convince themselves they had to be the perfect composite of Angela Davis and Diahann Carroll as Julia? You will be graded.

Perhaps I should tell you this is a sorrow song for my aunt Kimako who was knifed to death by a stranger in her Manhattan high rise because her doorman assumed that any man who was black like her and requested entry was automatically a friend.

This is a cover of *Upscale* magazine showing Janet Jackson, her skin lightened to the tone of Marilyn Monroe's.

Herein is an extended nappy-hair conspiracy theory as proven by remarks made in *U.S. News & World Report* concerning Lani Guinier, the law professor whose nomination as assistant attorney general for civil rights was withdrawn by President Clinton in 1993: "Strange name, *strange hair,* strange writing—she's history" (emphasis mine).

A fact, as documented by the television series "Eyes on the Prize, II," the fifth episode, *Ain't Gonna Shuffle No More (1964–1972):* The black consciousness movement at Howard University began in October 1966 when Robin Gregory became the first homecoming queen to sport an Afro. The writer Paula Giddings, interviewed in the documentary, offers this account of the homecoming coronation: "The curtains opened . . . the lights began to come up at the same time. Well, before you saw Robin, you saw . . . the silhouette of her Afro. . . . The audience exploded. . . . It was a wonderful moment. People started jumping up and screaming. Some were raising their fists. Then spontaneously a chant began . . . 'Ngawa Black Power! Ngawa Black Power!' . . . a chain was created and people started to march to the rhythm of 'Ngawa Black Power!' . . . [they marched] all the way around the auditorium and out the door and into the streets of Washington, D.C., past the campus, still chanting 'Ngawa Black Power!' and that was really the launching of the movement." The following school year students occupied an administration building to demand that Howard adapt a curriculum that incorporated, as it had not done before, black culture and history.

Believe it or not the following headline appeared in the *New York Times* on March 3, 1993: FOR A BLACK WOMAN, SPACE ISN'T THE FINAL FRONTIER.

Consider this a narrative in which we invent our own heroine, the Bulletproof Diva. A woman whose sense of dignity and self cannot be denied; who, though she may live in a war zone like Brownsville, goes out everyday greased, pressed, and dressed, with hair faded and braided and freeze-dried and spit-curled and wrapped and locked and cut to a sexy baldie (so she is all eyes and lips) and piled ten inches high and colored siren red, cobalt blue, and flaming yellow. She is fine and she knows it. She *has* to know it because who else will? Perhaps she is Marian Anderson singing her Easter concert on the steps of the Lincoln Memorial after the Daughters of the American Revolution prevented her appearance at Constitution Hall, because opera singer or no opera singer, no colored woman was gonna open her lungs and blow in their hall, not in 1939, no, no, no. Anderson, of course, became in 1955 the first Negro to sing at the Metropolitan Opera House in New York City, where she appeared in Verdi's *The Masked Ball* and blew. But you *know* that.

A Bulletproof Diva is not, I repeat, *not* that tired stereotype, the emasculating black bitch too hard for love or piety. It's safe to assume that a Bulletproof Diva is whoever you make her—corporate girl, teen mom, or the combination—as long as she has the lip and nerve, and as long as she uses that lip and nerve to raise up herself and the world.

This is also a search for home.

So I lied. It's an appreciation of several homes.

Accept this as a manual: How to survive a Jewish mother who thinks she knows how to cook collard greens better than you do and happens to be right.

This is what happens when you grow up listening to your father recite poems like "Beautiful Black Women . . ." and preach Sunday sermons at "Soul Session," where folks talk about revolution in between playing James Brown, the Temptations, and Billy Preston, and get to standing up, swaying, and clapping just like church. You develop, to borrow a phrase from Patricia Williams, "feelings of exaggerated visibility," which, later on when you attend an Ivy League university, are countered by feelings of exaggerated invisibility.

Evidently this is the result of having an aunt whose repertoire includes "black folks love Chinese food more than orgasm"; "They need to free Mike Tyson and put that Desiree girl in jail for rape"; and "America's a great country, but whitey's doing his best to mess it up."

This may contain a series of photographs of my handsome grandfather. Dark Gable, they call him. And these are his bowling trophies, his cigars, and his Negro League stories.

At last, here find a collection of love letters to my grandmother, who while she lived loved a good Snoopy cartoon as much as she did the Race; an Americanist who had not a blind faith but an intellectual engagement with democracy, who believed black folks built this country; an internationalist, lover of all who presented themselves to be loved.

Hello my name is Lisa Victoria Chapman Jones. Victoria after the queen, Chapman after my great-great-grandmother Delphia Chapman who was once enslaved in America, though she lived on past Emancipation until she was 105 years old, whereupon she died. But only because her house caught fire.

Welcome to my America.

one

how i invented
multiculturalism

how i invented
multiculturalism

It was easier than you think. First I arrived, fatter than an A&P chicken, just another black child in New York City born to a Jewish woman and a Negro man. Before race became my passion and my battle cry, the only thing I wanted in life was to be joined at the hip with my older sister. At the wee age of three I followed her to the Church of All Nations school on the Lower East Side. For many years I thought the entire world was a band of Latin, black, and Chinese children dancing around the maypole and singing "Que Bonita Bandera" and the few Ukrainians who served us lunch.

Picked up my first curse word, *maricón,* from Jesús,

born in the Dominican Republic, which was an island, he showed me, just across the river from our playground on Avenue D. Twenty years later I moved there, but someone had changed the name to Brooklyn.

Endured my first Toni home permanent at age six to have an Afro like Angela Davis. This continued for four years, then thanks to chemical overload or natural progression, my hair napped up enough to make a 'fro on its own.

Ate potato kugel and boiled chicken with Aunt Fannie, the only Jewish relative who didn't disown my mother for marrying a black man. Eighty-year-old Aunt Fannie stayed in Flatbush through the Caribbean migration and was known to have made only one comment about her niece's interracial marriage: "How do you wash that hair?" she said, leaning over her grandnieces, still in grade school, and their enormous globes of nappiness.

Metamorphosed, in the late sixties at age seven, as a nationalist poet. Appeared in the poetry revue *In Praise of Black Women* on stage at the Negro Ensemble Company Theater wearing seventeen braids and reading, in the style of the Last Poets, "Fried Chicken and Collard Greens/Gramma." My grandmother had me recite this masterpiece for her friends the social workers and other silver-haired belles of black Newark whenever we came across the Hudson to visit.

Named my cat Huey Newton. Named my dog Ho Chi Minh.

Grew dreadlocks at Methodist summer camp in New Hampshire. The camp counselor couldn't comb my hair. Hung out on a nude beach in Nantucket another summer realizing how black people's bodies put the fear of God in some white folks. Most memorable summer: 1969. Spent two blissful months in a cabin on the Jersey shore with a household of very opinionated and well-dressed black women—my grandmother, several aunts, scores of cousins, and my sister—riding bikes six in a row and lip-synching to Aretha. The townies thought we were some lost tribe of Amazons.

Went to high school in Chinatown. The yearbook lists my two favorite books as *Wuthering Heights* and *Native Son.*

Endured chemical relaxers to slay my Afro and curling irons in homage to Farrah Fawcett.

Gave up my cherry in Babylon, Long Island, in a trailer home owned by the Italian drug dealer. My first boyfriend was his son, a black kid with an orange Afro who sold reefer on the weekends in Washington Square Park. The kid introduced me to Jimi Hendrix and sushi. I gave him Chaka Khan and Caporel's Spanish-style fried chicken.

Took hustle lessons in the mid-seventies from a Polish DJ who grew up around Puerto Ricans and had a black Panamanian girl-friend. Became a regular at the Paradise Garage. Thought the "disco sucks" movement was a racist ploy backed by the Ku Klux Klan to keep folks of different cultures from dancing together.

Traveled to Trinidad the summer of junior year in high school at the invitation of seventeen-year-old pen pal Jenny Paul. Jenny's best friend Wendell was Chinese, East Indian, and African. Didn't bring back much Trini twang, though did learn how to wine like a Trini at Saturday night jump-ups in Port of Spain.

Worked in Greece as a mother's helper. Stumbled on a shrine of one of Europe's many black Madonnas on a tiny island off the coast of Crete.

Found my soul sister/best friend on an Ivy League campus in the late seventies wearing a red bandanna, booty-tight jeans, and five-inch heels. Once she cursed out the entire rugby team for advertising a "slave auction" fundraiser. "Puerto Rican" wasn't inclusive enough for Miss Two and a Half; she called herself "black Latino" or "Third World Woman."

Read Wole Soyinka, William Carlos Williams, and Gloria Anzaldua. Led a boycott against the campus store for tracking black male customers like prison escapees.

Cofounded the We Waz Girls Together Off-Campus Collective. Threw "After the Revolution" parties with Ghanaians educated in Britain, white women in "Warhol does Mao" T-shirts, Nuyoricans in Izod polos, white guys from Chicago who spoke "black English," black women from Compton who became prison lawyers, and Cubans in deck shoes who wanted to be rich whites and, in fact, were.

Lived in a North London squat with African-American rock & roll expatriates and a Scottish skinhead motorcycle gang.

Returned to New York in time for the premiere of *Purple Rain*. Wondered if black women—especially browner-skinned black women—would be missing from Afro America's new media facelift as sculpted by fellows like Prince and Michael Jackson.

Refused to endure a "California curl" so my hair could bounce, as promised by a stylist, just like rainbow-baby actress Rae Dawn Chong's.

Dug Jessica Hagedorn's collection *Pet Food and Tropical Apparitions*, about a Filipino-American woman coming of age to black music and California kitsch. Discovered the multiculti in me and loved her fiercely. Knew that cultural pluralism was more than a performance piece for well-heeled art house patrons, but an everyday life led by thousands of Americans, black, yellow, brown, red, and yes, even white.

Reborn as a race woman after Howard Beach. Joined the Make Black Film movement. Made Black Movies.

Reread Zora Neale Hurston, Kafka, and Nella Larsen. Rediscovered my mentors, Thurgood Marshall, Fannie Lou Hamer, Che, and Ida B. Wells. Have plans to revamp Dr. King's Poor People's Campaign in crack capitals across the country. But first I have to write my version of *Bonfire of the Vanities*. Instead of scratching each other's eyes out, everyone does what everyone has wanted to do all along: has sex.

Eventually I'll make it to the Motherland when I raise the cash. It's been a wonderful life, really.

1991

hair always and forever

We ate lunch, the tape recorder was rolling, and now the legendary jazz singer would tell me her life story. This was her preface: "When I was a little girl, about thirteen or so, they told me that a woman's pride and glory was her hair. Then they told me mine wasn't any good. I guess I went to war to absolve myself of this grief."

Not, "Back when I used to gig at the Five Spot . . ." or "Coleman Hawkins sure could blow . . ." but, everything I've done with my hair explains everything I've done with my life and my art. This wasn't an epiphany for me as much as a confirmation of something I've believed for a while. Hair is the be-all and end-all. Everything I know about American history I learned from looking at black people's hair. It's the perfect metaphor for the African experiment here: the price of the ticket (for a journey no one elected to take), the toll of slavery, and the costs of remaining. It's all in the hair.

People, mostly men, tell me I'm too strung out on hair. That hair is not political, that it doesn't matter what we do to our hair, that there's more to life than hair. But this is just not true. Like Jamaica Kincaid, who writes only about a character named Mother, I've decided to write only about hair: what we do to it, how we do it, and why. I figure this is enough.

Which is how I happened upon Charlene's, a place where women can go twenty-four hours a day to get their hair done. Now twenty-four hours really means Monday through Thursday till midnight and twenty-four hours on the weekends, but it doesn't matter. The idea still titillates me to no end: a place where you can go just about any time of day or night if your hair "turns back," which means, in case you didn't know, returns to its natural state.

Last year Charlene's, lit up in green and red like a Christmas tree, became the newest neon landmark on Flatbush Avenue, the Broadway of Brooklyn. Lest you thought twenty-four-hour hair was peculiar to the fashion victims of downtown Brooklyn, it's not. With eleven shops, three in the New York area, Charlene's is one of the largest black-owned salon chains in the country. Charlene's Fifth Avenue, in midtown occupies a swanky office building across the street from Lord & Taylor. If you're hair obsessed like me, you'll get a thrill from the familiar perm aroma that drifts down to the lobby from the salon on the second floor. Former model and football player Troy McSwain, now general manager of the New York–area shops, looks straight off the pages of *Ebony Man:* a fade with a crown of "texurized" curls—yet another euphemism for chemicals. (Yes, I identify everyone I meet by hairstyle.) Troy gives me the grand tour: twenty-two hair stations, five waiting rooms with burgundy velveteen chairs, and a supply room where hair products are doled out to stylists, depending on the job, by the ounce. Inventory control, says Mama, keeps costs down.

Mama is owner Charlene Miles, the Charlene of Charlene's. It's a tight-knit family business. Troy and the other salon general managers, who are the same age as Miles's oldest son, the company president, call her Mama. He wants me to speak to Mama herself because she is, after all, the inventor of twenty-four-hour hair.

While Troy calls Detroit, I check out the photos: Ms. Miles with Oprah, Ms. Miles with Jesse, Ms. Miles with Nancy Wilson, Ms. Miles in a new mink coat. Ms. Miles's soft voice on the phone reminds me of my grandmother, who took me at age six to get "straightened and curled" for the first time at the hair salon atop Bamberger's in downtown Newark.

Before cosmetology school, Miles did all kinds of work—"from cotton chopping on up the line." As a young woman in the 1950s she spent most of the decade on the road styling trade shows for Posner's hair products. With six chairs and three thousand dollars, Miles opened the original Charlene's salon in Buffalo, New York. The year was 1960. Her first employees were black beauty-school grads on welfare. White salons refused to hire them.

Spiritual daughter of Madame C. J. Walker, purveyor of the hot comb, Miles was an early champion of chemical relaxers at the dawn of the sixties. Later she boycotted the Afro. ("I lost money. In this business you gotta change with the changes.") Years of styling hair showed her how difficult it is for working women to make it to salons during the day, hence the twenty-four-hour hair concept. Late-night customers aren't sleazy, Miles will testify, just "family people; lawyers and housewives who leave the kids with their husbands."

And so went my night at Charlene's: I arrive just after nine on Saturday, and stylist Eddie Ogletree, a receptionist, and a janitor are the only folks around. Eddie has styled hair going on thirteen years; in the eighties at salons like Black Hair Is and Soul Scissors. He offers to give me a "blow-curl" while I wait for the games to begin. Late-night business at Charlene's Fifth Avenue has been slow since the city shut down half of its dance clubs a few years back, but the salon does have its after-hours regulars: "Your club crowd comes in from eight to eleven," Eddie breaks it down. "From two to seven, you have your postal workers" (from the main post office on Thirty-third Street). Wedding parties show up after three ("I do the bridesmaids, Jerome does the bride"), the church ladies after four. Then the sun comes up. Every Friday, for a few months running, Eddie saw a woman whom he believes was carrying on an affair: "She had a Mercedes, Jersey plates. I saw the car from the window. She'd come in around one. Her hair was always a mess. I'd curl it, but she'd style it herself. She didn't want to look too 'done.' "

Night manager Jerome Shavers rolls in with a bald head and ample panache to match his job title. In addition to his salon gig, Jerome does hair for musical revues like *Chitlin' Circuit,* now playing at Sweetwaters, a supper club near Lincoln Center. On the last day of every month, twenty wigs from the traveling sixties revue *Beehive* are shipped to him UPS. He has one day to style them and ship them back.

Jerome regales me with tales of "his nights at Charlene's," which he pronounces in an exaggerated lisp, as if recalling some infamous cabaret or brothel. He always asks new faces what brings them to the salon so late at night. One woman said she just couldn't sleep. Another swore her husband wouldn't let her back in the house unless she got rid of the "Afro beads" on her neck.

When Jerome the hair griot gets on a roll, he'll take you anywhere. Tonight it's back to Missouri, where he was "Curl King of St. Louis." As a young stylist he "pumped" two dozen curls a day for an old-school salon owner by the name of Master Metcalf. Jerome is ready to swear that Metcalf did cold waves on black hair to create a loosely curled effect twenty years before the Jheri curl. She sold fried chicken and fish out of the salon and would curse you out in a minute. Once a woman threatened to bomb the shop because her hair "went back" too fast. Metcalf cursed her under the table. It was Metcalf who kept Jerome off the streets when he was a teenager by giving him a job in her shop. Every time he twirls an iron, he thinks of her.

Charlene's is still empty at 2:00 A.M. Hours have gone by listening to Jerome. He's talking now about being "called" to do hair and why: to save his Mama and her girlfriend, Miss Orphelia, from being bald-headed. (The two burned each other's scalps regularly with head-over-the-sink perms.) This is where I belong forever, in Charlene's twenty-four-hour hair joint, listening to Jerome's war stories. Bury me under a hair dryer, Jerome can deliver the eulogy: "Here's she rests—fried, dyed, and laid to the side."

1991

my slave name

My name is owned by so many other people, I often think that I have not a name but a group moniker: the Freemasons, the Moonies, the Lisa Joneses. Ever notice that every year there's an *Ebony* bachelorette named Lisa Jones? (I hope to make the list in 1995 as Lisa Jones number 52.) My mother has this story she tells: When I arrived there was only one other Lisa in Manhattan—the very slender wife of a famous conceptual artist. Zillions of American mothers in the early sixties must have dreamt up the same story. The Lisa population, as you know, now outnumbers laboratory rats.

As *Ebony* bachelorette Lisa Jones number 52,

I would say, names are among my obsessions, or as girlfriend Deandra would say, my "issues." What's life without African-American names, nicknames, and naming rituals? Without folks calling other folks "out of their names"? Or of wondrously mythic stories involving names—like that of a friend's cousin who since grade school had gone by "Niggerman." He died in the electric chair. His crime? Shooting a white man for calling him "nigger."

The jazz dynasty is proof alone that names are divining rods: Mingus, Thelonious, Ornette, Coltrane. Even with all their urban newness, hip-hop names in rhythm and word play are reminiscent of the blues: Big Daddy Kane meets Blind Lemon Jefferson. And what of that gold mine of names as metaphor in Afro-Am lit? Bigger Thomas, Shug Avery, Milkman Dead, Jesse B. Semple, and Sula—possibly derived from the West African name *Sule*, meaning adventurous. New black cinema aches to be in the grand name tradition: *She's Gotta Have It*'s Mars Blackmon gets his name not from the candy bar, but from the filmmaker's great-grandfather. Here's the real question: The stank-breath character in *House Party* named Billal—is that a Muslim name or just a pun on bile?

We writers raid our family trees for names (Uncle Bubba, Aunt Gottlieb, Uncle Flat Top), then scavenge our friends'. (My friend Byrd—real name—has an uncle named Duck—real name.) But no one, I thought, could beat my great-uncle G. L. Russ. (G period, L period. Period.) Come to find that initial names were common among black men, like my uncle, born around the turn of the century. The Black Muslim "X" (signifying the absence of ancestral name) and hip-hop's initial as exclamation point (as in Chuck D.) join in to make another tradition: The name implied.

The field of names that young African Americans in the nineties draw from begs of excavation. A good friend teaches black studies to Ivy League freshmen. Her students, born in 1974, have names like Kenyatta, Rhasaam, Zuwena, Shakinah, and Rondai. Some are "movement babies" whose parents gave them African and Muslim names at the height of black cultural nationalism. Some converted from Anglo names as recently as the Afrocentric eighties. And there are those, like Shakinah and Rondai, whose names reach to Africa, if not for content, then for sonic inspiration.

Naming/renaming has been an "issue" for black folks on these shores since the slave ships docked. Following Emancipation, not only did families seek to reconstruct their ranks, but their names as well. Sixties nationalism made an expressive though shrill link between slave names, slave hair, and slave mentalities. It wasn't just Cassius Clay, Abbey Lincoln, and Stokely Carmichael who took African and Muslim names, but thousands of regular folk. While hippies baptized their kids Moon Unit and River Phoenix, folks named their's Kwesi and Latifah. Even Clarence Thomas's son, born in 1975, was christened Jamal.

Afrocentricity has brought back African name books, a fixture in black bookstores of the nationalist days. The slave-names-for-slaves doctrine is now gone; these new books appeal to spirituality rather than politics. They discuss African philosophical ideas about naming and offer names that reflect the continent's diversity, whereas the old books gave just Swahili names, or names identified only as "Afrikan."

I've seen over ten name books on the shelves recently. Four were published last year, including *Senkha-sen Ren-a (May They Mention My Name)*, a handbook of names in the ancient Egyptian language Metu Neter. (I chose the name *Amaumeru*, meaning, "I remember the heroes.") There's the popular *Book of African Names* by Dr. Molefi Asante, who coined "Afrocentricity." Asante's mission: to provide alternatives to the rash of African-inspired names that reflect, so he deems, "a half-understanding of the culture." His most colorful example is of a girl named Rhodesia after the former stomping grounds of strident racist Cecil John Rhodes.

Sheniqua, Twanda, Lakeisha—I call these the Watts, Africa, names; they sound African to some ears, yet they're made in chocolate cities like Detroit. Mattel's new African-American fashion doll line has two dolls with Swahili names and one named Nichelle, which falls in the "Frenchified" category of the Watts, Africa, aesthetic (along with names like Chante, Saute, Tanqueray). There's a R&B/pop category too: A friend just became aunt to nieces named Shalimar and Cameo. I admire the invention of these names, how boldly they announce themselves, how they aim for the singular quality of royalty. I try to imagine the world that they conjured up for the parent. Tanqueray, say, must have been less a brand of a gin made in England than a place like Tangier, with beaded curtains and sandalwood incense.

Watts, Africa, names don't get much respect from the intelligentsia. *Essence* ran an opinion piece a few years back dismissing them for being "cumbersome," "phonetically incorrect," and, presumably, low class. A buppie couple in their early thirties, asked recently why they chose an Anglo name for their child, said, "At least we didn't name her Toyota Corolla." (Some lump the contemporary African name movement, over twenty years strong, in with more fanciful Watts-Africanisms.) Then there are others, like Gordon Chambers, a twenty-five-year-old jazz musician, who sees himself as part of a "postmodern George Wolfeian generation of young boho and buppie African Americans." Black cultural awareness, he believes, is an "assumption that doesn't necessarily have to be proven anymore. We don't have to wear it as much."

I made peace with my slave name only recently, and have even found a measure of tenderness for it. Truth is, life would be empty without folks singing to me, "Me and Mrs. Jones" or "I got a love jones for you baby, oohoohooh." And how could I wean myself from spectacular nicknames like "Worm the Phi Slama Jama Hermaneutic" that compensate for the *Ebony* bacheloretteness of my name?

A tidy coda came last summer. Since I was eight I have considered taking an African name; more, back then, as a badge of blackness than to escape the baby-girl femininity of my given name. This is an irony to me now, given that all along I've had one of the most indelibly "colored" names in the book. I was late to work one day when a very skinny brother missing a few teeth asked me to sign a petition. As I signed it, he looked me over, "What's your national-lee-tee?" "Negro," I said, with plenty sarcasm. He had such a good laugh that I was nearly two blocks gone before his comeback. "With a name like that," he yelled out louder than anything on Flatbush Avenue that morning, "you just ought to be."

1992

never "auntie"

The perverted love letter from Jim Crow America that unnerves me most was white folks' fondness for calling mature black women "auntie," a keepsake from slavery days. One translation of this is that even a total stranger could stand in as a wet nurse and be good for a forgiving embrace; and that, somehow, though no longer cattle slaves, black folks were still the emotional property of whites, still to be counted among their personal effects. Like many African Americans of my generation, I first came across such expressions, and the images that accompanied them, in a history book. Having no firsthand reference, these words seemed camp and almost fantastical. Did white folks really say this stuff with a straight face?

You couldn't put a red bandanna, see, on my favorite aunt, Cora, with a ten-foot pole, or for that matter have her suckle Massa or brats. Damnation would be yours. This conviction I guess is a little like Eddie Murphy's gleefully ignorant joke about slavery being for those other nigras. Yet whatever auntie was, historical reality or figment of white folks' imaginations, Cora has never been. Of course most women weren't the stereotype either, weren't that auntie, even if they did auntie work. Still, I bring it up because the distance my aunt's life has measured from auntie's life continues to feel uncommon and extraordinary. I could watch television for a day and not know that women like my aunt really exist and have existed. At a time when portraits in American entertainment of black women as caretakers of white folks have resurfaced with creepy popularity, it's worth repeating: My aunt has never been your auntie. I will never be your auntie. Auntie yourself.

Tailored to the nines, the coif always in place, my aunt, Ms. Cora Coleman to you, cuts a mean figure even at sixty-five. Her tongue is a very sharp instrument, somewhere between a switchblade and a chainsaw. There's always that point in a conversation with her in which she'll have you grabbing your gut, bent double 'cause you can't laugh anymore. It usually falls halfway through one of her famous missives to America. Cora is among God's children who will never forget the African Holocaust or forgive the white man for poot, though she admits having known some "decent white folks" in her time. On the other hand, she is profoundly patriotic and might even be considered something of a jingoist.

The sitcom based on her life is still too hip for television: the closet Elvis fan who plays Nat King Cole when company comes; the retiree whose Scrabble partners, all lady retirees, meet each week to debate whether the latest injustice against black folks is indeed that or just the misdoings of the race's more triflin' members. Every episode, she ends up kicking the ladies out because they get too loud, tear up her house, and wake up her white neighbors. Then she sends the neighbors to bed with a piece of her mind, stays up for the national anthem, prays "To Whom It May Concern" (the God who looks out for colored folks when no other God will), and says good night till next week.

We are not related by blood or marriage, my aunt and I, but by friendship. Aunt Cora and my grandmother were best friends. Gramma passed six years ago, though the family that she and my aunt created has remained. Cora Coleman met Anna Lois Jones when Gramma was taking donations for the Red Cross in the Colonade Apartments, the newly integrated high rise in downtown Newark where my grandparents moved in the early sixties. Cora, a court reporter for Jersey's Essex County, lived down the hall. My grandmother worked for Newark's housing authority, was a lobbyist for education, and did trench work for many civic causes. The two became old friends immediately.

Beyond their involvement in Newark black politics (like holding fundraisers for future mayor Ken Gibson), grandmother and aunt shared an ethos about children—that they should be loved abundantly, exposed to everything, never stifled. Childhood upsets kindled this. My grandmother was a champion runner at Tuskegee on her way to the Olympics the year Jesse Owens competed. Her father, a stern race man and business owner, had to leave the South after threats from the Klan. He forbid my grandmother from entering the qualifying races, believing track was not proper race work for the daughter of a pastor.

Aunt Cora grew up in Depression-era Newark in an extended family led by her grandmother Cora Lee Helen Struther Rogers, a "beautiful, evil woman who sat on her hair and ran a tight ship." Too proud for Relief, Cora Lee had little Cora and her brother do their homework by gas lamp when the light bill couldn't be paid. Even in the hardest times, the children were sent to the junior museum to study natural history. Backward folks mumbled that Cora Lee was raising them white. My aunt recalls never wanting for anything except affection. When her mother died young of congenital heart failure, Cora, a sheltered eighteen-year-old, left her grandmother's house and joined the military. She visited Cora Lee once before shipping off for duty in Japan. Grandmother told granddaughter she was "allowed" one kiss, and pointed to her wrinkled cheek; it might have been the first and surely was the last.

Cora made it her life business that no little girl be without a doting aunt. Her "kids" now number close to twenty. Cora's aunt-ship also brought with it an extended family: Her brother Oscar, a career marine who taught in inner-city schools after the service, became our Uncle Flat Top. An old friend, Alice, took the mantle of sweet Alice, the aunt whose hugs went on forever. Our Jersey cousins were Alice's nieces and Cora's many kids.

The summer of 1969, the cousin-nieces were rounded up for a month at the Jersey shore with Gramma and Aunt Cora presiding. Every morning us recruits fell in line for inspection by Sergeant Cora. The day began with her marching orders: "Look alive, *tafadali!*" By using the Swahili word for "please" in such a context, my aunt both endorsed and poked fun at the nationalism of the day. Cora has always been one of those folks who can't help but signify.

Easter, Christmas, Fourth of July, we shuttled between houses. The family embraced relatives from four or more blood-family groups, friends, the single and divorced, the gay and straight, a few conventional nuclear families, and a few white folks (including my mom who, missing an older sister-friend, found one in Cora). "We don't choose our mothers or fathers," Aunt Cora told me once, "but we can choose our families"—wisdom that sounds New Age, yet properly in line with her up-South, old-school preachifying.

The history you save may be your own. When I was holed up in Minneapolis, Minnesota, last summer, my aunt came to cook me succotash. I knew as a girl that Cora was "in the service." Though a photograph of Aunt Cora in uniform stands guard above my writing desk, the details were still hazy. Almost thirty years after we were united as aunt and niece, I asked Cora about that photo.

I come from a family of Negro Historymakers, so it didn't surprise me that my spirit aunt would be one in her own right. Cora was a Black WAC. Truman signed an executive order in 1948 to integrate the armed services. The deed wasn't done, it turned out, until four years later. When my aunt enlisted in 1949, she found herself in the last segregated company of the Women's Army Corp. Company B was a no-mess bunch from up North that placed first in the marching band competitions. They almost served some scalps one night in Camp Lee, Virginia, when the white women in Company C broke into hateful southern swan song ("In the moonlight you can hear those darkies singing"). Cora remembers the black female captains and lieutenants who looked out for the recruits. These career officers joined the service in the early forties before it became the Women's Army Corp; often they were nurses who enlisted because civilian America wouldn't give them jobs.

Trained as a court reporter, Cora was sent to Yokohama, Japan. There she earned three medals and stayed on for a year as a reporter in the army's civilian employ. Occupied Japan she describes as a surreal place with its fog and rickshaws and its American-imported racism (nightclubs with signs that forbid "niggers and dogs").

Black Americans, it's been said, are the true patriots. Still it's always disarmed me that my aunt's patriotism could coexist with a sublime hatred of all that whitey is and all that whitey does. (I use the arcane "whitey," because she means it in the sense of whitey, the great institutional animal.) I finally made sense of Cora's marriage of the two through stories of her life in uniform. This is her remembering retreat:

"You're walking alone in a lonely field when retreat blows and there could be nobody around you for miles. You could just be out there picking straws, but when you hear that bugle, you salute. There's such a pride you have standing there. It's a very secret pride. You could still go back to the base among your peers and say, 'I'm only in here for what these honkies can do for me,' but you had your moment in that field. You forget everything that's wrong and have this sense of belonging to this great society called America. If you think about it, what else do we have to belong to?"

Also in Minneapolis, I had the unsettling opportunity to stand up to one of my heroes. The City of Lakes, Minneapolis is advertised as a liberal oasis between the coasts. Naturally when my aunt shows up it is anything but. In one week she is treated like a suspect while shopping at a progressive-chic *parfumerie;* she witnesses a black man getting beat on the head by four white cops; and she sees enough Debbies curled up with Sam to let loose an avalanche of historical memory about Debbie's debauchery and psychosis being the true root of the race problem. The Debbie thing was shaking me up. I too had seen enough Debbies curled up with Sam in Minneapolis to last two lifetimes. Then again, if one Debbie hadn't curled up with Sam, I wouldn't be on this planet. I had a headache.

At a restaurant one night we argue. It's great cinema that in this restaurant of cloth napkins we are the only black folks. Aunt Cora's position has racism defining everything: that whitey's massa plan rules the world. Mine is that whitey holds the purse strings, though racism isn't the only way of explaining the universe. I raise my voice, it cracks, I steer it steady. This is not casual rebellion. I am my mother's, still, I am very much my grandmother's child. I was willed this sense that your elders are your gods on earth. I would have walked behind my grandmother carrying an umbrella if asked. This voice raising is not easy, but I want her to know about my inheritance. How this power is only made possible by her life and what she endured—the grace and intelligence with which she endured it and the anger and history she never forgot. If I feel more mighty than whitey, it's her bequest. Aunt Cora taught me that knowledge works. That it could get you, like the Isley Brothers sing, to the next phase.

It feels good to have spoken up. But the next day's headlines drive nails into my little victory: lockout of Haitian refugees, forced famine in Somalia, Nazism's new clothes in Europe. Maybe my elders know something I don't. Perhaps in the massa plan my doormat days are fast coming.

Do you know who speaks through you? Early in my aunt's career as a court reporter she was assigned to a judge who thought it appropriate to sentence a man on his hospital deathbed. Aunt Cora doesn't remember the details, the man's plea or the severity of the crime he was charged with, just the venom of this white judge as he castigated this black man who lay motionless, tubes connecting him to an oxygen tank. Cora stood beside the judge and silently took the record. For several days afterward she was sick. Her own muteness, she said, had poisoned her.

"You can imagine a person like myself, sitting there, recording the facts. Being seen, but not heard. All we could do was sit there and burn. Our hands were tied. We were trying to make a living. We were proud to be court reporters, doing the best job we knew how, and then we had to watch our people get railroaded time and again. During the riots, when blood was running down Springfield Avenue like a waterfall, black folks were coming into court with their heads split open, looking at us like we were traitors—we burned then too. Either you became cynical or you just didn't hear. You wrote words, not sentences; it helped you do your job."

My aunt would have been a writer, my grandmother too. My mother is a writer who came to it later in life after raising and supporting children on her own. All three indulged me, I realize now. Aunt Cora has been announcing my profession since I was seven and carried a pad and pencil to record family conversations. My mother typed my poems. Summers at my grandparents' house Gramma set up a desk and called it "Lisa's office."

Those who don't know me assume that I write because of my celebrated writer father or my less celebrated writer mother. Or that I do it in spite of them or to spite them. But when I sit down, the voice that stays in my ear is my aunt's. It's merciless, it laughs a chill up my spine, it never forgets. It's taken me years to know that voice was my aunt's. The voice that never got to speak in court. I listen for her now. She urges me to speak with her, through her, and, when necessary, back at her, to get to the truth that the day demands.

1993

mama's white

Just another rainbow baby on the IRT, that's me, handing out flyers modeled after Adrian Piper's seminal art piece, "My Calling (Card) #1" (1986):

Dear Fellow Straphanger:

My mother is white. And I, as you may or may not have figured out, am black. This is how I choose to define myself and this is how America chooses to define me. I have no regrets about my racial classification other than to lament, off and on, that classifications exist period.

Actually the mystery of my background is really

not much of a mystery at all, despite those taboo-love-child stories you read in *People* or *Jet*. If you boned up on your world history, you'd know that unions between people of different racial classifications, such as my (white) mother and my (black) father, are not a recent phenomenon. Entire countries in South America are peopled by the offspring of such relationships. Even our own country is more of a creole outpost than we are ready to acknowledge.

Are you still staring? Let me guess. My white mother presents a different set of enigmas to you based on your own racial classification. Those of you who are black might find "evidence" of my white parent reason to question my racial allegiance. For those of you who are white, evidence of my white lineage might move you to voice deep-seated feelings of racial superiority. You might wonder why I would choose to identify as "fully" black when I have the "saving grace" of a white parent. I have no time for this sort of provinciality either. I realize both sets of responses display an ignorance of our shared cultural and racial history as Americans.

I'm sorry you're still staring. If you care to, I'll gladly engage you in a lengthy conversation about this subject at another time. But right now I'm having just another "attitudinous"-black-girl day on the IRT, and if you keep staring, I'll just stare right back. I regret any discomfort my presence is causing you. Just as I'm sure you regret the discomfort your ignorance is causing me.

Yours (More Truly Than You Think),

L.J.

This is the story of Emily Sohmer Tai and Hettie Jones, two women who don't know each other and whose only connection is the melanin count of their skin.

Recently Emily Sohmer Tai, who describes herself as the "white female half of an interracial marriage," wrote a letter to the *Village Voice*. The letter is worth returning to as an example of the closeted superiority trip I mention above. And what I mean by superiority trip is the type of thinking that assigns whiteness highest value (and upholds white people as the only viable arbiters of experience), though this thinking may at times be draped in the gauze of liberalism.

I had written a sentimental tribute to my sixty-five-year-old Aunt Cora for a series the paper ran for Black History Month. In one section I recount my aunt's visit to Minneapolis, where I was living at the time, her brushes with racism there, and her reaction to the large number of white female–black male couples that coexist there alongside this racism. I sized up these couples as "Debbies curled up with Sam"—to allude to the lady-stud legend that burdens them and, at the same time, to pry it apart. I was sure to note, in the same breath, that if one Debbie hadn't curled up with one Sam, I wouldn't be around. Clearly I was saying that these duos tangle up my emotions; I look at them as a child of an interracial marriage, but also as a black woman who has witnessed the market value put on white femininity.

Tai seems to have got stuck on one word, "Debbie," and looked no further. Her letter responds to my entire essay as if it were merely a personal attack on her and other white women in interracial relationships. Tai never once mentions my aunt. In effect, she completely erases Cora's story. What I got from this is that there is nothing I could say about my aunt, her amazing life, and our feelings as black women about interracial relationships—some shared, some not—that could be as important as Tai's outrage as a white woman measuring herself against a stereotype. Nothing, simply, was as worthy of readers' consideration as Tai's story, Tai's version of history.

There's a shrillness to Tai's letter, and it seems to come from the fact that I don't accept her view of what interracial identity means. She rather smugly assumes, in fact, that she can define this experience for me. To Tai, this identity is a haven from racialized society; to me, it's not. And Tai assumes again that such a safe house is indeed something I have political or aesthetic interest in embracing. I've been called "nigger bitch" more than once in life, and I wonder if Tai would advise that I handle it by shouting back, "Actually, guys, my mom's white, so call me half-white bitch, or how about mongrel bitch, since it's better rhythmically?"

Left unsaid, though lurking in the margins of Tai's letter, is this amazement that I, as a woman, would claim "black" over "interracial" or "white." The implication being that choosing black was somehow a settlement, a compromise following a personal identity crisis, and not a much larger cultural-historical calling or even just sheer love, romance, and respect for blackness (in all its permutations), for better or for worse, amen. Would Tai's mouth hang open if I told her my story? That, among others, it was my (white) mother who raised me to think politically about being a black woman?

Could Tai picture this complexity as well? That I'm a writer whose work is dedicated to exploring the hybridity of African-American culture and of American culture in general. That I don't deny my white forebears, but I call myself African American, which means, to me, a person of African and Native American, Latin, or European descent. That I feel comfortable and historically grounded in this identity. That I find family there, whereas no white people have embraced me with their culture, have said to me, take this gift, it's yours, and we are yours, no problem. That, by claiming African American and black, I also inherit a right to ask questions about what this identity means. And that chances are this identity will never be static, which is fine by me.

Tai's reaction to this "racial persona" of mine is nothing I haven't come across before. White women in particular have trouble seeing my black identity as anything other than a rebuff of my mother. Deep down I wonder if what they have difficulty picturing is this: not that I could reject, in their minds, my own mother, but that I have no desire to be *them*.

Friends of mine, who are also rainbow babies pushing thirty, have had similar run-ins, and sometimes we sit around and compare notes. We're not disinterested in our white "heritage," even though most of us don't know our white relatives (apart from the parent who raised us), or we were given up for adoption by a white biological parent and have never had white family. In my own case, my mother's parents, first-generation American Jews, disowned her for marrying black. When she announced she was pregnant, they begged her to have an abortion. On hearing that in her third year of marriage my mother was pregnant with a second child, again they begged her to abort.

We of the rainbow persuasion joke about whites' inability to imagine why we would want to see ourselves as people of color and as African Americans—how connected this makes us feel. What could they possibly think is *in it* for us to be white people? Would it extend refuge or protection, provide moral directive? If it helped us get better jobs and higher salaries, would it offer spiritual community? Would it bring us family?

Forget everything that the Emily Sohmer Tai example tells you about race, and meet Hettie Jones, author, poet, teacher, and my mother. Her memoir, *How I Became Hettie Jones,* revisits her life as a woman among the Beats as the starched-collar fifties gave way to the guns-and-roses sixties. It also tells of her marriage to my father, writer Amiri Baraka, and of her own coming of age as a writer. If you want to know more, the book is in paperback. I will share this: The most dreadfully cute fact about my mother is that she has taken to checking "other" on her census form. In the line slotted for explanation she writes, in her flowery longhand, "Semitic American mother of black children."

Fans of *How I Became Hettie Jones* include young African Americans, many of them women, who seek me out at public events to express how the book touched them. They are moved by the woman-finding-herself-amid-the-ruins story, but they relate also to the story of Hettie, the white woman who *stayed behind,* or *stayed on,* or was just plain *there,* raising the black children while the brothers went where their muses took them. They know women like Hettie. These women live in their neighborhoods. These women are the mothers of friends. Sometimes these women are their own mothers. They're pleased someone is telling this story.

Her literary endowments aside, my mother is my mother, and I'm very protective of her and of our relationship. I find myself in this amusing little bind at times, which reminds me over and over that what I am, I guess, for lack of a more sexy and historically complex word, is a humanist. This is the bind of explaining that my mother is white, though I am black, then getting pissed when people reduce dear Mom to the calling card of "your white mother." Negotiating all this continues to be one of the challenges of my intellectual life. I'll crib from Greg Tate on this one: "The world isn't black and white, it just feels that way sometimes."

I owe Mom a couple of solids. One for being strong enough in her own self to let me be who I was gonna be. My pride in being a black woman actually brings me closer to my (white) mom. This identity gives me a stronger sense of history and self, and I can come to my mother as what the New Age folks might call a "fully realized person." If I called myself "interracial" (in my mind, and I know others see this differently), I would need her presence, her "whiteness," to somehow validate my "half-whiteness."

Another solid. Mom's bohemian from way back. The journey she's made as a woman, as an artist, making herself up in America, has been useful to me as a black woman living outside of society's usual paradigms of femininity. Mom knew that we—my sister and I —needed black female relatives and role models, and she made sure these ties were in place. She never tried to substitute for these; what she gave instead was her own DNA, her own boho Mama-in-the-black-stockings self, and she trusted that this would be enough.

Solid number three. My mother, more than anyone I know, has taught me difference as pleasure. Not as something feared or exotic, but difference as one of the rich facts of one's life, a truism that gives you more data, more power, and more flavor. These are the sort of things you needed to get by: a black South Carolinian grandfather who did the Moon Walk before Michael Jackson (though he called it the Camel Walk), a mother who speaks Yiddish and jazz, a

Caribbean boyfriend to make you rice and peas, and a sister who's a Latin American art scholar so you won't lapse into thinking you're God's gift to all knowledge as a North American Negro.

Today my mother is in town from Wyoming, where she's teaching for a stint. We hug, I cook her tofu and collard greens, we swap clothes, watch TV evangelism for a goof. We talk about race as the world places it on us. We argue sometimes, but we don't stumble on it. When our differences in age and race make themselves felt in how we see the world, it doesn't butt against our love, our trust.

I've got my pad and pen out and she's laughing at my official-ness. Mom, not *how*, but *why* did you become Hettie Jones?

"After the breakup of my marriage," she explains, "people asked me why I didn't change my name, why I didn't, quote, 'go back to the Jews.' There was no going back to something that denied you."

And why was it important to you that we be black and not "biracial"?

"I was not about to delude you guys into thinking you could be anything different in this country. And, frankly, I didn't think that being anything other than black would be any more desirable."

Mom, what you say in the book about black people's anger in the sixties being necessary to America, how did you come to this?

"Some people think that I'm dishonest and that I'm a martyr for saying that, but there's a certain time in your life if you're a white person and you have black children that you have to see that the world is ready to take them on. I love my children and I just sensed that the world had to go through this period in order for it to be a better place for them."

Motherhood has been more than a domestic chore or emotional bond for my mother. It's a political vocation—one she's taken seri-ously enough to go up against the world for. She always stands ready to testify about how her children and blackness have broad-ened her own life. In the music—jazz, blues, the language—she found her own.

Mom's headed back to Wyoming. The cab driver offers to put her backpack in the trunk. "May I take your parachute?" he asks. People of all ages and backgrounds say fetching things like this to my mother. She's led, as she wrote once, a "charmed life in the middle of other people's wars," and it comes through in her smile. When Mom sends the mojo his way, the cab driver lights up like New Year's Eve on Forty-Deuce. I'm reminded, right then, that there is no place that I'm ever gonna go (by way of geography or ideology) where I can't bring my mother, and where I can't bring myself, which she has in large part made possible. And, as Adrian Piper would have me ask, what are all you—black and white—gonna do about that?

1993

video soul
(and salsa)

You used to go to clubs with names like Buttermilk Bottom and Paradise Garage. You used to wear very short skirts and, when you danced, move your rear end in such a way that many people who didn't know you at all would want to get to know you right away. You would do this until eight in the morning. Afterward, you'd go eat French toast on Second Avenue, catch the F train to Coney Island, and sleep all day in the sun. This was known as a night on the town.

Now you have a job. Maybe you have two jobs. Maybe you have two jobs, a very small apartment you pay lots of money to rent, and heavy philosophical questions to consider like, "How come my man doesn't answer his phone at nine o'clock at night?" Because of all this, it is quite likely that the only going out you want to do on Friday night is to a video store. And this is how you meet Tony Smith, who owns Tompkins Square Video on Avenue B near Tenth Street, and Carmen Montalvo, who runs the joint when Tony's not around, and all the folks who hang out there.

If you're lucky one Friday, you might catch Tony and Carmen working the store together. Tony and Carmen make you feel like multiculturalism was born on the Lower East Side, and is alive and doing quite well, thank you. Tony's slim with a crooked smile. He's got a Nuyorican accent, though he's black, as in black American. Carmen's healthy figured and Puerto Rican. In a former life she was a Jewish mother. Carmen's motto is: "Once you go black, you never come back" (except don't tell her I told you).

Tony used to be a deejay. He made a vow to leave club life before he turned thirty, so a year and half ago he opened his own video store, where you can rent movies like *Black Orpheus, Diary of a Chambermaid, The Jetsons Meet the Flintstones,* and *Cleopatra Jones.* The distribution outfits that supply Tony told him that mixing "black and Puerto Rican videos" with "white videos" wasn't good business. Tony didn't care too much what they thought, that's why you can go into Tompkins and find *Slaughter's Revenge* displayed next to *My Dinner With Andre.*

A typical Friday night around nine: Tony's playing house music at club volume. The TV's on with no sound, and Michael Jordan and the other guys in Chicago are making one last push against Detroit. Instead of viewing a new arrival like *Crack House* ("Getting in is easy, getting out is hell"), everyone in the store—a dozen people at the moment, Latinos, blacks, and whites—is leaning on the counter as if they're in some sports bar, witnessing the Bulls get played. Above the counter is a movie-marquee-style signboard that Tony's carpenter installed this afternoon. It's supposed to list new arrivals. Instead JESUS WAS HERE is printed out in neat block letters. "Who's Jesus?" a customer asks Tony. "Oh," he says, "that's my carpenter."

"Sexual harassment is not a problem here, it's one of the benefits," reads a sign behind the counter. If there's anyone harassing people, it's Carmen. "We're up to nine hundred customers now," Tony boasts, "and Carmen still remembers all their names and their numbers." "Like Roman, 1504?" she bats her eyes at Tony, "you know that guy?"

Classic Carmen: She barks, with hands on hips, at full lung power, "I HAVEN'T SEEN YOU IN AGES!" at some guy who just came into the store. You think he's her man or something, but he's just another customer. An Asian punk, in a T-shirt that warns us "A Mind Is a Terrible Thing to Waste," returns *Beverly Hills Brats* and *Paperhouse*. Carmen hollers politely, "Thank you, Mama." This is Carmen addressing a favorite customer: "You know your girlfriend brought someone in here who looked just like your brother. I think she's playing you dirty."

"What kind of mood are you in?" Tony asks a customer, "Suspense, action, or horror?" He sends Luis to pick a few titles. Luis, the third man at Tompkins, could be a hard rock if you go by his broad shoulders and scowl, but he's just a shy sixteen-year-old kid. Tony and Luis cut a deal. As long as Luis stays in school, there'll be a part-time job for him at Tompkins. *Total Recall* opened today, and Tony, Carmen, and Luis have announced that after they close the store, they're headed to the midnight show. Twenty minutes later, six people from the neighborhood stop in to ask if they can go too.

"My mother calls me Mr. Public Relations." This is Tony talking. "If anything happens on the block, I know about it. The other day, a white customer was being followed, so he came in the store, and I had someone walk him home. . . ." You can't hear the rest of Tony's story because Carmen is shrieking, "DON'T LET IT HAPPEN AGAIN!" at some brown-skinned cutie with long eyelashes who's returned *Switchblade Sisters* a couple of days late.

Near closing time, Tony performs Operation *Harlem Nights* on a copy of the Eddie Murphy movie that got stuck in a customer's

VCR. A half dozen people are still wandering around the store looking for the perfect nighttime companion. A kid in a "Ninja Turtles Rule" T-shirt flips through the Nintendo file. "You got any new games, Tony? I'm sick and tired of what you got."

"What's your problem, Seymour? There are 130 games—what about *SuperContra?*"

"Oh, I didn't see *SuperContra.*"

"That's 'cause you're buggin', Seymour. Now go outside."

"I can't go outside, Tony, it's boring outside."

It's Luis who gets to scream now: "THEY TOOK JORDAN!" The entire store gathers around the TV to say good-bye to Chicago. Carmen then ushers customers out with their videos and their very own dose of tough love ("GET OUT ALREADY!") so that the Tompkins crew can make it to *Total Recall* in time.

After exceptions are made for latecomers who use creative tactics to gain entry, like swishing their faces against the store window, Tompkins Square Video is finally, officially closed for the evening. Carmen counts receipts. Tony counts money. Together they pull down the iron gate, on which one of the Lower East Side's many muralists has spray-painted a portrait of a lone videocassette. Carmen paces the sidewalk. "I hope we can get a cab to the movies. Tony, do you mind changing your skin color, so we can get a cab, PLEASE." Tony puts his keys in his pocket and lights a cigarette. "Sure Carmen, anything for you."

1990

east river's edge

No one has a name for it, but it's been going on every summer, every Sunday, for ten years. And for the last three of these ten years, DJ Louie and DJ José have lugged their fourteen crates of records and fifteen stereo speakers to East River Park, just across the overpass at Tenth Street and FDR Drive. They suspend a piece of green tarp between the limbs of a sturdy tree and a playground fence, and set up their turntables underneath. DJ José spins records, mostly salsa and merengue (with one hour of "English music—you know, standard disco—and classics from the fifties") and DJ Louie sweet-talks into the mike. People come from all over Loisaida, even

Brooklyn, East Harlem, and Jersey, to cram into the small space between the playground and the ballpark, which becomes an open-air dance hall lit by two street lamps. This goes on from one in the afternoon until sometime after midnight, every Sunday, every summer, without fail.

Some come to eat (vendors sell homemade rice and beans, *pasteles,* and *alcapurrias*). Some come to drink *(cerveza fría* sold from garbage pails filled with ice). Some come to bet on dice and cards (under single, naked light bulbs in makeshift tents nearby). But most come to dance—under very few stars, the smog, the heat —to what DJ Louie (a bright-eyed human cannonball) and DJ José ("the guy in the long hair who looks like Jesus," says Louie) have to play for them. All ages and shades of brown pack in together. Mothers leave strollers on the sidelines and partner up with their babies. Old ladies missing a few teeth stand alone rotating their hips like clockwork. Young men in long shorts and baseball caps dance together without touching. Couples grind furiously as if all things to come depended on this one good sweat. The Tenth Street overpass becomes a balcony, the best view in the house.

Even though the DJs try to keep things even—50 per cent merengue, 50 salsa—the battle between *salseros* and *merengueros* rages all night. "I don't want to be racist," confides Louie, a native Nuyorican, "but Dominicans and Puerto Ricans are always fighting. Puerto Ricans are mostly salsa people, and Dominicans are merengue people. See, salsa is like soul and merengue is like rock and roll. I give Dominicans credit for their music, but they try to act too macho about it, like it's the best."

Louie and José aren't on salary. "What I make here is what the people give me," says José, who's been spinning records since the "days of the 45s." Vendors pass the hat for the DJs and dancers give them money to announce their families or dedicate songs. Miguel Maldonado pays to hear "La Soga" by V. Rogue and La Gran Manzana because he just turned seventeen: "I want to dedicate it to my own self 'cause I love this record so much."

"Llegó la hora," Louie announces. "What will it be, *una*

salcita?" Half the crowd yells "No!" "Or *un merengue?"* "No!" the other half calls back. José plays *"Devórame Otra Vez* (Devour Me Again)" and after the first few beats, objections from the merengue corner die down. A woman selling sodas dips a handkerchief into her ice bucket and squeezes it over her head. Then she grabs a man by the neck and forces him into a kiss. A middle-aged man with a mustache, and a tattoo on his arm showing two hearts pierced by a knife, watches his wife dance with a young bodybuilder.

The last dance is not a merengue or salsa, but Frank Sinatra's "New York, New York." Some folks line up like the Rockettes. "I want to wake up in a city that never sleeps," Franks sings, while a sleeping man near the turntables cuddles a can of Budweiser between his thighs. Someone standing in the middle of the overpass waves the Puerto Rican flag in time to the music. "It's time to say so long," Louie croons, pressing his lips against the microphone, "but we'll be back next Sunday. Even if it rains, I love you."

1990

the outback

The gospel of cultural pluralism brings me to Utah. I've been speaking at colleges around the country as a journalist and coauthor of "Spike Lee books." Once I live through the pure terror, I'm glad to do the talks. Glad to be that beam of color for p.o.c. youth roughing it in the still snowy white collegiate outback. Glad to be a diversity moment for others. Better me than Professor Griff. Better me than Patty Buchanan.

In Utah I find what one finds when one travels in any direction or looks under any rock: people of African descent and variations on that theme. Four meet me at the airport; a surprise because a college rep warned on the phone, "We don't have many minorities and stuff like that here." And what a bushy-tailed "them" they are, full of questions such as, "Should history books be rewritten?" and "What do you think, as a *sister*, about the *Jungle Fever* phenomenon?" Or the usual, "Did you have an identity crisis growing up *interracially mixed?*" (which, put that way, sounds like inbreeding Pan-American style).

I dub them the Fab Four in honor of Michigan's spunky Five: Melanie, twenty-one, student senator, zoology major, future chiropractor, has lived in Utah since grammar school; Dennis, twenty, from "somewhere near Tupelo," Mississippi, came to Utah to study automotive design ("before there were women, there were cars"); Belva, nineteen, moved in junior high, and now studies respiratory therapy, and is, among other things, an albino who wears her platinum-blond "black hair" in a permed wedge cut; and army brat Zack, twenty-two, known as "DJ Ivory," but is changing his name to "the Visionary" to get away from "all that mighty-whitey business." Before college, Zack did time in the Gulf. Even in Colin Powell's armed forces, Zack will tell you, white guys like him still get called "nigger lover" for hanging black.

The Fab Four's repertory of black media culture is as up-to-date as any hipster's from Brooklyn Tech. They've got the latest Queen Latifah, watch *A Different World,* admire Oprah and Toni Morrison. Zack plays Farrakhan's speeches on his radio show. Dennis, who plans to design his own line of cars one day, relates to Ice Cube's take on black self-reliance. Arguing about new black cinema is a favorite pastime. They question whether air-head comedies like *Livin' Large* "trivialize the black experience." I wonder just what black experience they mean? The one they see in music videos or the one they live in Utah?

It's spring at Weber State University, a large commuter school just outside of Salt Lake City, and the young Republicans are leafletting the quad. Their dramatic backdrop, the Utah mountains, sharp white peaks against a true-blue sky, is very close to the illustrated rocks of ages you see in hymn books; the Mormons couldn't have ended up anywhere else.

Weber is courting diversity, and with numbers as low as 150 students of color out of fifteen thousand, it still manages to have the most realistically "all-American" student body in the state. A poster announces the Miss Indian of Utah pageant ("contestants must have at least one-fourth Indian blood"), and style around campus—big hair, suntans, zoot-suit jeans—makes everyone look Hispanic-by-Hollywood. Student-run KWCR touched more than a few racial nerves when it switched formats to become the only rhythm and blues–based station in Utah, with a full Sunday of hip-hop programmed by Zack. ("Geez," said a student, "don't you think it's getting *too* black?") Belva got sick to her stomach in a faculty/student meeting when a professor argued that a rhythm and blues–based station "wasn't multicultural enough" and went against Dr. King's dream.

There's my speech, a luncheon, then the Fab Four and I go for an opinionated tour of Salt Lake City and surrounding territories. We drive through the one-drag town of Ogden, home to Weber State, Hill Air Force base, and most black Utahans. African Americans migrated to Ogden for railroad work starting around the turn of the century. Alberta Henry, the spry seventy-two-year-old president of Salt Lake's NAACP, came from Kansas in 1949. Henry says, "Utah kept all the black codes of the South" until the late sixties. The state still has no unified civil rights bill and was the last in the union to pass hate crimes legislation. The Fab Four have their own stories of race hate in Mormonland. Rocks and "nigger calling" welcomed Belva and her twin sister to public junior high in the mid-eighties. Dennis has come to accept regular harassment from cops for "being the wrong color."

Twenty minutes on the thruway and we're in Salt Lake cruising the campus of Weber's competition, the University of Utah. The Fab Four play the old game of "Look, There's a Black Person." We pass a honey in a four-by-four. Belva's not impressed: "That's an athlete, you can tell from California plates, but they usually date only the white girls." Lounging on the grass are a black man and woman, a rare sight in Utah, to hear Melanie, our driver, tell it. She almost swerves off the road to get a good look.

Our last stop is the Crossroads Plaza mall in downtown Salt Lake. The Fab Four say it's a typical Utah mall—department stores, food court, movie theater (playing *White Men Can't Jump*)—still, nods to the cultural rainbow, at least in consumer items, would get a rise out of even the most jaded East Coast multiculturalist. Filipino fast food, Latin American textiles, a Japanese gift shop. We stop at an African art shop that also sells "African trade beads" to kids who see them on models in *Elle.* Asian and Latino teens parade around the mall. In Salt Lake, you'll find gang members from the Samoan Crips transplanted from L.A. and upwardly mobile Mexicans who prefer to be called Hispanic.

On the plane back I'm trying to fit my Fab Four into all this talk about post–soul culture and fragmented black communities of the nineties. Nothing, I think, will define their sense of black community more than the ideological battles to come around interracial relationships and mixed-race identity. What they've come to call the *"Jungle Fever* phenomenon" is setting off Scud missiles in their psyches. All seem torn; it sorta feels politically incorrect, but they've got too many ties to white folks to believe it's flat wrong. Belva is most opposed to interracial relationships, though she takes heat from blacks for being albino, is engaged to a Mexican American, and has many white friends. Zack criticizes men whose "rhetoric celebrates the black queen, while they sleep white," but his own race complicates his critique. Dennis has no apologies for dating across race ("Who's the sellout, me or the guys selling drugs to your little sister?"), yet he'd consider adopting "endangered" young black males before having babies with the woman he lives with, who is white. I was taken with how honestly they spoke of their conflicts, their choices. The Fab Four are not members of a race-ambivalent middle class growing up alienated outside of the hood. They belong to an expanding body of young Americans, race identified but grappling with new definitions of community.

"Do you still want to change the world?" Zack asks, as we pull into the airport. In my speech, I talked about being their age and on my way to law school to become the next Morris Dees, exterminate the Klan, and change the world. Then I read Gayl Jones's *Corregidora*. Jones, equipped with nothing save lyrics and her own version of the American story, disarms the psychological vise grip of slavery. I was driven to rethink my tactics. I'm lost in a thought bubble, taking in the fertile cultural moment that brought me to Utah to talk about my grandmother, my mother, Thurgood Marshall, Chuck D., cultural pluralism (without racial apathy or loss of community), and Shades of You makeup.

But I'm thinking also of Charlayne Hunter-Gault, who returned in 1988 to deliver the commencement address at the University of Georgia, which she and fellow student Hamilton Holmes integrated more than a quarter century earlier. Hunter-Gault was the first black person to deliver the address in the university's 203-year history, and resisting the comforts of tokenism, she urged those assembled not to pretend that "the events of the past twenty-five years, even my presence here today, have transformed our peculiar world into one that is beyond recognition." African trade beads in the Salt Lake City mall? Cute, but not even close, and no cigar.

"Well, do you . . . ?" Zack's sounding worried now.

"What?"

"The world . . ."

"Yeah. Definitely"

1992

tragedy becomes her

Don't hate me because I'm still tragic and beautiful (after all these years). Isn't it true I work best for you as a tragedy? You have your moment of showy guilt, then I'm out of your hair for another decade, until the next movie. You never have to face that this Frankenstein of yours is you also, is us, is America. Yet how could you? That would render even you impure. So let it remain just me and my tragedy. The toxic mix of my blood.

Somebody get an exorcist! I'm being haunted by a miniseries that aired months ago—Alex Haley's *Queen*, as scripted by Hollywood screenwriter David Stevens.

Caught up, as we were, in the questions of authenticity and plagiarism surrounding *Roots,* Queen snuck by without a hard glance. The series was such a monument to a nineteenth-century brand of racial determinism, those who did brave the six hours of flagellation still have the shakes. Perhaps Black History Month should be renamed Black Future Month, so we won't be subjected to any more TV fodder that, rather than presenting ground-breaking interpretations of history, feels like an excuse to see black people lynched, raped, or chased by the Klan on national television. America's racial violence is reenacted without any new way of understanding it, absent any hint of black folks' resistance or agency. The moral here? History tells us black Americans were run to the ground like Georgia mules, why should the future hold anything different?

Queen follows the life of Haley's grandmother, Queen, daughter of a master and a slave. The miniseries was marketed as a work of New Age racial healing, out to probe miscegenation with sensitivity and frankness. Turns out it was more akin to American film's tragic mulatto narratives of yore—a foreboding parable of race mixing and the race mixed. Skim off the melodrama and these films are cautionary tales about interracial sex and, more acutely, integration and black parity. In these days of furious cultural commingling and mixed-race scholarship and activism, *Queen* plays as an endorsement of an older racial order.

At the same time *Queen* romances the past, it manages to be cock-and-bull revisionism of the cheerful sort. Picture Halle Berry as the rosy-cheeked Queen, a formulaic house nigra so devoted to the plantation she volunteers as an overseer during the hard times of the Civil War. Leave it to Queen to have the mistress in the fields picking cotton as she, Queen the slave, eggs her on with a whip! Is this priceless moment meant to suggest that the Africans who became slaves were just as abusive to whites—and therefore just as culpable for slavery?

In fact modern day plantation dramas like *Queen* seem intent on erasing from our minds that there were such things as masters and slaves. We were just one big happy family back then, with a few codependency issues to work out, but no big deal. Slavery days were some of the best days of our black lives, these tales suggest. We were well fed, we didn't have to compete in the job market, we got to prance around in those off-the-shoulder plantation sundresses. And certainly we didn't worry much about the black man shortage, 'cause, like Queen's Mama, Easter, Massa was always willing to slip us some, all we had to do was holler. What *Queen* boils down to is *Roots* for the self-help generation: Racism is and has always been just a black self-esteem problem. If black folks would get over their demons already, so says *Queen,* America would treat them just fine.

Back to the tragic mulatress text: Not only does *Queen* drag out mulatto clichés from every B movie and paperback, it luxuriates in them with eerie aplomb. The trailer described Queen as having "raging blood" that tore at her insides in the same way that the Civil War was tearing at her country. *Queen* producer Mark Wolper, whose father David Wolper produced *Roots,* told *Entertainment Weekly* that the hardest part about filming the miniseries was finding an actress "who is as white as [I am] but yet is black. And she had to be a hell of a f———ing actress"—as if there weren't scores of chillun who fit the bill running around Hollywood. One can only guess that Wolper and the other creative types behind *Queen* weren't up on the tragic mulatto genre, so much so that they were hell-bent on reinventing the wheel.

Vessel of desire and pity, martyr or redeemed heroine, the tragic mulatto has been a Hollywood standard since the silent era. (*The Octoroon,* made in 1913, may have been her earliest screen appearance.) Each decade she resurfaces with a new wardrobe: the postwar "moral mulattos" (seen in *Pinky* and *Lost Boundaries),* who taught white America compassion for the Negro Problem, gave way to the island half-breeds of the 1950s. (Dorothy Dandridge carried the weight of this imagery in movies like *Island in the Sun.)* That the tragic mulatto is almost exclusively a woman isn't hard to unravel. A man might work his tragedy out through violence, whereas a woman can be plain doomed, attractive, and worthy of clemency.

As relief from the conservatism of the eighties, the tragic mulatto was resurrected yet again in films like *Angel Heart* and *Mona Lisa,* where she appears as the predictably tortured exotic. In the nineties she has been less of a cipher and more of a player in the likes of *One False Move* and *The Crying Game.* Though now front and center to the narrative, the character remains true to blueprint —a lost child. She no longer seeks to pass, yet she still hasn't found a home.

Apart from being such a throwback, there's a reason why *Queen* is still squatting in my psyche. It's a paragon of the lessons the mulatto and her tragedy oblige and why America clings to her so dearly:

Miss Tragedy is the morbid personification of integration. Those raging bloods of hers will explode one day, as will America's if it keeps mixing up bloodlines. Mono-race communities are the only place to find love and shelter. Don't cross the tracks.

The mulatto's alienation is ultimately her own psychological illness—neither socially constructed nor shared—and she should bear it in silence. Or, in the case of the latter-day pop mulattoes, she must market it as a fable of caution, like the warning label on a pack of cigarettes.

Miscegenation is still black folks' problem, best dealt with across the tracks and behind closed doors. While Queen ends up in the loony bin, rejected by her slave-owning family, the whites never suffer a moment of remorse. Far from addressing miscegenation with any new complexity, *Queen* did the usual and let white folks off the hook. Like satisfied johns, they're allowed to put their jays back in their pants and sneak back to the big house. The "stain" remains within black folks.

Tragic mulatto has two choices: get black or die. And her redemption—because all this is really her own fault for daring to be born—is only possible when she admits she's a Negro (which, in *Queen,* is like owning up to your codependency). Queen doesn't decide who she is in any way that embraces African-American culture, or even her African and Irish roots. She accepts where she belongs—which is vastly different. Her sense of self is not truly addressed, just society's pressure.

If you dig deep beneath the melodrama and the psychosis, the tragic mulatto on film has been a tangled metaphor of black resistance. The dissatisfying thing, at least on the symbolic tip, about her being "returned" to the black community, as she is in *Queen* and most of the other narratives, is she is stripped of her rebel spirit. She loses her power to rock the racial boat, to question race-based class hierarchy, to expose both the white and black world's creole underbelly. And like any other po' plantation chile, she's left singing what Michele Wallace calls the invisibility blues.

How do you like me now? I could be heroine, I could be healer. I talk back. I refuse complicity with any of you if I can't speak the truth that is mine. On my body is inscribed the future. I'll keep my hands around your throat until you claim me. I am yours. I am yours. I am.

1993

is biracial enough? (or, what's this about a multiracial category on the census?: a conversation)*

Who are you, what are you, where are you from, no, where are you really from, where are your parents from, are your grandparents Americans? Are you from here, what's your background, what's your nationality, where do you live? Are you black, are you white, do you speak Spanish? Are you really white, are you really black? Are you Puerto Rican, are you half and half, are you biracial, multiracial, interracial, transracial, racially unknown, race neutral, colorless, colorblind, down with the rat race

* This was a speech given to "Common Differences," a conference of interracial student groups sponsored by Wesleyan Interracial Pride (I-Pride) and held at Wesleyan University in May 1993.

or the human race? Who are you? Where are you coming from? Who are your people?

THE IDENTITY FAIRY: Excuse me, before you get all up in my business, don't you want to know my name?

Should we keep it simple or run the extended-play version? I hail from the Afro-rainbow tribe. Papa's black by way of Newark and South Carolina, Mom's Jewish by way of Brooklyn and Eastern Europe. Ethnically I'm African American. Politically I'm a person of color. My résumé: Womanist-theater producing circa the eighties; day jobbing at an alternative newspaper, looking to define the role of race woman in the multiculti nineties. My faith is strictly rhythm and blues. Still hung up on soul music, poetry and jazz, sixties girl groups. Air guitar to the Isley Brothers and Living Colour. Marley heals my soul. Al Green and Sting wake me up in the morning. I go to Aretha and Joni Mitchell when I need to cry.

I know a Panamanian-American computer technician who is deep brown as a Senegalese and ethnically Latino. He speaks Spanish and Brooklyn-Italian blue-collar English. Ask him what he is, he'll tell you black Hispanic. I know a Caribbean-American architect who has lived on three continents, calls soccer football, and has a white great-grandfather and a Chinese great-grandfather, though he himself is gingerbread brown. This guy is from Grenada originally, though he identifies politically as African American. I also know a music promoter, black, who was raised by his mother, Jewish, in the suburbs of San Francisco. But from the way this guy swaggers and curses you'd think he was gangsta straight out of Compton. Trust me, all three guys are cute.

Say I marry one of these guys, will our children be multiracial, multiethnic, African American, black, people of color? Will they be called "niggers," "cocos," or "spics"? Will they live in an America where race, as Cornel West reports, still matters? Will they live in a war zone like Bosnia, where ethnicity, culture, and religion still matter? Or will AIDS and toxic waste cut their lives short before they can begin their pontificating, philosophizing, awfulizing, agonizing, rejoicing, preachifying, and signifying over just who they are in this shaky home we call the Americas?

Last night I had dinner with a group of friends who are Asian, Latino, and African American, and combinations of the above mixed with European. I love us dearly. We take David Dinkins's gorgeous mosaic quite literally and we aren't alone. We value the ethnic histories, rituals, stories passed down to us from our families of origin, from our families of choice, and from our book learning. We swap these traditions, make up new ones. At home, we identify each other by turf: Peter is Miss Mott Street, I'm Miss Bowery, Miss Dorado Beach is Maria. Yet we'd probably be more comfortable with the public monikers black, Latino, or Asian, than with "biracial" or "multiracial."

Most of us just hit the big three-oh. We saw the sixties as grade-school kids. We memorized TV pictures of dogs sicced on black folks in Mississippi and stories our grandparents told of Japanese internment camps out West. We can tell you about the years before English-as-a-second-language programs, when little girls like María, Margie, and Gladys were thrown into English-only classrooms and left to sink or tread water. We got to Ivy League colleges thanks to affirmative action programs. Corporate America hired us under diversity initiatives.

The idea of a "multiracial" category on the census fills us with ambivalence. Is this just one more polite, largely academic game of identity hopscotch folks are playing while Los Angeles burns? Still, we're keeping our ears open.

What do you know about the groups that are behind this census movement? Are they a multiracial, interracial Mafia? Biracial Rambos and contras? Are they white parents of mixed-race bambinos bartering for a safety zone for their café-au-lait kids? Or are they regular folks searching for a new way to identify their families?

THE IDENTITY FAIRY: This is what I know so far. There's the Association of MultiEthnic Americans (AMEA), a nationwide confedera-

56

tion of interracial/multiethnic support groups based in San Francisco. And there's Project RACE (short for Reclassify All Children Equally), a lobbying organization out of Atlanta that campaigns on the local level. As of May 1993, due to the labors of Project RACE, three states have passed and two are reviewing legislation that adds the category "multiracial" to school forms.

AMEA and Project RACE are at the forefront of the census movement. This June these groups and several others will converge on Washington at hearings before a subcommittee on the census. If their efforts pay off, "multiracial" will replace "other race" on census forms in the year 2000. What this will mean, no one's sure. Could there be a massive flight from the categories Hispanic and black? Will the 9.8 million Americans who checked "other race" in 1990 switch over without a hitch to "multiracial"? By the turn of the new century, will the numbers in the "other race," now "multiracial" category, have multiplied dramatically? Will America have become the brown stew pot that *Time* and *Newsweek* have been warning us about since the mid eighties? And call them black, multiracial, or Hispanic (another ethnic appellation concocted by politics), will the majority of these brown ones still be poor folks? Or might all Americans check "multiracial," finally recognizing their heritage for what it is?

Give us your off-the-cuff take on this census movement.

THE IDENTITY FAIRY: I haven't been to any meetings, but I did speak at length with several organizers and foot soldiers, including, among others, Carlos Fernandez, president of AMEA, Susan Graham, executive director of Project RACE, Kendra Wallace, Project's vice president in California, and Michelle Erickson of Chicago. Erickson pulled her five-year-old son out of the public school system rather than choose between existing racial categories. (She identifies Andrew, her son, as biracial.) Instigated by Erickson's letter-writing campaign and the lobbying of Project RACE, the state of Illinois is now considering the "multiracial" category.

Many in the census movement see the bottom line of their

crusade as a fight for the self-esteem of their children. Graham of Project RACE, who is a white mother of two, as she calls them, "multiracial kids," says children are psychologically healthiest when they have accurate racial labels at their disposal. But what on earth constitutes an accurate racial label? And if the census movement is ultimately out to do away with such sacrosanct labels, will creating new ones accomplish this?

Beyond the children's self-esteem issue, the movement's larger agenda and philosophical goals registered blurry. Race is configured as choice, as a category on a school form. Race is not seen as a political/economic construct, a battleground where Americans vie for power and turf, but a question of color, a stick-on, peel-off label. If there *is* an end goal to the census movement's efforts, it appears to be assimilation. I don't mean this in the didactic sense of chiding others for wanting their piece of American pie; I mean it as finding a place to fit in, creating a space of comfort for self, away from the choke hold of race. The business as usual of discrimination, against the have-nots, who are usually shades of brown, and in favor of the have-sos, who are usually shades of pink, is left undisturbed.

When I heard that all state legislation for school forms would remain symbolic until the Congress and the Office of Management and Budget vote to add multiracial to the list of official categories, I scratched my head. And when I heard that the activists couldn't agree on whether those who checked the "multiracial" box would be considered a disadvantaged minority deserving of federal protections under the Voting Rights Act, I scratched some more. Why was this movement—potentially a vital movement for the acknowledgment of hybrid cultures/lives—being tied to a kite that no one could steer?

Do you have other concerns about the census movement?

THE IDENTITY FAIRY: Let's look at a few:

Is race (and racism) left intact? Instead of fighting for a new racial category, if the end goal is, as census activists say, to do away with the biological pseudoscience of race, why aren't they in the trenches casting stones at institutional racism? Anna Deavere Smith's *Fires in the Mirror* quotes an interview the playwright did with Angela Davis. Davis says she feels tentative about the meaning of race these days, but not tentative at all about racism. People of color, whether they call themselves biracial, Swirls (as they do in Fostorio, Ohio), or zebra Americans, are disproportionately members of America's underclass. Here's a meaningful contrast: Ohio became the first state last year to adopt the multiracial category on school forms. This year, Ohio saw a bloody uprising at the Lucasville state prison. Almost 60 percent of prisoners there are black men, though African Americans make up barely one quarter of the state's population. Will the symbolic recognition of multiracial identity reverse numbers like these?

I was struck that the census movement had no alliances with progressive organizations representing other people of color. None of these organizations had staged a teach-in or protested over the miscarriage of justice in the Rodney King case. Was biraciality being constructed as a less progressive stance than identifying as a "person of color," that catchphrase invented in the eighteenth century, then popularized in the seventies, as an expression of solidarity with other p.o.c.s worldwide?

Cape Town, U.S.A.? It's been asked before, and until I hear a good comeback, the question stands: Would "multiracial" be akin to South Africa's "colored" caste created under apartheid? Carlos Fernandez of AMEA believes that an "in-between" racial category isn't racist in itself, it is how such a category is used. Yet why wouldn't multiracial/colored by mythologized or positioned politically any differently in America?

Are we special? The census movement and its "interracial/biracial nationalists," as I refer to them playfully, claim biraciality as a mark of "racial" singularity, one that in America (where most racial groups are multiethnic and multicultural) has little grounding. Their insistence on biraciality's unique status borders on elitism. They marvel at the perks of biraciality: That biracials have several cultures at their disposal. (Though don't we all as Americans?) They say things like "biracial people are free of bias because they embody both black and white." Can you fight essentialism with essentialism? Are we to believe that all biracials are chosen people, free of prejudice, self-interest, and Republican Christian fundamentalism?

By proclaiming specialness aren't biracials still clinging to the niche of exotic other? "How could we not love them, they're so cute," boasted one white mother active in the census movement of her biracial children. Minus butter-pecan skin and Shirley Temple curls would they be less of an attractive proposition?

The nationalist vibe. The writer Kristal Brent-Zook calls nationalism a search for home, for family, and for sameness. Young movements of any kind are prone to nationalism, yet it's hard to forgive the biracialists for indulging. A large part of why they disassociate themselves from traditional ethnic communities is just *because* of their hybridity, their lack of purity.

Is there now to be a biracial party line to tow and a biracial lifestyle to upkeep? *Interrace,* a magazine chronicling the census movement and interracial and biracial social life, called the actress Halle Berry's choice *not* to marry interracially a "cop-out." (One guesses they made this judgment about the race of Berry's husband, baseball star David Justice, based on photographs. A few issues later, when *Interrace* found out that Justice happened to be "Afro-European," they laid out the biracial carpet.) Are those of us who marry the same, "mono-race" partners now retro, antiprogressive? Have the interracial/biracial police determined that the only way to change the world is to breed a "new race?" "Like it or not," read a letter to *Spectrum,* the newsletter published by Multiracial Americans of Southern California (MASC), "racially mixed people are the most beautiful people of all." The new Stepford people.

What's history got to do with it? As black/white biracials, when we distance ourselves from the African-American freedom struggle, from aging, though historically critical, ideas like "black power" and "black community," do we fail to honor a history that brought us to where we are today? Is biraciality political sedition? And if it feels that way, and it shouldn't, how can we make it feel less so? Are there ways to be responsible to a history that we are indebted to without being imprisoned by it?

I found the generalizations the census movers made about African Americans disturbing. Resistance from some blacks to the multiracial category was translated into resistance from the entire African-American population. Aren't some of the parents involved in the census movement African Americans? The bills to add the "multiracial" category on the state level have all been introduced by African-American legislators. The census initiative has garnered support from local chapters of the NAACP. *Essence* magazine and other black publications spread the word about AMEA and fellow interracial groups long before their white counterparts.

To say that biracials have been cold-shouldered by African-Americans throughout history, as some activists suggested, is selective ignorance. Black communities have always been shelter to multiethnic people, perhaps not an unproblematic shelter, yet a shelter nonetheless. Black folks, I'd venture, have welcomed difference in their communities more than most Americans.

Nothing but a photo-op? Watching biraciality gobbled up so eagerly on the Donahue and Oprah circuit makes me pause. If it weren't such a fashionable and marketable identity these days would so many folks be riding the bandwagon? (And like the hip-hop club, media darlings of the late eighties, the biracial lobby comes across on television as having have no agenda other than its own pride politics.)

Are biracial people being offered up as the latest market ripe for exploitation? *Interrace* magazine sells T-shirts inscribed with Webster's definition of biracial. The ads urge buyers to "Wear the Right Thing" or to "end racism . . . advertise in *Interrace.*" *New People: The Journal for the Human Race* hawks ceramic wedding figurines in your choice of complexions. Not unlike trade or hobby magazines, both publications look at the world through one prism: biracialism.

Are we family? Shouldn't we ask what makes biracial people a community? What holds us together other than a perceived sense of our own difference from the ethnic mainstream? Consider if the Mexican-Samoan kid in San Diego has the same needs as the black-Jewish kid from New York's Upper West Side? Maybe politically as people of color, but do they share a definitive mixed-race culture? And if they do, should we call it "biraciality" or should we call it "American culture"?

Does blackness remain a stigma? As my telephone travels made clear, the census camp is not minus attitudes of: "If you had a choice you'd be anything but black." Biraciality was posited by some as an escape from the "blemish of blackness." Chicago mother Michelle Erickson asked me quite innocently if I knew how de-grading it was "to be attached to categories like black or Hispanic." Kendra Wallace, a biracial woman in her early twenties, pro-nounced rules of membership in the black community to be too stiff —based, she feels, on such criteria as "hair texture and whether one speaks proper English or not." (Is African-American diversity still that invisible to the world? One could have come away with a picture far more complex by watching a week's worth of sitcoms.)

A moment of cruel and unusual irony took place in a conversa-tion with Project RACE's Susan Graham. During Black History Month, Graham's son returned home with some materials on Lang-ston Hughes. Graham was disappointed that the school had failed to focus on "Langston Hughes's biraciality." I reminded Graham that African Americans as a whole were a multiethnic and multiracial folk, and that Hughes never hid the fact that he had white family, yet he "cast his lot," as the expression went back then, with his darker kin. Hughes's writing, one can safely say, celebrates, if not romanticizes African-American culture. Graham seemed irritated. The one-drop rule was the only thing that kept him in the black community, she insisted. If Hughes were alive today, he would choose to be multiracial, he would identify first with mixed-race people and the work of her lobbying group.

People of all races and cultures should feel free to claim Hughes as an idol, but wasn't Graham aware of a rather painful history? One where black people have had their every gift confiscated and attributed to others? Would this now happen in the name of multiracialism?

Seems like you've exhausted the critical tip. Did you happen upon anything constructive in your telephone encounters with the biracial movement?

THE IDENTITY FAIRY: Carlos Fernandez said something that made sense. Official recognition of multiracial identity may not end racism; it is, however, a necessary step. If we refuse to recognize that any material reality exists between black and white, we do nothing except enshrine these social boundaries—and enshrine the political divide that upholds them.

Certainly the daguerreotype of mixed-race people as freaks of nature could use a long overdue slashing. If the biracial lobby can help in this regard, bless them. Says Kendra Wallace: "We're invisible or our identities are always problematized and sexualized." Our "bloods" are at war inside of us. If mixed race were made normal, we could look forward to the comic mulatto, the introspective, the slovenly. We might one day come to miss ye olde tragic mulatto, the world's pet mule.

As much as I found myself resisting the biracial nationalists, to deny a group the right to identify as they wish to seems equally reactionary. In October last year the San Diego Unified School District, known for its conservatism, balked at admitting a little boy to grammar school until his mother, Patricia Whitebread, who is black, assigned him an "appropriate race." (Unlike many school forms nationally, San Diego's has no "other" designation.) Whitebread refused. The school district admitted the child anyway. Later the district classified her son as black without Whitebread's permission.

The activists I spoke to framed their cause as a civil rights movement. Perhaps one not as transparently vital as a movement for equal opportunity in employment or fair access to housing, but certainly one consummate with religious freedom or freedom of expression. In *Interrace,* psychologist Francis Wardle, director of the Center for the Study of Biracial Children, a clearinghouse in Colorado, makes a passionate appeal for interracial family networks not to been seen as a threat to African Americans:

"We are so aware of the need to improve conditions for so many blacks in this country that we are very puzzled some high profile blacks spend time and energy fighting us.

"We are not the enemy. . . . Don't insist we must raise our children to belong to a distinctive (and arbitrary) racial or ethnic category. Don't say that history and society must define who we are and what we want our children to become."

Perhaps the arrival of the biracialists might finally drive home to traditional ethnic communities the need for more proactive coalition politics. Kendra Wallace thought biracial organizing would allow people to leave racial enclaves, build bridges, and in time, return. In the lore of the passing novels, those who "passed for white" (or in this case "stood for colored") always found their way back to the black hearth. Of course the black hearth, as we approach the twenty-first century is more fragmented and scattered than ever.

At the dinner table last night we gathered, not to discuss the dainties of identity politics and the census, but to remember a close friend who died a year ago from AIDS. I could tell you that AIDS is an equal opportunity killer and I'd be telling the truth. I could also tell you that more and more of those who die from AIDS are people of color; that would be true too. This speaks reams about race and the very real equation of power, poverty, and privilege.

I like to think of Eduardo Mejia, the friend we lost, as a multiculturalist and global citizen cut from the cloth of a W. E. B Du Bois. To Eddie, unlike Kendra Wallace, *black* embraced every ethnic community that wished to claim it (a belief he shared with the Pan-Africanists of the sixties and the British Asian-Caribbean-African coalitions of the seventies). Would it surprise you that Eddie was a fair-complexioned Puerto Rican? A gay man and nurse, "the Queen," as we called him, was a street-shrewd philosopher who studied race all his life. He identified as a black, as a person of color, as Latino, as Puerto Rican, as a New Yorker. No one identity canceled out the other. Knowing Eddie, "biracial" would have been a label either too precious or sterile. He would have told you in one breath that he was "a Puerto Rican from a Haitian block in Brooklyn, who stands for gay rights and the freedom struggles of people of color around the world" before he would describe himself as biracial. It wouldn't have been fierce enough, specific enough, or ultimately progressive enough for Eddie in his day. But that would've been Eddie's choice; you may decide otherwise. Eddie, I'm sure, would have loved you and claimed you just the same.

What's your idea of art and scholarship that politicizes multiracialism?

THE IDENTITY FAIRY: Certainly the visual art and writings of Adrian Piper provides keen example. Piper works genius at demystifying the political economy of what she tags "racial classification." Her call to American whites to face up to their black heritage (and to blacks to do the reverse) takes multiracialism/multiculturalism beyond politically correct arts programming and into the realm of configuring a new American identity.

The work of writers and media artists Guillermo Gómez-Peña and Coco Fusco also stands out. In her contribution to the anthology *Black Popular Culture* Fusco tells us that in Cuba, where the black people in her family come from, there's an expression that goes *"Chivo que rompe tambor con su pellejo paga,"* which translates literally, "The goat who breaks the drum will have to pay with his skin." The phrase has another meaning as well: "The troublemaker turns him- or herself into the instrument to continue the music." Fusco argues that "black popular cultures, especially musical cultures, have generated an abundance of archetypes that embrace dissonance and contend with internal difference; these [are] semantic residues of histories of contradiction and conflict. Maybe one of these days our intellectual debate will catch up with our popular cultural ability to engage dissent, without the defensiveness that continuously rears its head."

Gómez-Peña's work takes on America in the "intercultural crisis." Writes critic Richard Schechner: "Interculturalists [such as Gómez-Peña] refuse utopian schemes, refuse to cloak power arrangements and struggles. Instead, interculturalists probe the confrontations, ambivalences, disruptions, fears, disturbances, and difficulties when and where cultures collide, overlap or pull away from each other. Interculturalists explore misunderstandings, broken messages, and failed translations—what is not pure and what cannot successfully fuse. These are seen not as disasters, but as fertile rifts of creative possibilities."

Any last words of advice to those swimming in the identity pool?

THE IDENTITY FAIRY: As you get older, chances are you will define yourself by your alliances with a multitude of communities. No one community will speak for you completely and no one community should be so static as to not let you share in others.

As for the biracial nationalists and their movement: Check them out, debate them, start your own. Don't accept any position—be it biracial/multiracial/interracial/African/Asian/or Latin American—as a political catchall.

Challenge all your communities to live up to you. The late poet Audre Lorde, African American, Caribbean American, feminist, gay, and supporter of the global causes of people of color, always spoke as a member of all her many homes.

In coming to self, balance individual identity with a responsibility to and critical eye on history. I'll never forget visiting the Afro-American Cultural Center at Yale as a prefreshman. I wandered around the building looking at the posters and murals, remnants of the late sixties, of the days when black students were admitted to mainstream universities in sizable numbers, of student protest for admission and retention initiatives, of sit-ins for ethnic studies departments. Alone, I walked the rooms of the House, as we call it, and felt the spirits of those students. A priceless moral and intellectual inheritance was being passed to me. On the train back home, I wept all kinds of tears: angry tears, tears of pride, gratitude tears. Later I would move away from the House and find other homes, but I always took the House and that inheritance with me.

Welcome to America. It ain't as airbrushed as a Benetton ad, but it's a happening place. Hope you brought your Rollerblades *and* your Air Jordans.

two

bring the
heroines

bring the heroines

Wanted: Women, single, married, with kids/without, lovers of men, lovers of women, generous hips and butts preferred; to lead housing rights movements, voter registration drives; to be inventors, blues legends, moguls, vigilantes, soothsayers, mystics. Hair not an issue. Method actors or naturals okay. Call immediately for a screen test.

Film and TV may have taught us a black heroine ain't nothing but a sandwich; still, we hope on. Picture our anticipation last month when the previews for *Stompin' at the Savoy* hit the decks. Rare—monumental even—

for the lives of black women, four in this case, to make prime-time, network viewing. A "motion picture for television" (ooh, just the sound of that evokes progress). Set in Depression-era Harlem. And, yes, the women were, you guessed, domestics, but we deserved a catch: life outside of Missy Anne's hot kitchen.

We holed up in front of tubes across the nation, with our combs and hair pomade, our bottles of Clearly Canadian, our checkbooks to balance, our knitting. All's aglow at first. A luscious cornucopia of skin tones from stars Lynn Whitfield, Vanessa Williams, Jasmine Guy, Vanessa Bell Calloway. Nice camera choreography from director Debbie Allen in the opening scene. Nice acting from Jasmine Guy in a speech that plays against the tragi-mulatress type. Nice near minstrelsy when Allen, doing a cameo as an "attitudinous" prostitute, is threatened by Whitfield brandishing sizzling curling iron. Nice, nice, nice for television.

Then the ending—and our defeat. Guy finds herself a fine yet poor black man, only to drop dead soon after from tuberculosis. Calloway gets her own pad downtown and a white lover; then he ditches camp and she goes crazy. Williams, an aspiring singer, loses her nightclub-owner sugar daddy to Whitfield and is reduced to gigging at pit stops in Jersey. Whitfield, the most driven, sees all her material dreams come true, yet is left alone. So we sit back, once again, and wonder when black girls on screen are gonna get something other than a bum deal on life. (Excuse us, 'cause we got the sassy-catty-black-women-alone-again blues.) Whitfield is warned: "You want too much and you're gonna be disappointed when you don't get it." And, by hook and crook she gets it all, except she ain't happy. Nothing like a fashionable postfeminist coda.

Savoy fits a trend: pop images that depict black women's ambition as solely materialistic and ill serving the community. We've seen it in the "boyz" movies. Professional women—a/k/a working women—are too busy to raise kids right, says *Boyz 'N' the Hood.* The selfish, scheming buppie chicks of *Strictly Business* lose their empathy for black men, along with their "soul," in bed. A neat companion legend was at work in the vilification of Anita Hill: Flash cards provided by Clarence Thomas crony John Doggett III at the hearing drew Hill and black professional women like her as desperate lunatics who live that *Fatal Attraction* life.

So we hear that success will turn you bitch, turn you antimale/family/race, turn you crazy, turn you *white.* Quite a fallacy if you crack some history books. Black women's ambition, I'd wage, has been linked primarily to community uplift. Look at all the social workers, teachers, antilynch campaigners, antipoverty workers, the church activists. The field hands of every black political movement, the editors and typists of every black arts movement. Now suck some teeth.

In the world of *Stompin' at the Savoy* even sisterhood is bankrupt. Whitfield is left not just without a man, but sans friends. Williams goes back to distrusting women after Whitfield shimmies away with her man. And only after the fact do the girls find out Guy caught TB and was buried a pauper. Director Julie Dash said once that she sees no reason to make films about black women hating each other. It wouldn't involve any tasty dramatic risks for her as an artist and intellectual. Others have done so well with backbiting she-devils, why impose?

Watching *Savoy* brought back shades of *Mahogany,* the Diana Ross–fest of 1975, directed by Berry Gordy. La Ross stars as a fashion model/designer who risks losing her man—and her Black Card—by frolicking as the glamorous Negress in Europe. *Mahogany* is out on video now, and recently I found myself at a brunch where it was playing on a big-screen TV as a stylishly retro background visual. The whole room groaned when Bille Dee delivered the film's famous line: "Success is nothing without someone you love to share it with." Another struggling woman artist and I were loudest; nervous perhaps, deep down, that we'd be gagged one day with the same scenario. *Mahogany* ends with Ross running home to Chicago and Billy Dee the grass-roots politician. (But not without that white mink coat.) Not retro at all, so it seems. Almost twenty years later, *Savoy* tugs the same motto: Nothing you will ever do matches what a man—very specifically a black man—can bring to your life. In this day and age, art that tells us the only solution is a good man is way simplistic, detached from our lives, and plain lazy. As for many of us—by choice or the numbers game—this is not an option, nor should it be a requirement.

I know a successful art dealer in her late twenties who admits to being a closet cult fan of *Mahogany;* she owns two video copies and the soundtrack. Dana's middle-class parents wouldn't allow her to see blaxploitation-era films. They made the exception for *Mahogany,* since it featured that cinema rarity, a glamorous black woman who wasn't a prostitute. Never before, says Dana, did a brown-skinned woman have so many costume changes. Though now she has a problem with the moral, that a woman's success happens at the expense of a man, Dana often crawls into bed and loses herself in the film on a PMS day. In what other movie can Dana see a black female character travel around the world, start her own business, and never wear an apron? When it comes to black women on-screen, *Mahogany* is still better than most. The pickings continue to be that slim.

Panning *Savoy* was not my assignment here. It's encouraging that the gigs went to director Debbie Allen and screenwriter Beverly Sawyer. The piece actually helped me clear up some thoughts on how art functions in my own life. Not fond of the rigid "positive-image" approach, I still crave heroines. In art and fantasy I want to win. I want power, even as I ride off a cliff. I want art to show me what I can do, not what I can't. And I don't want to waste seven bucks to be told that my tragic flaw is that I am a woman, I am black, and I have expectations. I can get that in the street for free.

1992

venus envy

I take butts very seriously. And butt theory too—from actress/comedian Phyllis Stickney ("Power of the Boo-tay") to Audre Lorde ("Uses of the Erotic: The Erotic as Power," her manifesto on pleasure and black female agency). So seriously, that a few weeks back I was roused, for the first time, to express my two cents via the *Voice*'s letters page. But one sarcastic little stab at fashion writer Anka Radakovich—for pitching girdles to those of us who are cursed, she feels, with "bulbous rear end[s]" and "big ol' butt[s]"—wasn't enough. Radako-vich's butt baiting needs to be "read," as we say in the vernacular, some more.

More interesting than Radakovich's history-blind tribute to a girdle's ability to "flatten your fanny" was the juxtaposition of her piece with an ad for padded underwear that appeared on the following page. No more "flat, sagging" buns, the ad promised; these briefs can simulate what "nature may have neglected." Here stands another example of the Eurocentric aesthetic's attraction/repulsion to the buttocks. (Ooh, says Freud, look at those tushes; females are more anally inclined, more, yikes, primitive!)

A veritable butt revolution has swept America in the last two decades—brought to you by black music, designer jeans, and MTV. (Once you've seen Janet Jackson gyrate to "Black Cat" can you really go back to Twiggy?) Could it be the rump is edging out legs and boobs as the preferred female fetish commodity in the eye view of mainstream white culture? Butts, yes, but just a champagne-glass full, *s'il vous plaît*. Listen to the alarms that sound right before swimsuit season: Butt alert, hide those heinies! (Even in a hotbed of correct sexual politics like the *Voice*, large derrieres have been likened to cows' asses.) What's all the hullabaloo? Fear of the big black butt?

A recent spread in *Elle* caught my eye (and those of a few male friends who announced benevolently that they had discovered, at long last, "the butt of life"). Most black models you see in *Vogue* and *Elle* et al. have pouty, little, pocket-size booties not much different from their Caucasian sistren, or if they do have some butt, it's not featured. Enter sixteen-year-old Beverly Peele, dashing solo around an eight-page layout styled like an English country garden. (My, times have changed, no chain-mail midriff, no bone through her nose?) In one drop-dead photo she stands, in profile, clutching flowers to her breast; a beaded jacket rises above her waist, exposing gently poked-out belly, arched back, and skimpy bikini thong. All eyes are led to her near-nude rump, which really *is* taking no prisoners. Breathtakingly endowed, Peele's cheeks seem to stretch horizontally for more than a foot. Hers is what's known as a "high butt," an outie, a shelf, and she wears it with an expression that mixes solemn pride and innocence.

In profile. Mmmm. Haven't I seen this image before, another time, another place? In an anthropological textbook, maybe, as an illustration for an ideologically charged concept known as "steatopygia." Webster's calls it "an excessive development of fat on the buttocks esp. of females that is common among the Hottentots and some Negro peoples." Mercenary scientists and cultural theorists, whose fascination with the trait dates back to when Europeans first hit the shores of southwest Africa, called it "abnormal," "genetically base," "malformed." Nineteenth-century etchings of Hottentot women were rendered in a style that's purposely cartoonish—as if the subjects were she-devils, Loch Ness monsters, missing links. There's a sense of alchemy at work, stretching truth for profit.

Isn't Peele lucky to be a young black woman posing for a fashion spread in America circa 1991—while Negro bodies and self-expression are in vogue, marketable, and represent some vague notion of visual equality, in lieu of political and economic power? With a resplendent derriere like hers, in another era, Peele could have been the legendary Hottentot Venus herself: the twenty-five-year-old woman from the Cape of Africa, known in Dutch as "Saartjie" (little Sarah), who in 1810 was exhibited naked in a cage in London and Paris. When Saartjie died five years later she was the subject of a famous dissection that was used to support almost a century's worth of myths of white racial superiority. Today you can find the revered "Hottentot apron" (her pendulous labia minora) in Paris's Musée de l'Homme. Her genitalia float in a jar of formaldehyde, a shelf above Broca's brain. In a country where we can crown three black Miss Americas but almost fail to pass a civil rights bill, perhaps Peele is the Venus's twentieth-century incarnation.

The Hottentot Venus became the dominant icon of black femininity in the nineteenth century, reduced in the European imagination to her two sexual "attractions"—butt and apron. (And her disembodied buttocks live on. Peek at the album cover photo of 2 Live Crew's *Me So Horny*—black women don't have faces or souls, just big ol' butts.) Representing sexual deviation and disease (the Hottentot apron was compared to the syphilitic vaginas of European

prostitutes), she was an allegorical deterrent to the Continent's rising tide of miscegenation. Maintaining this notion of the black female sexual "other" became crucial to doctrines of racial purity in
both Europe and the antebellum South. Fear of big black dick?
Public Enemy and others want to keep this bit of race lore fresh in
our minds, but what about fear of big black ass? Wasn't the rape of
African women during slavery a form of castration, of conquering
the "sexual beast"?

Among the young African-American womanist intelligentsia,
the Hottentot Venus is being resurrected as a cause célèbre and
bestowed with a Frida Kahlo–like martyrdom. Last year visual artist
Renée Green did an installation at Clocktower Gallery in New York
based on Saartjie's story. (Observers were invited to stand on a
platform and be displayed.) Patricia Hill Collins's *Black Feminist
Thought* (1990) argues that the treatment of black women's bodies
in nineteenth-century Europe and America (a most chilling example being the Hottentot Venus) became the blueprint for contemporary pornography's objectification and dismemberment of women's
bodies.

The title poem of Philadelphia-based writer Elizabeth Alexander's first poetry collection, *The Venus Hottentot* (1990), begins with
the voice of Georges Cuvier, the man who dissected the Venus
("Science, science, science/Everything is beautiful/blown up beneath my glass"), then segues to Saartjie's ("Since my own genitals
are public/I have made other parts private"). Not only does this
Venus have a point of view, but Alexander as the modern black
woman artist/translator holds court, navigating through these two
versions of history. As horrific and oppressive a symbol as the Hottentot Venus became under Cuvier's knife, she is now reclaimed
and offered as an homage to black female resistance. When I called
Alexander recently to talk shop, she told me that legend has it that
the African women exhibited as Hottentot Venuses—there were
many—were the inspiration for the bustle. (*Fairchild's Dictionary of
Fashion* tracks down the bustle to 1830, just fifteen years after
Saartjie's death. Could be!) Alexander says the legend rings true to

her: "That which you are obsessed with, that you are afraid of, that you have to destroy, is the thing that you want more than anything. Black culture has been expropriated in this manner for centuries. Those who have expropriated it have utter contempt and disregard for the people who represent this culture. Detached from those who inspired it, culture is siphoned off as 'style.' I daresay European women walking around in bustles weren't thinking about the Hottentot Venus, just as American women in 'Bo Derek braids' weren't thinking about cornrows."

1991

gold digging
the skeezers

A young woman we know writes:

There was a time in my life when I too derived power
from using my body to manipulate men. This was in
the late seventies, a few years before the second
coming of the miniskirt, when being naked in public
still meant something. Nowadays, it's just one big
meat market out there. Even on TV, a tit here, some
ass there, nothing registers on the Richter scale. I
blame crack. In the crack ecosystem, women's bodies are the lowest commodity. You can try to make a
cute statement like Madonna and walk outside in

your bra and panties, but the irony will be lost on the guy who offers you a dollar for a blowjob. Every day I'm surrounded by hateful images of women and hateful language—*gold diggers, skeezers* (women who screw for status), crack hoes (women who screw for a fix). Is it my imagination or are women playing along with it? I mean, has anyone stood up and said this devaluation of our bodies and our humanity has got to stop? No, we just get on "The Party Machine" with Nia Peeples and gyrate to the beat. I'm a feminist, or a womanist, or pro-woman whatever, but I swear, I'm about to borrow an Uzi from my neighbor the crack dealer and shoot the next traitor I see in a Lycra mini. Surely this is misplaced anger. Can you help?

First of all, don't annihilate any innocent young black women—AIDS and teen pregnancy are doing that work for you. You're right about one thing: These images are everywhere. They reign in hip-hop, which brought us the word "skeezer." In the tabloid circuit, if it isn't Sandra Miller Reese called a gold digger for pressing charges against Mike Tyson for fondling her in a club, it's Vicki R. Long, called a skeezer for bedding an archbishop. You'll even find them in that cutting edge of creativity—black cinema: not just in a newfangled *Superfly* flick like *New Jack City* (where a skeezer named Uniqua gets between the brothers), but in a family movie like *Five Heartbeats* (where a skeezer named Tanya gets between the brothers).

The woman-as-gold-digger image is as old as the hills. The *Oxford English Dictionary*'s first reference is this from 1920: women who "dig for the gold of their gentlemen friends and spend it on being good to their mothers and their pet dogs." By way of rap etymology, skeezer comes from the verb *to skeeze* (to fornicate; particularly a rap entourage with groupies on the road). An early cite would be UTFO's single "Skeezer Pleaser" from 1987. In the concert film *Raw*, also 1987, Murphy's paranoia about crafty American dames and "bush bitch[es]" taking half of his empire became a standard for nouveau-riche hip-hop's depiction of women. And if a clothes hanger–abortionist gangsta rapper like Ice Cube weren't enough to stop the stream of women trying to stymie men with sex, we now have male-produced female decoys like H.W.A. (Hoes Wit Attitude) and B.W.P. (Bytches With Problems) to pass off bite-the-bullet negativity as empowerment theory.

As a black woman, you may be particularly sensitive to the skeezer image and not know why. This might have something to do with its affinity to another age-old stereotype, the black female as Jezebel, the sexually loose and aggressive figure who justified rape by white men during slavery. Later this delightful image was transmuted into the parasitic welfare mother (who feeds on the system) and, finally, the skeezer/gold digger (who feeds on brothers with bank). What might make the skeezer an even more painful thorn in your side is that, unlike its forerunners, this type is manufactured primarily by black men. And just as Coco Fusco questions whether *Mambo Mouth*'s John Leguizamo is "Broadway's latest primitive . . . stomping verbally on the women he shares an ethnicity with" for ticket sales, one wonders too whether the misogyny so rampant in skeezer imagery and black male pop product in general is also a kind of primitivism milked for consumption by the white mainstream. (The pop success of records like N.W.A.'s new offering of gangsta rap—featuring such beauties as "One Less Bitch" and "To Kill a Hooker"—is one of many clear signs that the market for this music is larger than just young black men.)

When you dig behind the skeezer/gold digger character you find a storehouse of male fear and insecurity. Men deal with women they can "buy" presumably so they can control them, though when "bought women" exploit the situation, men, caught in the logic of their own game, cry victim. Music videos that feature skeezers are more successful as portraits of male ineptitude than paeans to machismo. EPMD's "Gold Digger" begins with the rappers in a group therapy session with a white shrink. Later the guys twiddle their thumbs while axe-toting women, spray-painted in gold, work the EPMD gold mine.

A typical defense of skeezer imagery is that it speaks to "realness." But whose realness? (Clearly this is realness as defined by certain individuals and not by natural law.) And why the assumption that realness equals good art? Unfortunately life mimics bad art too: Could N.W.A.'s Dr. Dre have taken their song "One Less Bitch" a little too seriously when last January he allegedly beat up Dee Barnes, host of Fox's rap show *Pump It Up!*, for giving the group bad press?

If this all depresses you, let me recommend an empowerment pill: Hunt down a copy of the feminist film journal *Camera Obscura*, number 23, and read Tricia Rose's "Never Trust a Big Butt and a Smile." Rose positions women rappers like MC Lyte, Salt-N-Pepa, and Queen Latifah as important feminist cultural critics. "By expressing their sexuality openly and in their own language," Rose writes, black women rappers challenge their male counterparts to address women as equals. And by conducting their dialogue with men in the open, they move an issue once characterized as domestic into the public, hence political, arena. Rose recalls an MC Lyte video where the rapper reads her man in a subway car in front of his boys, i.e., the community.

I called Rose recently to swap skeezer stories. (Rose: "How does a skeezer let you know she 'did' Al. B Sure!? By mentioning in passing that the brother has flat feet.") The saddest thing about the skeezer/gold digger character, Rose pointed out, is that it reminds us how in a market society we are all commodities. But it's also a twisted testament to female power.

If you pursue this thought, then Robin Givens—according to her commodity value—is the most powerful woman in America. She "took out" millionaire Mike, the most lethal man in the world. Dogged for being a gold digger when she divorced Tyson after nine months of marriage (and alleged physical abuse), Givens went on to redeem herself in the eyes of some of her critics with *A Rage in Harlem*, in which she plays a character very similar to her media persona, though does it on-screen, in a tight Lycra dress, for everyone to consume. After seeing the movie, a friend—an intellectual man, I thought—said, and I quote verbatim: "Givens is not a bad person after all. And her ass! She was pretty talented. This gave the Tyson thing a context. She deserved the conquest. And she didn't even have to go ten rounds with the brother."

1991

supermamas
revisited

You pink-ass, corrupt honky judge, take your little wet noodle the hell out of here. And if you see a man anywhere, send him in, 'cause I do need a man.

                                   —Pam Grier as Foxy Brown

If you're looking for heroines in all the wrong places —like your video store—check out the gun-toting, karate-kicking, sass-spitting supermamas of the seventies blaxploitation flicks. It's "bad black chicks" like Pam Grier *(Coffy, Foxy Brown)*, Tamara Dobson *(Cleopatra Jones)*, and Jeanne Bell *(T.N.T. Jackson)* up against crooked white cops (pigs), crooked black politicians (sellouts), and lecherous drug dealers of all races (the pushermen). The black girls serve justice the American way, vigilante style, with bare breasts and sawed-off shotguns. When a pimp called Doodle Bug finds out Cleopatra Jones is back in town, "Man," he whines, "that broad is just ten miles of bad road."

Of course these films are "negative image" superfests. All we do in these movies, and by inference life, is sell drugs, sell our bodies, and shoot each other. For home-video release, they should come with labels. "Warning: This film contains oppressive images of blacks that may be unsuitable, unpleasant, and downright unfit for some viewers." But even a label wouldn't prepare you for this scene from *Foxy Brown:*

"Crawl over here, you no good nigger bitch," demands a European heroin dealer of Foxy Brown, who's posing as call girl Misty Cotton. "I know I'm not good enough for you, but let me have your precious white body just once," pleads Foxy. When the dealer spits on her, Grier pulls out a .45 and points it to his temple: "You want to spit on me and make me crawl, white motherfucker? I'm gonna piss on your grave tomorrow." She does.

Supermamas have their share of personal problems. Coffy's relatives are all druggies, dealers, number runners, or in the hospital with brain damage. Cleopatra Jones is forced to leave behind Rufus, a righteous black man with a vast Afro (played by Bernie Casey), to go on special assignment in Hong Kong. T.N.T. Jackson's new man (Stan Shaw) turns out to be her brother's murderer. Foxy Brown shoots her brother's ear off because he has her man set up by pushermen. (Says a white pusherman in *Foxy Brown,* "maybe these people don't believe in family loyalty.")

Blaxploitation's favorite pusherman pimp is Antonio Fargas. Fargas, as Link, Grier's no-good druggie brother in *Foxy Brown,* sums up the genre's male problem this way: "I'm a black man and I don't know how to sing and I don't know how to dance and I don't know how to preach to no congregation. I'm too small be a football hero, and I'm too ugly to be elected mayor. I watch TV and see all them people in those fine houses they live in and all them nice cars they drive, and I get all full of ambition. So tell me, what am I supposed to do with all this ambition I got?" Star in blaxploitation flicks, naturally.

In their own contorted way, roles like Cleopatra Jones and Foxy

Brown raised Hollywood's threshold of black female visibility. Whatever you say about Cleo and Foxy, they are not shuffling mammies, teary-eyed mulattoes, or boozy blues singers. They talk back. They are political in that they are about ridding "the community" of drug slavery and corruption. They take the law into their own hands (vigilantes Foxy and Coffy) or they *are* the law (special narcotics agent Cleo). *Get Christie Love!*, a supermama spin-off that ran for one season in 1974, starred Teresa Graves as television's first black female cop.

Despite the confines of genre—dim-witted plots and motivations, racial stereotypes, and slaphappy nudity—these actresses have moments of transcendence, of "attitudinous" rebellion; moments when they win the image war. When a crooked cop calls Cleopatra Jones "dark meat," she chuckles at his insolence: "Baby, I think you'll find this meat rather tough."

Life as a supermama isn't gonna be easy. But consider the advantages:

What you'll get to wear. Low-cut silver maxidress with a cropped white-mink jacket, red-plaid bell-bottoms, seashell choker, beige knit mini with beige, high-heel, thigh-high suede boots, eight-inch curly Afro wig, twelve-inch nappy Afro wig, mane of loopy, processed curls, feather halter, black leather bells and matching jacket with wide lapels, powder-blue maxidress with ruffled split up to the crotch, sunshine-yellow pantsuit with brown piping and canary-yellow applejack, and the classic combo: rabbit fur jacket, red turtleneck, and black bells.

What you'll get to do: Shoot a man while his pants are around his ankles; become a pimp's leading lady by fistfighting with his stable of whores; hide razor blades in your Afro wig; shoot your boyfriend, a right-on politician, in the nuts when you catch him with a white woman; tell a pusher, "There's no such thing as light shit, brother Snake," and flush his stash down the toilet; castrate a pusher and present his software in a pickle jar to his old lady; ride a motorbike; burn a thirty-million-dollar poppy field in Turkey; and fight (and beat) a tribe of ninjas in Hong Kong.

Things that will happen to you: All the righteous black men in your life will get shot in the back while you watch. Then you'll meet some brothers from the Anti-Slavery Society, a neighborhood antidrug group, who'll help you get revenge.

Songs they'll sing about you: "Coffee is the color of your skin/ Coffee is the color of the world you live in" *(Coffy);* "Baby, you're so fine, loving you just blows my mind" *(T.N.T. Jackson);* "Sweet as a chocolate bar/No one knows who you are/Such a rare black pearl in a very big world filled with tragedy and tears" *(Coffy).*

Who will write these songs: Willie Hutch, Roy Ayers, Joe Simon, and Millie Jackson.

The names men will call you: Black trash, chocolate, darkie, goddamn nigger cop fink, goddamn black bitch, big-jugged jigaboo, nigger bitch, lucky nigger junkie broad, crazy black bitch, spook, sweet pickaninny, jive jungle freak.

The names you'll call men: Lousy stinking pig, white motherfucker, ugly prickless white faggot, whitey, super honky, fatso.

How they will market you: "A one-woman hit squad on a trail of vengeance lined with hitmen, prostitutes, and thugs"; "In the bedroom and out in the open, she revs up the action so no one is safe from her wrath"; "She's a one-mama massacre squad."

Why wait?

1990

girls on the strip

The comic strip that is my life might be perfect material for Barbara Brandon's "Where I'm Coming From," if it weren't so, damn, excuse me, X-rated. Like Brandon's strip, mine has a dozen *dames de couleur* ("the girls," Brandon calls them) who run around with piled-high hairdos and argue all day, usually on the phone, about racism or sexism on the job, what a dog boyfriend has been this week, and whether Clarence Thomas will suffer a nervous breakdown by the year 2000. Why my girls won't play well in the *Des Moines Register* is because, when it comes to boyfriend's p-size or beating the yeast monster, they find it hard to hold their tongues. I tell them, you girls won't play in Albuquerque until you wash your mouths with Lysol. But who listens to me?

Barbara Brandon, however, has been playing in Albuquerque, Harrisburg, Pennsylvania, and a dozen other cities. As of last November, Brandon became the first black woman cartoonist to be syndicated nationally so she's getting plenty ink. *Glamour, People,* and *Time* have all descended on her little studio in Brooklyn's Fort Greene to have a peek.

Brandon has mixed feelings about being, in the nineties, a "first black something." Though with the prospect of seeing her characters on T-shirts, calendars, and greeting cards by fall, thrill is winning out. "Girl," she says, in stylish outer-borough girlfriendese: "Don't we just *need* greeting cards? I'm tired of coloring in those faces."

The girls have been making noise in Brandon's head since college. *Elan,* a black women's magazine, bought the strip in the eighties, only to fold soon after. Her next stop was *Essence,* where they needed a fashion writer more than a cartoonist. Brandon took the writing gig, as it beat dressing mannequins for JCPenney. Eventually she sold the strip to the *Detroit Free Press,* where it has appeared weekly in the life-style section since 1989. Getting by on seventy-five dollars a week from the strip and the odd freelance job, she left *Essence* to devote 24-7 to her girls.

Cutting a syndication deal, Brandon's next move, was no weekend at Virginia Beach. The strip was criticized by potential buyers for its Feiffer-style talking heads. Put the girls in real environments, they said, draw some male characters, make it a daily. Brandon stood ground, and finally signed with Universal Press Syndicate, where she's in good company with "Doonesbury" and "The Far Side," and is encouraged to be as political as she can get away with.

Fifty papers have signed on so far, yet some, like the *Minneapolis Star Tribune,* may have done it to beat the local competition— they've yet to run the strip. "Where I'm Coming From" is as far north as Calgary, Alberta, and as south as Houston. New York City papers, though they serve a majority nonwhite population, are holdouts. Is it a question of space (an old cop-out) or are Big Apple dailies not ready for women who talk loud about pregnancy out of wedlock, affirmative action, and racial identity?

"I'm personally insulted," says Brandon, "if a paper is not interested in the strip because it only features black women. Does that mean my existence can't teach anything? Hey, I didn't grow up with a community of ducks, but I read 'Donald Duck.' And I don't live with a dog, but I read 'Marmaduke,' and I understand it too."

The girls of "Where I'm Coming From" are twenty- and thirtysomething and have names like Lekesia, Nicole, and Alisha. Lydia, who owns a business, named her new baby Aretha. Judy wants to be a novelist. You won't see "cleavage or hot pants" here, says Brandon; the emphasis is on minds for once, not rumps. As single women, the girls are inevitably compared to "Cathy," queen of the coffee mug and greeting card set. With due respect to creator Cathy Guisewite, this is Brandon's comeback: "Buying a bathing suit and worrying about when we'll be size six again, we all trip like that, but I don't want to in my strip. I think I have more of a responsibility." Instead of one character being the repository of every stereotypically female neurosis, Brandon offers a balance. If a strip shows Nicole going on about boyfriend, then Lekesia is on the other end of the phone rolling her eyes.

Brandon's critique of hetero relationship-obsession is an ongoing theme. She takes digs at women who have blinders on when it comes to everything but their man. That men appear in the strip only as voices on the telephone speaks to their complicated presence and absence in the lives of black woman of Lekesia and Nicole's generation. These male phone voices, disembodied and shown in blownup and cluttered type, remind me of the adults in "Peanuts," who are represented only as high-pitched garble.

Brandon is a walking library of black comic-strip history, having grown up putting in Letratone (the dots that suggest Negro skin) for her father, Brumsic Brandon, Jr.'s strip "Luther." In 1969, the year Barbara turned eleven, "Luther" became the third black feature to go national. Images of blacks in American comics have paralleled those in film: Step-in Fetchit characters ruled until pioneer strips by black artists, like Morrie Turner's "Wee Pals" and Ted Shearer's "Quincy," won syndication in the sixties. By the eighties, newspapers lost interest in efforts to integrate the comics. After fifteen years in newsprint, "Luther" was dropped. Brandon traces her lineage to Jackie Ohms, a black woman cartoonist whose character Torchy Brown, a girl reporter, ran in black newspapers like *The Chicago Defender* in the 1930s, ten years before the debut of "Brenda Starr." Torchy dealt with "sexism, racism, and her man," so Brandon preens, and was way ahead of her time.

A *Mad* magazine kid who didn't care much for the Archies, Brandon kept a Feiffer strip tacked above her bed in junior high. In a house that doubled as a gallery for her father's comic art, she was never at a loss for black images in the medium. I, on the other hand, remember combing newspaper strips, cartoon shows, and comic books for little black girls—and drawing a blank. It seemed we couldn't be imagined on screen as live characters or on paper as illustrated ones. I ask one of my foul-mouth friends to confirm this, and she comes up with "Josie and the Pussycats," a 1970s television cartoon that followed the escapades of a female rock group. Remember Val, she asks, the black girl who played drums? Didn't you feel liberated by Val?

Brandon's strip and the commercial recognition of other women whose humor has intelligence and political bite, such as comedian/ actress Phyllis Stickney, performance artist Rhodessa Jones, and novelist Terry McMillan is more than welcome. (You have to make it to Stickney's live show at the new Cotton Club in Harlem just to hear her call Clarence Thomas the "jungle fever judge.") In mainstream comedy, black women have been familiar whipping posts. We are the female image, says bell hooks, that everyone is allowed to show contempt for. It's about time girlfriends get out there and return the compliment.

1992

soldier in the style wars

You're a smart girl, concerned individuals tell me, write about the Gulf war or Lee Iacocca shooting spittle on Japan or how a gang in L.A., the Crips, got tight with some dictators in Latin America, the Medellín drug cartel. But why style? Isn't it . . . too . . . *fem* for you?

I've always admired the way the Crips did a leveraged buyout of the color blue and would shoot in cold, red blood anyone found wearing the rival gang's color—red—on Crip turf. This conjunction of style, power, desire said so simply, so precisely, everything one needed to know, really know, about the human tribe. Style is political, of course:

It's about danger and choices, who is made family and who is made slave.

Put race in the mix and you've got (mis)representation (who gets to take the pictures) and the now heated, ever muddy waters of appropriation (who gets paid). Madonna cashes in on a dance style created by black and Latin gay men, frames it as a homage to white, female glamour queens, and the dance originators are left without a wooden nickle. Do we ignore this and wiggle our butts to her music, smack her, or applaud her marketing genius? And why do the critics who salivate over Madonna and her womb of symbols never mention Josephine Baker? With her body, style, and the adulation of her white fans, Baker wrote entire treatises on how the "primitive" functioned to the repressed who invented it. What of Grace Jones? You can talk about gender and power when you're dressed in Marilyn Monroe's garters, sure it's safe, yet what if, like Grace, you throw gender to the wind as a uselessly polite, bourgeois restriction, and dare all of us—no, command us—to want you still? Now *that's* signifying chutzpah. In a magazine recently I read Grace Jones described as "the woman Jean-Paul Goude invented." Yeah, and the Greeks gave birth to Egypt.

Style is where I want to be right now. I feel like I'm listening at the bedroom door of all your psyches. Feminism puts me there, too. For black women without access to the room of one's own to make leisure-time art, our bodies, our style became the canvas of our cultural yearning. It has been, in recent history, not just a place of self-mutilation, but a place of healing. Racism wounds us in gender-specific ways. Men, an elder once told me, are made to feel stupid, and women to feel ugly. Claiming beauty (and the power in that), and the dissemination of it to the young women who follow us, is serious, in my mind, serious as boys pointing cannons at oil wells.

I get these large ideas about style from visionaries like Coreen Simpson. At the threshold of womanhood and in search of a God, I happened on one of Simpson's photographs: a cook, a black woman with an expanse of hip and breast, standing in the kitchen of a restaurant. The face she presents is regal and unexpectedly sensual.

American cinema's pictures of mammy as mere bosom for white woe, mammy as woman with no personal stake or ambition, were dashed right there. I realized how important one's own eyes, Simpson's in this case, were to transformation. Just in a gesture, this woman's hand on her hip, I found a reservoir of cultural history—a history of pleasure and a history of self-defense—and it was all so close to home.

Coreen Simpson, for those who haven't seen her shuttling around New York City with her cameras and sack of treasures, is a visual artist—a fine-art photographer and jewelry designer—known on the international fashion scene as the midwife of the Black Cameo. Simpson is doing her usual quota of three things at a time: adding a new item to her accessories line (the Black Cameo Scarf, a pattern that combines the original Black Cameo ancestress, cowrie shells, and sea horses), having dental surgery, and preparing for a solo show of her photo collage, inspired by hip-hop style and Romare Bearden's jazz paintings. As we unravel her life, I take pictures in my head; not photos, because she moves so fast, I take music videos: of Simpson rushing between life locations, with her melting-pot voice—Brooklyn black, been-to-Europe, Upper West Side Yiddish—as narration.

The photographer and her younger brother were foster kids growing up in the 1950s. At age six and five they were removed from a middle-class home on Long Island and placed in a Manhattan orphanage. The two were eventually taken in by a family in Bed-Stuy. Simpson recalls the trauma of being uprooted, but also how she was "floored by the style, bravado, aura of the people in Brooklyn. There was this guy who walked around in an orange suit; everyone was outdoing each other with these outrageous ensembles. At the orphanage, you never had your own coat, you had to pick one from the community closet. So I was always aware of clothes." A visit from a social worker in "mink pom-pom balls on her suede boots" is still vivid: "I had never seen a black woman like her before, and I was enchanted."

Simpson "took the back door" to photography, first writing lifestyle pieces for small magazines like Vy Higgensen's *Unique NY.* She brought along a camera to control the look of her stories and soon was known more for her images. In the eighties Simpson became one of the first black female photographers to cover the European fashion collections. Impressed, she was not: "You did see black representation on the runway. Iman was working. All the *girls,* but fashionwise, there's more on the street."

For her hip-hop series, begun in 1982, the photographer set up a portable studio in downtown clubs, Harlem barbershops, and braiding salons in Jamaica, Queens. "I knew there was more to it [hip-hop] than these cute little dance steps that were being played up in the media," she says. "The style element was very important; very African and very American at the same time. I connected it to the way people dressed when I was growing up in Brooklyn. Black folks, as far as style goes, we're the leaders. I think it's important to document this. That's why I did the hip-hop photos so big, because I wanted viewers to confront that black America originated these styles."

Simpson has had a jewelry jones since she can remember. She went to Puerto Rico as a teenager to study Spanish and ended up selling costume jewelry door-to-door. As an adult, Simpson came to jewelry design to supplement her income as a freelance photographer with two children to raise. After three years of selling her one-of-a-kind pieces on New York streets, her work was picked up by retail shops and featured in fashion magazines.

A futile search for a black cameo led Simpson to design one of her own in 1989. Later research told her that the art of cameo making was thought to be inspired by Egyptian glyptics, carvings on precious stones. Likenesses of black women were made in the seventeenth century by Italians, who were the first to mass produce cameos. These cameos are rare, many are in European collections or museums.

"If you look at most white cameos, the model holds her head down in a demure way or seems vulnerable," Simpson explains. "With all the problems we have as black women, I knew this cameo had to look up." Demand for the cameo has been so steady that Simpson continues to expand the line. I went to a dinner party in Minneapolis recently where the hostess's Black Cameo was displayed on the table as a centerpiece, right next to the gourmet black-eyed peas.

In my fantasy music videos of Simpson, one location is the factory that manufactures her cameo. It's her first visit and she explains to factory managers, all short white guys who ressemble Rick Moranis, the importance of getting the features right—long neck, twisted locks, and full-bloom lips—since, Simpson stresses, this will be the "first American cameo of a contemporary woman of color." Later for Lee Iacocca or the Medellín drug cartel, this is history. The soundtrack is the Isley Brothers' "Who's That Lady," the 1964 version with the wild samba feel. Simpson profiles an asymmetrical hat that would have Catwoman at her knees and bangles on each arm up to the elbow. No one can keep their eyes off of her.

1992

this is faith

The college boys are trying to make sense of all the leg and thigh rising and rising above them. Seems like Christo has staged another environmental art hoax: the Twin Towers smothered in black Lycra. This ain't the World Trade Center though; these are the gams of Felice Rosser, a six-foot-tall black woman with a bass guitar. And this ain't two miles from CBGB; this is Toad's Place in Ivy League New Haven, a frequent stop for big money tour buses.

Tonight's bus belongs to headliners Living Colour. But back to the woman with the bass guitar, not that we could ever lose her, as she's nothing short of magnificent with that river of dreadlocks cascading past her shoulders and that cocoa belly exposed to the wind; locked as she is knee-deep in a groove that says all at once, quite loudly, rock/reggae/funk/you-guess/does-it-matter, and standing, as she is, at the very edge of the stage, just straddling and straddling that groove until hell or kingdom come. In the face of this Cleopatra electric, the college boys are backing up, bewildered, straight-up lost in a collision of fear and desire. This bass woman is by no means fitting their picture of band leader, bass guitar player, lead singer, date, hairdo. What do their eyes see? Death or a warm wet place, or both? And what are they forced to confront? Their mothers, their guitar gods, their country?

Standing on a bar stool in the back, I'm lost too. It's that rush that hits the clit of your very soul when you're witnessing something for the first time that will define you for years to come. Where can I buy this, where can I see this again, where can I bathe in this? The vocal harmonies are working the Middle East, the I-Threes, and Laura Nyro duets with Labelle. The music is getting hard and soft in all the right places. And all this image/text/sound is being mainlined straight to my brain, my crotch, and that pumping thing under my T-shirt.

Who are these urchins of the diaspora? The keyboard player/vocalist might be a rare Ethiopian miniature or just an East Village fashion plate in leather hot pants and sturdy shoes. The drummer has the long neck of a Masai and is slamming the bass drum upside the head like a metal-head's mama. And the tiny guitar player with that cabbage of dreads sprouting over his head is giving me all-blues. He cradles his axe to his pecs as if it's his woman, not his johnson, then fingers it till it wails pleasure. The college boys have no more room to back up.

Living Colour plays a powerhouse set, complete with a spine-numbing "Amazing Grace," perhaps to lay a little church on the redneck vibe fogging up the club. I'm still with the new kids who call themselves Faith. You can see why. With their instruments held together with gaffer's tape, it's probably all they have. It's October

1990. I had come to New Haven trailing a man, but ran into something a little more lasting, an aesthetic. I found a band called Faith, and I'm head over heels involved.

this is a photograph, 1992

The view up Broadway from Soho to Harlem is all water towers and gargoyles, those details the aerial shots in movies don't catch. A photo session is about to begin on this eleventh floor loft around the corner from the Time Cafe, hanging post of the glam and glamy paid. Writer Malu Halasa, Felice's girl since college, and her husband, Andy Cox of the Fine Young Cannibals, live here, though as usual they're offering it to Felice and her band. The loft has seen much of Faith, from after-gig parties to baby showers, and everyone's nostalgic today because Malu and Andy are giving it up for London. The bass lady herself walks in pushing an empty stroller, all flustered 'cause she lost her rock & roll costume bag on the D train. Her old man and manager, Buzz, brings up the rear with the kid and that constant smirk of his: That Felice, if she weren't so talented, if I didn't love her so goddamn much.

Felice Rosser has a lot on her mind these days. Drummer Garry Sullivan is on the road *without* the band. Poached a few days ago by the B-52s, he'll be gone for six months, or maybe for good. The other Faithfuls aren't here, either, and may not be; something about a tiff last week. Though soon they file in; anything for the band. Guitarist Rene Akan, last, is full of ginseng and happenstance: His clothes are missing, his cat's sick, he wants a Bob Marley tattoo. Keyboardist Diana Baker rolls her most deadly weapon, those Ethiopian poster-child eyes. Rene plays uncle, lullabying the kid with James Brown tunes, then takes his place in the frame.

They decide against sunglasses and in favor of natural light. Leaning against each other to balance Felice's gift of height, they look like who they are: a Brooklyn family of choice, not some folks out to storm the rock citadel, though they are that too. Malu, just another Arab-American rainbow baby, be-dreaded Buzz with his Coke-bottle specs, the drooling kid, and finally, the skinny British photographer, are dragged into the shot too. Aside from the drummer, the only missing person is comanager Nicole Payen, who compares her day job of human-rights work for Haitian refugees to managing a black rock band in search of a record deal. Click.

dance for the industry

Like any number of New York local bands hard up with dreams, Faith has a sizable following and a name with club bookers in the city for putting on a feisty live show. From their first gig in 1988 at a squat in Alphabet City, things had inched forward, for the most part, though now they feel they're circling the runway. Joining the Black Rock Coalition (BRC) and playing Coalition-produced showcases in 1989 was a turning point. Living Colour guitarist Vernon Reid asked them to take part in a benefit concert for homeless New Yorkers at the Beacon Theater that summer, along with Stevie Ray Vaughn and John Cougar Mellencamp.

So in their first working year as a band Faith had played a two thousand–seat theater. Soon they were opening at clubs like Wetlands for every big act that came through, "but only on the black side," says Buzz. Industry scouts began slinking around after the Beacon benefit. Showcase hell followed, as the band strutted, usually early evenings in the dark hole of CBGB, for independents like Pow Wow records and majors like CBS and Epic. These were funhouse events: maybe twenty people in the audience, along with perplexed record company folks. And our four African Americans on the auction block rocking until they bled. Pure funhouse, but no deal.

Other doors opened and closed. Faith passed on chances to contribute to small-label compilation discs, holding out for major-label deals that hobbled along, then never happened. Word came back from the sniffers: This band's not ready (though how to be "ready" was never outlined). Or the songs aren't there yet. (An odd one: You go to a Faith gig and what you get *is* songs. "Felice has that camp-fire ability," says a BRC member. "Anyone can sit down with an acoustic guitar and sing along to her music.") Or, the most frustrating: We don't know how to market this band. This is usually a code for "weird, unclassifiable black folks don't sell; there's no audience for them," which American artists have had to prove wrong time and again. The question was fast becoming not whether Faith was ready for the industry, but whether the industry was ready for them.

tribal grunge

Brand naming their music has always been a problem for Faith. "I don't know what we call it, tribal grunge, or something?" pipes Rene, followed by a laugh track. Felice uses "rock" to shock people who assume she plays reggae because of her locks. The term "black rock" doesn't work for anyone in the band. To Rene, it's as redundant and insulting as "Jamaican reggae." Ah, the lovely semantics you do battle with as an African American aching to stretch outside of market trenches and gimmicks and just do some art. Let's all move to London.

You'll hear the odd novelty-reggae song from black American artists. For Faith, reggae informs everything they do, including their "rock" songs. Their reggae palette sets them apart too. Not the fad of the moment, dancehall, it's a softer-edged groove that recalls the seventies. Even at their hardest, Faith seems to come from a peaceful, wise place. Though Rene says he's "addicted to distortion," his sound is not aimless industrial noise; it's closer to a primal human voice. Faith's cover of Funkadelic's "Cosmic Slop," say, comes off less as guitar pyrotechnics than the mating call of leopards.

Then you have the image wall. (Unless, of course, you are, know, or live with people like Faith, and you take your/their identity as "normal" for granted.) The locks alone set off a series of puzzlements: Felice, Diana, and Rene are neither the fashion-dread adolescents you see in Sprite ads these days, nor are they practicing Rastafarians. The Faith women have long locks well matched to their womanly bodies. Just the act of wearing locks uncovered sets them apart from most women working in reggae, who wrap at least the crown of their heads for spiritual reasons.

To boil it down, you have a major style war happening on stage: Says BRC cofounder and longtime Faith enthusiast Greg Tate, "Faith doesn't fit any of the clichés of what it means to be a rock band. It's fronted by a big sister with dreadlocks who plays bass. The music is very soothing vocally, then they rupture that. They're about as comfortable with being benignly psychedelic as they are with being straightforward dubwise. Basically, they shatter all conventions of what genre is."

"Yeah," says Diana. "A & R people try to figure us out and they get a big headache."

pow wow soundbite

Eight days into January 1991 and it's cold as a witch's tit outside and not about to let up. Onstage at CBGB though, we're frying pork rinds. This must be a showcase because the feedback is so vicious it stings. Tonight is for Pow Wow Records, who are close to making an offer. The band's apologizing for tuning up onstage, while Garry tries to cover with nervous fill-ins on the high hat. The bass lady doesn't make it to that knee-deep groove of hers until the final song. Then she's *on* stage, legs spread, humping each bass note, her locks doing a mad Krishna dance of their own. She takes a lyric up like Chrissie Hynde, then oozes it down like Nina Simone. The posers glance up from their beers and dig, at last. Felice never looks at them. "This morning I had no money to pay the van, no clothes to wear to the gig. This ain't no glamorous shit, this rock & roll. But I believed, I prayed, and I'm here." The small audience claps hard for an encore. Felice finishes in grand rock decadence, her body exhausted and bent over like a rag doll, her locks coiling around the power cables on the floor. But the moment is lost. God at the lighting board has aimed the spotlight somewhere else.

the bass lady

Felice Rosser's mother recorded a 78-rpm record at a Woolworth's in Detroit in the 1940s, then put it in the basement for thirty years. She types letters for a judge now. Her father, a real estate broker, and her grandfather, a factory worker, only listen to country music. "Sunday nights my mother always had the radio preachers on," she says. "I told my grandmother I wanted to be a preacher, 'cause I loved the way those preachers talked. Jesus, ah huh, Jesus. They'd make those Bible stories come alive, like Elijah going up in a flaming chariot and Moses. The magnificence of it all. Then the Beatles on Ed Sullivan was the next big thing, and of course Kennedy got shot. I went on a Beatles quest for the next ten years."

Home was Russell Woods, a black middle-class enclave in Detroit. Being a too tall, too smart black girl in public school made you an easy target. Felice was shipped off to Roeper City and Country in the suburbs, where it was "okay to be smart and like rock music." At Roeper she hung out at bar mitzvahs, sang in a madrigal group, and met her first black beatnik. A first guitar came next, and at night Felice locked her bedroom door and taught herself to play Joan Baez songs.

"In 1968, the hippie movement started, and of course you didn't send your daughter to an expensive private school so she could freak out, but that's what was happening. After ninth grade I was back in public school—and just continued freaking right out. There was a whole contingent of black people who were freaking out, and white people too. We'd go see concerts a lot.

"Jethro Tull played six nights in Detroit and we went every night. Saw Zep, Sly, name it, we saw it. Only thing, we didn't see Hendrix, but we did see the Moody Blues the night he died. Hitchhiked to the Toronto Jazz and Blues Festival 'cause I was getting into the blues. I was struck by the Wolf. Something about him, he laid a vibe on me.

"At the Michigan Palace, this big rock club in Detroit, the New York Dolls changed my life. David Johansen had on these clear plastic pants and some big old clogs, and Johnny Thunders had on these really tight pants, and all this hair. It was more aggressive and glitter. Everybody was styling hard. The bass player, Arthur Kane, had broken his arm, and he was just standing on stage with this cast looking really mean, while somebody else, the roadie or something, was playing the bass. They played only two or three songs, then the P.A. broke. We were hanging around the backstage door, of course. The Dolls were long gone, but their manager was around. He said, 'Where can you get a drink in this fucking town?' It was 12:30, and I remember thinking, he wants to get a drink! I'll never forget that. I *had* to go to New York."

Anthropology, Faulkner, and reggae awaited Felice at Barnard. Her literary magazine, *Upstart*, published classmates Jim Jarmusch, Luc Sante, and Darryl Pinckney. (Pinckney's novel, *High Cotton*, has a character etched allegedly from Felice's life: The black girl in Paris with the white boyfriends.) She remembers being "totally unconscious on a black tip. I just wanted to have fun and go to concerts. I didn't know the world was such a racist place until I started going on job interviews." Felice made her way downtown eventually, to Indian food on Sixth Street and new kinds of rock, mainly Patti Smith and Television. Rock in Detroit had meant large arenas. At CBGB she found out the music could be personal (though still loud, fast, and guitar based). And punk was saying anyone could do it.

Felice took punk at its word. But first, senior year abroad (digging Arabic music in Paris and London punk) and dead-end secretarial work for CBS Records (she was "passed to black music" because the rock music department wouldn't hire her). Then she headed downtown for good. Felice jammed with fellow East Villagers like painter Jean Michel Basquiat, who made clarinet music into "pure noise." Deerfrance, a good friend who worked the door at CBGB's, played guitar, so Felice picked up bass. The bands piled up: Cargo, V. (after the Thomas Pynchon novel), the Blue Picts, the Wild Wild West. In between all this came a book contract with Simon & Schuster and a move back to Paris to work on her novel. The novel is still unfinished—the music snatched her away.

By 1987 Felice had done two years in a "real musician's gig," an all-women reggae band based in Brooklyn. She was exploring Rasta, letting her hair dread, and learning more about her instrument. The band was nurturing and she loved the music, but those power chords were calling. After being told for years she couldn't sing, that she had a "sixties voice," Felice made three brave moves: ignored everything, allowed her musical souls to copulate, and started her own band.

fem-rock, not

A Marshall amp is dressed in a Marcus Garvey scarf and a belt of cowrie shells. Botanica candles are burning onstage. Faith the rock band is honoring Malcolm X this evening, February 21, 1991, on the twenty-sixth anniversary of his murder. There's no announcement. This is just something between the man and Faith. Felice has other concerns to get loud about. Tonight's gig at the Knitting Factory made the *Village Voice* as a weekly choice, though the band is close to livid about its assigned moniker. The bass lady grabs the mike close as a security blanket. "Contrary to *Village Voice* opinion, we are not a fem-rock band. We've got two very handsome young black men up here. And I'm not a fem, I'm not a butch, and I'm not a bitch. I don't know what I am." Rene stomps the pedal and lets loose a Molotov cocktail of distortion. Faith is gonna play hard tonight.

What fem-rock is, we don't know, but Felice has made it clear it's not her cup of goldenseal. There's friction within Faith about what a band led by a woman should symbolize. (Diana thinks it's "unfortunate" that a woman leading a band should be seen as exceptional.) This isn't so much ambivalence about feminism, though womanism would probably be the preferred term, as it is a feeling that the band shouldn't be colonized by any flag.

Leaving behind straight reggae in the eighties, Felice also left the concept of an all-women unit. It'd be easier to get a deal if Faith were a girl group—there's a market niche for that. But Faith's gender balance is something all the musicians revel in and want to uphold. Rene talks about the "perfect chemistry" of the band in terms of male/female, lightness/heaviness, soft vocals over hard guitar and drums—and how the soft/hard dynamic doesn't always break down by gender.

This symmetry certainly sets Faith off from the rigid gender divide in black popular music. Arrested Development breaks through this too, but band leader Speech still stands as the father figure/swami of the hip-hop commune. In Faith you have a strong woman, leading a band of men and women, and no one's energy is diminished because of it. We may assume the reality of this in our own lives. In pop imagery, though, it's a new moving picture, and a statement in itself; one that counters all sorts of au courant artifacts of black men and women lunging at each other like cannibal pit bulls.

The gender breakdown is also the root of the band's understated but rushing sensuality. Malu Halasa, president of the unofficial Faith fan club, is still trying to nail it: "It's not lick-my-dick rock. It's not the Victoria's Secret catalog. It's more the kind of sensuality and sexuality that real people have. 'Earthy' sounds too much like Janis Joplin. It's earthy and steamy too. I mean, look at Rene. If that's not walking hot sex, I don't know what is. Look at Felice: She's wild, she's beautiful, she's distinctive. They drive everyone insane with their adrenaline. It's almost like they can see the future."

The yin yang of Faith notwithstanding, the music is pushing some womanist science, whether band members articulate this offstage or not. Women in the audience connect with obvious, loud pleasure to Felice running the show. (Songs are dedicated to Blanche DuBois and Winnie Mandela, but also to Magic Johnson and the "brothers in prisons.") They get happy over Diana and Felice's between-song call and response. This is typical: Rattling her bracelets, the bass lady coos, "I got to take some of this shit off. If you're a girl you've got to have this stuff. It happens all the time, your heels get stuck in the street. We women gotta do what we gotta do." Diana answers with a line from the black girl's canon of nursery rhymes, "Bra too tight, booty shaking from left to right." Women also hook into the songs, most written by Felice: about affairs with younger men, self-reliance, being in love and in power struggle, and the wear and tear of love games on your ego. These offer up a complex portrait of black femininity. Usually we come off as all powerful or all vulnerable in pop music. Felice seems to say we negotiate both verities.

In the band's rehearsal space, with a wooden bass on her thigh, Felice talks about bringing a new sensuality to the pop panorama, where the ruling black female icons are the sequined R&B queen or the desexed folk singer. Felice doesn't find the focus on sadomasochism in music these days to be transgressing any taboos, or even much of a turn on. She's after a "comfortable, mystic sensuality" that she finds in the imagery of "southern blues," a legacy from her grandmother, who eloped to Detroit from Georgia. But this doesn't mean gingham dresses: "I want to rock, and I want to rock hard, so I'm not gonna be wearing flimsy outfits and fancy clothes. I just want to wear pants 'cause you can rock hard in pants. I can't stand there with no dress on and my legs open. You know, I gotta do stuff with my legs."

"My whole life I never thought I was beautiful," Felice continues, her voice quieter now. "I was too tall, too dark, nose too big. But musicians are always talking about rectifying past lives. This is what I'm doing, I guess. This music makes me feel beautiful. I love how sexy the bass sounds. I'm finding out more and more, it's nothing you can buy. Before these shows I used to run around the Lower East Side, going crazy with my little twenty dollars 'cause I had to get a shirt or something for the gig. But now I realize that there's nothing you can buy, 'cause I bought everything, and it didn't work for me."

Rene joins Felice in the studio and the two trade off images of black women in music like baseball cards. Rene: "What about Chaka Khan, Aretha, Billie Holiday?" Felice: "Yeah, Billie Holiday. There was that sense of her own self-exploration. Chaka Khan has that too, but Billie Holiday! To a society that denies that we as black women have an inner life, Billie Holiday said, This is how I think, this how I speak, this is how I look. She wasn't just a natural sister, she was *magic.*" Watching Felice move (with the awkward grace of an antelope), and speak (in that Detroit, up South, "ed-ju-macated," Village-hipster drawl of hers), and sing (with that richly textured voice of blues and triumph), you get some of that magic too.

the man from sulfur-8

Into the Chinese restaurant on lower Broadway came walking hot sex. Rock imp Rene Akan is picking at his egg foo young and reminiscing about superheroes. The homemade kind, with names like Supersonic, the Human Fly, and Sulfur-8 (after the hair pomade). These were his confidantes, growing up in the Williamsburg section of Brooklyn, an oddball, gifted kid in a family of Jehovah's Witnesses. Rebellion snuck up with adolescence. Soon he was hanging with white kids from Brooklyn Heights and hopping trains bound for Washington Square Park.

"I started cutting school to check out the street musicians. There was this one wicked guitar player with a lazy eye playing Hendrix stuff and Santana. Since forever, I have been into Santana. That tone on 'Black Magic Woman'! From the time I was seven, I knew that was the way a guitar was supposed to sound. You hear one note, and that becomes your note for life."

Rene made it through high school and went to work for the phone company. Nights he studied political science at Hunter College. At twenty-one and still sheltered in many ways, he happened upon *The Autobiography of Malcolm X*. The raging had only begun. It continued with the Michael Stewart and Eleanor Bumpurs murders, and the Move bombing in Philly. Arrested for standing on the wrong street corner with the wrong attitude, he spent three days in jail: "I knew I needed another outlet. I got into guitars in a heavy way, lost my job." Slapped with probation for playing "Voodoo Chile" on the roof of Hunter, Rene split college too. He was drafted into a reggae band fronted by a bass player who was once a roadie for the Bad Brains. Rene stayed for a while, then moved on to East Village hardcore.

"I was playing with this band of Ukrainian guys, then went to one guy's house and found out he was a Klansman. That was bizarre. I was doing this hardcore thing, but getting into all sorts of other music: Fripp, Eno, African music, the blues. What I dug about hardcore is that it's visceral. Something about that fuzz and that chunky sound. But in terms of the content, I thought it was kinda stupid. I wanted a voice for the guitar that could pull together all the different types of music I heard in my head."

Wanted: Guitarist for a reggae-rock band. Rene answered Felice Rosser's classified ad in the *Voice* in November 1987. "An hour after auditions were supposed to begin, time I was paying for, Rene comes strolling in with his ripped-up clothes and a little hat," Felice remembers. "Everyone else was dressed nicely. I said, Who is this person, he's late and all. Well, Rene plugged in and started playing the blues like Muddy Waters. Four notes in, I said, that's my guy."

Rene's in full regalia today: a magician's top hop (missing the top, so out sprout, very coyly, his dreads), his metal-boy and Afro-chic talismans, combat boots, and tuxedo tails. On the iron horse to Brooklyn he's railing about the image politics of rock & roll. You should look at the musicians-wanted classifieds sometime, they all say "image important" or "long hair a must," he yells. "Not only is Faith out here, not really playing reggae and not really playing rock, but we don't look the part. Not just Felice and Diana as women, but me as a guy. I'm not blond. I don't look like Slash or Lenny Kravitz either. I'm a dark-skinned man. How are they gonna package me as a guitar god?"

nubian soundbite

The Gods, the young ones from the Five Percent Nation (and those who like to style as if), are being frisked with metal detectors. They've come to see their boys, Brand Nubian, rising sons of East Coast hip-hop, at Wetlands in lower Manhattan. This is Black History Month, 1991.

With Gods packed in so tight, there's little breathing room in this small club. The opening band—yet another lost tribe of aboriginals—files onstage and jaws drop like dominoes. Felice and Diana have their locks crimped. It's a look that melds love child Lisa Bonet and Medusa, and it leaves the baby-faced Gods scratching their baseball caps. When Felice straps on her bass, a God shrieks, giddy with disbelief, "Oh, shit!" His boys in the back fall out.

Having started rowdy, the crowd keeps it up. (One God blows smoke straight at Felice's throat for the entire set.) But the music creeps up on them. Bodies are moving, just a bit, as if Gods don't want other Gods to know they're really down with such weirdness. Before "Cosmic Slop," Faith's parting anthem, Rene, who rarely talks on stage, grabs Diana's mike and shouts, "Rock & roll is black music!" The Gods, who can dig nationalism packaged in any torch song, roar.

Rap shows being short, the club asks Faith to play a second set following Brand Nubian. The crowd is down to a handful; most are Faith junkies, bohos of all creeds and colors, though a few Gods are hanging too. Felice, who never sways from under her constant halo of light-love-humanism, prefaces her younger-man song with a smile and story. "A little God," yes he did, tried to rap to her between sets. Diana isn't impressed. Introducing "Cosmic Slop," she plays a nursery rhyme on the keyboard. "Hey, Mommie," she whines along, doing her best God imitation, "What's a Funkadelic?"

on keys

Diana Baker's got a bachelorette pad in Alphabet City. She calls herself "an African woman living on the Lower East Side," so you'll know the difference between her and everyone else slumming in their renovated flats. Hers in an old building on a block known for crack traffic. A sign in the hallway warns tenants not to let their kids eat the rat poison.

Like the rest of the band, Diana comes from middle-class or aspiring folks who preached hard work and education—and had fabulous record collections. And same as the others, she did higher education, East Village rock & roll, and, along with Felice and Rene, Rasta. Diana grew up in Pontiac, Michigan, and South Plainfield, New Jersey, the only child of a schoolteacher and a jazz musician. (Her father, who passed when she was young, played tuba in the Air Force One band. They flew around the country with the president and played whenever he landed.) In high school she made all-county, then all-state choral groups. Her dream was to go on the road with a modern, black-boho version of the Andrews Sisters.

Back in Michigan, music wasn't as "segregated" as Diana finds New York radio to be. "Parliament-Funkadelic was the standard. Groups like Parlet and Brides of Funkenstein were enormous. We listened to jazz like folks listen to Hot 97. There was even a black radio station that played rock. That's how I found out about the Bus Boys. I thought they were huge nationally, then I came to New York."

Diana transferred from a Jersey college to the New School in Manhattan to be closer to the downtown club scene. Her family freaked out when she left school to play music and started locking her hair: "First I cut it all off. I went over to my grandmother's house. She told me how cute it looked short, but then she looked closer and said, 'But you're not combing it!' I know what Grandma was thinking, 'My God, she left college, she's not combing her hair, she's probably not bathing. The child's going to the dogs!' "

Rene brought Diana in as a singer shortly after his audition. Drummer Garry Sullivan, raised up in local Bronx metal bands, came next, answering another of Felice's classifieds. The four got on so well, they edged out their keyboard player and gave Diana the job. Faith is Diana's first band; she'll tell you every road story: from the broken-down vans to almost getting killed that time Faith's driver fell asleep at the wheel en route to Virginia for a gig with fellow rockers, also black, the Good Guys. Once Faith played a private party in Darien, Connecticut. When the music got a little loud for Darien, cops showed up to cart off the band, not the family who hired them.

Asked whether there is any image of black women in pop music that she identifies with, Diana screws up her face: "They're all Whitney Houston clones. There's not even a black woman out here with her own hair. No one is comfortable with or can sell her own image. That's the beauty of Faith, it's just us up here, we're not gimmicks in miniskirts. That's why the record companies are so scared of us. The independence we project is even scarier than the strength. They don't have any precedents for us." How about Tracy Chapman and Joan Armatrading? "They're solo artists and their music is mellow and palatable; as folk signers they're easier to package."

And what of the long line of black women "in rock": Tina Turner, Betty Davis, Pauline Black of Selecter, Rhoda Dakar and the Body Snatchers, the women of the Family Stone, Poly Styrene of X-Ray Spex, Neneh Cherry in her punk phase; and bands like Labelle and Isis; or Chaka Khan, the women of Graham Central Station, Merry Clayton, Taka Boom, Joyce Kennedy from Mother's Finest, Nona Hendryx, Grace Jones, D. K. Dyson of Eye & I? (Felice's list includes Bessie Smith and Memphis Minnie, who wrote "When the Levee Breaks," covered on *Led Zeppelin IV*). Foremothers, yes, but few and far between. Largely they've been ignored by rock criticism as innovators in the genre, and are thought of as anomalies. No one has bothered to chart lines of influence, or note that their audiences have included like-minded boho chicks. Even the BRC's revision of rock history, as quoted and mythologized by the pop-music press, leaves them out.

mystery soundbite

We're back at CBGB, and it's spring now. Faith is in showcase mode again, this time for Forty Acres and a Mule Musicworks, Spike Lee's new company, distributed by Columbia Records. Label director Lisa Jackson fell for the band and has brought Lee to see for himself. On stage Faith is dishing their sexy best. Felice introduces Rene as "our guitarist, the cute guy over there showing his nipples." But tonight it's the songs that really stand out. Felice's younger-man tune, "What Should I Do About You," is sweating up the bar stools. "It's a strange, strange acid life," she sings, "He was 19/She was 35/ . . . He came so quick the first time/Then they tried a second time." The band debuts a new piece, "Race," which Felice describes on mike as "the sad story of the pulling away that happens between black and white friends": "Your reality is so different than mine/See, they follow me around in stores/And I've never had a job where I could use my mind/ . . . Now you call me long distance to ask how New York City has been/But I've got nothing to tell you/Because when we talk about race, you don't understand."

Felice is working the hair overtime tonight, swinging it 360 degrees around her head, like Marley always did. So busy watching the hair show, some folks missed the main event. "My God," screeches an A&R type at the bar, "what's that growing under her blouse?"

heavy with child

And somewhere in between, our heroine gets pregnant. Not unlike your period, it always happens in the middle of some painfully important, big male moment, like standing on the verge of a record deal after you've busted your butt for four years. Think about the courage it took Felice to stand on that stage at CBGB, black and pregnant, playing rock & roll, the sacred text of white-boy angst, and being gaped at by A&R suits and skirts. And doing it in a black-lace tunic and Lycra pants, and having the gall to announce, "Lately I've been exploring my sensuality."

All comanager Nicole Payen had to say was, "It's lucky big tops and leggings are in this season." The pregnancy, though unplanned, was welcomed. Felice and Buzz had been together as a couple since the band was born. And Felice, over twentysomething and counting, felt it was her time. The summer of 1991 was turning out to be Faith's busiest yet. Averaging three or four shows a month, the band stayed onstage through Felice's eighth month.

For Felice this meant not only performing, but dropping tapes, renting vans, rehearsing, booking shows, sales clerking at HMV Records, prenatal checkups, Lamaze classes, cleaning, cooking, bass practice, working on songs after midnight, and combing the city for rock & roll maternity wear.

Seth Malik arrived December 20, 1991. Seth was the third son after Cain and Abel, a gift to his mother after hard times and tragedy. Malik, an Arabic name, is Buzz's contribution. It had been a long year.

let's make a record deal

The summer of '91 also had promised a miracle. After seeing the band live, Spike Lee and Lisa Jackson were ready to sign them to Forty Acres and a Mule Musicworks. Then a snag: The A&R attachés at Columbia saw a Faith showcase shortly after and were dead against a signing. Musicworks pitched Columbia a low-budget deal, but after nine months of wrangling, it fell through too.

Lee wasn't pleased with the outcome. Faith, in Lee's opinion, "deserved to be signed." Apparently word came from as far up as Columbia president Don Ienner's office that the band had, among other things, an image problem. Says Lee, "They just didn't like the way the band looked." Lisa Jackson, who has a mane of locks herself and has been in the record business for a decade, backs Lee up: "I can't say I got this verbatim from Columbia, but this is my feeling: Columbia's biggest objection to Faith was the fact that this was a rock band led by a black female. And not only is it led by a black female, but not your typical petite rocker. They weren't prepared to promote it."

Everyone staggered back to their day jobs: Felice to the record store, Diana to teaching nursery school, Buzz to his messenger gig, Nicole to human-rights work, and Garry to playing drums in the subways and passing the hat. Rene got a new "slave," musician slang for day jobs, as a model at the Art Students League, where Charlton Heston and Madonna once bared their torsos too. The lady retirees who paint him often linger after class to inquire if he's a musician. Sometimes they even ask to touch his hair.

"One of the wildest moments," Felice remembers, "was when I read that Sinéad O'Connor was pregnant when she got signed. She actually made her record during her pregnancy. She was so glad it happened that way, she said, 'cause she felt so powerful and creative. When we started talking to Forty Acres, I was pregnant. I was thinking, great, I'll be pregnant, make my record, and have some money in my pocket. When the deal fell through, here I was with this baby coming, scrambling, thinking, how am I going to live, how am I going to survive?"

The A&R factory workers who checked out Faith must have wondered how they could sell the band as a rock rebellion fantasy to the white adolescent market when Faith's image didn't involve them. Felice, the consummate humanist, would probably disagree. Once she opened a set with a very polite, "Fuck racist white America." A white guy yelled back, "Right on!" Black folks in the audience kept silent.

Why was it easier to sell Ice Cube's letter bombs to white America these days then a band like Faith, who grew up in the college boys' backyards, went to school with them, and speaks their language? "The face of black rebellion now is KRS-One and Ice Cube," a colleague reminds me. "The powers that be have decided that that's our safe space. Even in our rebellion, motherfuckers want to ghettoize and contain us."

faith ever more

The phone rings, it's Felice. She doesn't want the band to be portrayed as black artists victimized by the system when she herself doesn't feel like anybody's victim or anybody's cliché. The record industry isn't most people's idea of an equal opportunity wonderland, but she knows what she's up against. It took six years for Vernon Reid to get a deal for Living Colour. (Of course Reid had to be a virtuoso guitarist, make friends with Mick Jagger, and start a political movement first.) Even Funkadelic and the Beatles, Felice reminds me, were turned down many times. Hendrix had to go to England. Punk and hip-hop snuck in on small labels. It's a racist, sexist, corporate migraine, but she can handle it.

Faith has decided, in the do-it-yourself tradition, to put out their own seven-inch single and see what bites: Maybe the majors will come sniffing again, maybe more gigs, a tour. While Felice and Rene are auditioning drummers, Buzz is running around town with Seth on his back, having their DAT mastered and pressed. With

Garry's exit and deals falling through, Rene felt like the band was "hemorrhaging." This isn't just a record, says comanager Nicole, "this will be our Grammy. We're giving it to ourselves. We needed it."

"Not too many things come around in life that you really believe in." We're in Brooklyn today at Nicole's place, close to the projects in the less chic rump of Fort Greene. A Haitian-American boho in her twenties, Nicole is talking about hooking up with Faith, though she knew nothing at the time about managing a band. She saw one Faith gig and pledged her life.

"Excuse me if I'm not blond or blue-eyed, but I'm a rock & roll chick. If someone would sit down and talk to me and see who I am, it wouldn't seem so farfetched. My experience isn't the project girl, but it isn't the black middle-class girl either. And En Vogue doesn't represent me as a black woman. In fact, they represent something that I'm trying to get away from.

"Hendrix, the Doors, the Yardbirds, that's part of my culture too. All this stuff about Malcolm X is cute, but people like Faith, we're products of integrated schools and integrated neighborhoods. The civil rights laws changed the country completely. Certainly they had to expect changes in the music, which is what American popular music has been about from the get go. And we represent some of those changes.

"There's more than a record deal at stake here; this is about our lives. Are you saying my life, my experience, isn't a valid as Nirvana's or Ice Cube's? Whether or not the industry is ready to deal with *this* America, we're here. Whether or not they're ready to play it on the radio, it's being felt. And it's not gonna go away just because they don't understand it."

subway to heaven, october 1992

"Unity and peace is pussy and soft/Black people don't like white people/And white people don't like black people/And I guess that's the way we want it." This is a warning from Bushmon, a post–Fishbone, post–Living Colour type of crew on stage at Space at Chase, a bar near NYU's village campus. They look just out of high school, these guys, some with dreads, some not. The drummer's Asian, another kid's a rainbow baby. Quite the new world order rock band.

Bushmon is sharing the bill tonight. Faith is like an old guard to this set, and there's a sadness to that, given the band still hasn't made it to the promised land yet. This gig is something of a test. It's their first since Garry's departure and they're anxious. When Felice makes it to her knee-deep blues, the worries pass. The groupies are worshiping at Rene's wah-wah pedal. Diana and Felice's harmonies wrap over and around each other like silk ribbons. Faith tonight is larger than the missed record deals and the lost drummers. Much, much larger.

The band is on my mind, as usual, on the train back to Brooklyn. There's an ad for Virginia Slims across from me. It pictures a petite rocker, in the Bananarama vein, with a flashy new red guitar, not like Felice's muddy brown thing patched with gaffer's tape. "Life's like rock and roll," the ad tells us. "It's more fun when you take the lead." I want to deface it and write, "Rock supremacist pigs and your impossibly slender-hipped, female mirrors DIE." But I don't. I've got Faith.

1992

For information on Faith, contact Lionhearted Management, 17900 Goddard, Detroit, Michigan 48212.

the invisible ones

The silent witness I carried with me throughout the Thomas/Senate/Bush *v.* Hill showdown was the judge's sister, Emma Mae Martin. In Pin Point, Georgia, that Moon River township we now know so well from the legends told of her brother's great escape, Martin still lives in poverty. She supports three of her four children and one son's pregnant fiancée on her salary as a hospital cook. Her run-down frame house has a hole in the roof.

You might know the judge's sister through his now infamous public castigation of her as a welfare dependent ("She gets mad when the mailman is late with her welfare check"). He used sis as an example of all-gone-wrong with liberal handouts and civil rights leadership. Serving up such a portrait of his sister turned out to be a shrewd career move for Thomas. It was this speech, made to a conference of black conservatives in 1980, that caught Reaganite ears and led to Thomas's quick ascent in the Reagan/Bush new American order. Though his comments came back to haunt him briefly during the confirmation process, they were buried under the pile of issues dug up by Hill's harassment charge.

In the scramble to get to the bottom of Thomas, a few journalists talked to his sister. Not surprisingly, the story of Martin's life as told by Martin offered quite a different picture from Thomas's soundbite. No welfare addict, Martin was forced to seek assistance during a family crisis, a common scenario for women. Married with kids right out of high school, her man walked out on her. While Thomas was at Yale Law School in the early seventies, Martin worked two minimum-wage jobs to support her children. When an elderly aunt who minded the kids suffered a stroke, Martin left work to care for both aunt and children. With her meager income and no child support, she found, as many women do, she couldn't afford a nursing home and child care. Welfare was a last resort. After four and a half years on public assistance, Martin returned to the work force. She reports to her hospital job most days at 3:00 A.M.

Martin's story becomes an even more telling parable of women and the poverty cycle once you find out that her life has mirrored her mother's. Leola Williams was also left by her husband with three young children to support. She got by picking crabs at five cents a pound; then came a crisis—fire destroyed her home and possessions. With an extended family in place, Williams was able to manage without welfare. She sent Thomas and his brother to live with their grandfather, Martin to stay with her aunt, and worked as a live-in housekeeper for rich whites. Today she's a nurse's aide at the same hospital where her daughter cooks.

Martin isn't a typecast welfare queen sucking the nation dry, as Thomas seemed to suggest, but a single woman like his own mother, who worked low-paying jobs without benefits to support her family and turned to relatives for help. (Where was Thomas, the lawyer, the federal agency chair, when his sister fell on hard times?) Thomas's distortion of his sister's life says a lot about him, yet it says even more about America. No child- or health-care system, dead-end jobs, dysfunctional schools, yes. But what of the political and media value put on the lives of women like Martin? Especially black women like Martin. The Martins of this country are pigeon-holed as sub-American, subfemale, and often—in renditions of the new crack-addicted underclass—dangerous and subhuman.

It's not just women like Martin who are ignored, stereotyped, and often scapegoated, it's families like Martin's. Among African Americans, single women head nearly half of all families. And over two-thirds of all black children under eighteen are being raised in these households below the poverty line. Poverty figures come not just from income, but from an individual's "dependency burden." Less discussed than the cost of children is the cost of care for elderly relatives. When old ones fall sick, it's the women of the family who care for them at the expense of their own personal ambitions. (And in most African-American families, for financial and cultural reasons, this care-taking happens at home.) It's the Emma Mae Martin syndrome. While Thomas was pulling himself up by the bootstraps, *self*-helping himself, Martin took care of auntie, because who else would? And for this, he calls her a welfare queen.

Law professor Patricia King was among those who gave testimony opposing Thomas at the confirmation hearings. King's statement centered around Martin and Thomas's ignorance or willingness to overlook the compounded hardships faced by women like his sister. Her remarks were treated summarily by the committee. Others raised the Martin issue, but it fell on deaf ears. Legal scholar Kimberlé Crenshaw made the point in a roundtable discussion in the journal *Tikkun*, only to be countered by Catharine McKinnon, who argued that gender shouldn't be the only factor in the Left's criticism of Thomas. This was a month before Anita Hill and sexual harassment, perhaps to some a more appealing "middle-class" women's issue than welfare rights.

Mainstream media circulated Thomas's nasty cliché of his sister as ammunition against his nomination. For the most part, though, the cliché was left undisturbed. The failure to look behind the stereotype sanctioned it. Scarier than the idea that Martin and women like her are disregarded—by Thomas, by the country, by the press—is how easy it is to disregard them. Who pickets, who lobbies, who screams? Used as a cutout for both pro- and anti-Thomas arguments, Martin remained just that.

As Emma Mae Martin was rendered invisible, so was Anita Hill, though in a more enigmatic way. Hers is the "postmodern variation on black women's 'silence' " Michele Wallace names in *Invisibility Blues*—in the frame, yet only when uncritical or mute. This is ironic when you realize that in the last month Hill has been the most visible and discussed African-American woman since Tawana Brawley. (This shows you, more representation, more screen time, doesn't always translate into more power.) Discredited for speaking as a woman and as a black person, Hill was rendered invisible as both. Looking for positive fallout from the hearing, many said that the black professionals on parade made appealing role models. And Anita Hill—shunning victimhood, though somewhat reluctantly—is admirable. Yet what happened to Hill sent a more forceful message than her face on the tube: Speaking out doesn't pay. A harassed woman is still a double victim, and a vocal, critical black woman is still a traitor to the race.

Despite his loud and repeated insistence that he was being persecuted by stereotypes, Thomas and the committee did more than any gangsta rapper to refocus attention on rancid formulas of black femininity. The stereotypes that blanketed Hill were far more insidious and destructive than the Big Black Dick myth that Thomas shouldered, a comic image kept alive by the pornography that he allegedly consumes. Try the Black Bitch—the emasculating matriarch, calculating and bitter. Or her younger sister, the male-deprived black professional woman caught in a "fantasy," as if the reality of a relationship with a man like Thomas, his sexual interest in her, or potential to be threatened by her were beyond her intrinsic worth.

Or the Handicapped Intellectual. Often Hill's legal education, powers of reason, and ability to articulate herself were on trial or the source of curious, as in disbelieving, interest. Or the Black Woman With a Color Complex. You might not have caught this stereotype as it zoomed by so fast. Thomas went so far as to speculate at one point in the hearing that Hill's motive for depriving him of his natural right to sit on the Supreme Court was her jealousy that he dated a light-skinned woman and promoted one at the EEOC.

There was also the Sexually Available Woman prototype, the one we can't shake. After all it was practically legal to rape a black woman up until the second half of this century, and still remains, as recent New York cases and media coverage attest, less newsworthy a crime. In an exquisitely backward op-ed in the *Times*, sociologist Orlando Patterson defended the alleged harassment as a "down-home style of courting" done while Thomas had his "mainstream cultural guard down." Thomas, Patterson argued, "may have done something completely out of the cultural frame of his white, upper-middle-class work world, but immediately recognizable to Professor Hill."

The battle of Hill/Thomas also taught us how invisible we (black) women are as black people. It's always been our burden: The community depends on our silence, and "race" is often used by our brethren to keep us from speaking critically. When we do, we're tagged as agents of the oppressor, devaluing anything we have to say as coming from a black perspective, from black people. Among its many achievements, what the Thomas/Bush lynch strategy did was promote male experience as the only black experience. (More working black folks saw prime-time Thomas than daytime Hill. And after Thomas's lynch speech, support for him among African Americans, according to *Time*, jumped from 60 to 70 percent.) But if we wanted to reduce history likewise: Was not the "rape" of Anita Hill by this process a definitive black experience?

———

A young civil rights lawyer confided to me recently that the Thomas hearings were the source of the most painful experience in her professional life. A month before Hill, she did an anti-Thomas teach-in on WLIB along with influential black New Yorkers, among them *Amsterdam News* publisher William Tatum and State Senator David Patterson. Callers were supportive of her. A day after Hill's allegations were made public, she was invited on WLIB again, this time with three other female lawyers. The lawyers didn't say unequivocally that Hill was telling the truth, only that she deserved to be heard. The tone of the call-ins changed radically. The panel was vilified. The word "feminist" was a curse worse than "bitch" and associated with female shame and the betrayal of black men. The last caller, a woman, said that the community should be happy that Thomas went after a black woman.

Some of the most virulent anti-Hill voices I heard during the hearings came from black women. But this hostility is easy to trace: Who loves or abhors a black woman more than another black woman? The little value we have for one another is yet another enabler of our invisibility. What's the source of this? We rarely see each other in positions of power, know few role models. For those of us who are heterosexual, media images have us fighting over what statistics warn is a dwindling supply of black men. The old "I'll cut you if you look twice at my man" posture is trotted out in every film from *Pinky* to *Livin' Large*. (At Thomas's swearing in, John Doggett III, the man you'd think would be every black woman's worst enemy, was pounced on by young women after his autograph.)

In the middle of the Hill/Thomas live-action morality play, I accompanied a friend to an abortion clinic. The assisting nurse, a black woman, chatted on as she hooked my friend's legs into the stirrups. She disagreed with Thomas's politics, yet didn't believe Hill one iota. Why? Just didn't trust her. Certainly lingering beyond the hearings is the stench of our distrust for one another. Those who know how sisterhood saves have a heavy responsibility to pull women of the "Video Music Box" generation up by the garter straps. Raised on video's business-as-usual violence against women, they have, as a shield, internalized distrust of other women in ways that seem unparalleled in my adult life.

Black women need feminism more than ever. Who else, after all, has a stake in our visibility—in an affirming community, in our power and representation—but ourselves and all those children we're raising? The cost of blind race loyalty will be our lives. With the Thomas nomination and hearings, Bush has set an ugly new standard for cunning manipulation of race and the black community. No doubt he'll continue to do the slick thing, vetoing legislation like the Family Leave Act and an unemployment benefits bill while pulling the wool over our eyes with opportunistically black politicos like Thomas.

That Anita Hill spoke at all, despite efforts made every step of the way to deny her voice, despite the mud or the consequences, was in the spirit, I'd like to think, of an older, more valiant generation. How many more African-American women, though, share Emma Mae Martin's story? Educational and economic barriers and the weight of family responsibility keep us silent, keep us from challenging the political process and discourse that boxes in our lives. Though absent from the harassment proceedings, at the confirmation hearing Martin sat behind her brother, head bowed. Whatever personal hurt she felt from his public smear of her was submerged, as she closed ranks with the family. Martin's family loyalty seems analogous to what race loyalty often means for black women: protecting the honor of men and the race before self.

What we have to realize as African-American women is that gender is not just a "self" issue. We are the community. (With the great numbers of female heads of household living below the poverty line, we definitely are the underclass.) It's on us to challenge the community with our concerns. Given the state of civil rights organizing now—its vacuum of leadership, lack of agenda, and loss of target constituency—this is an ideal moment for black women to create a popular movement to fill the void.

Working through existing channels could be a start. Last July the National Association of Black Journalists elected its first woman president, as well as four women to a five-member executive board, through the clout of a two-thirds-female membership. In her acceptance speech, new president Sidmel Estes-Sumptner, an Atlanta television producer, told the group she was putting the newsrooms of America on notice about their hiring practices. "They haven't heard from a black woman before. Especially not a black woman from the South," said Estes-Sumptner, bringing the women in the convention hall to their feet, hands in the air and far from silent.

1991

she came with the rodeo

I come with a dowry. Four boxes of props, most notably a construction hat, plastic pork chops, and several unused diaphragms poked with holes. Two boxes of costumes, among them a half-dozen pairs of black leggings well worn at the crotch. One box of faded press releases announcing the Rodeo Caldonia High-Fidelity Performance Theater. An album of photographs showing young women outfitted as urban witch doctors in faux-leopard skirts, lace veils, and the occasional cowrie-shell ankle bracelet. A black leather motorcycle jacket brought brand-new for twenty dollars from a junkie on Astor Place—its side pockets now caked with bits of Jolly Rancher water-

melon candy and missed birth control pills, its breast pocket permanent home to a small tin of rum raisin lip gloss, a New York City
subway token from 1986, and a crumbled copy of the last page of
Shange's *Spell #7*. The play's final line is circled in red: "crackers
are born with the right to be alive/i'm making ours up right here in
your face/& we gonna be colored & love it."

I am a Caldonia and these are some of my personal effects.

We decided against the Warm Leatherettes and took Caldonia, fan-
cying the inheritance of B. B. King and sundry blues songs that told
of "hardheaded" brown girls with pretty lips. Caldonia, B. B. sings,
why is your big head so hard? A rodeo brought folks together to stir
up dust. Shange herself had moved to Texas and was riding bare-
back. We were impressed. Rodeo Caldonia, it was. Twelve women,
sometimes more, in our twenties and giddy with our own possibility. We were gonna do theater. Performance pieces we were calling
them. We didn't care much about genres and structures and things.
Our need was to get out in public and act up; to toss off the
expectations laid by our genitals, our melanin count, and our college degrees. Rodeo heralded our arrival: young, gifted, black, and
weird (so we thought), and in search of like souls.

*We splurge on a cab to carry props. Me, Celina, Derin, and our
caravan of shopping bags and backpacks. First stop at a drugstore to
buy spray paint and Tampax, then to Sweetwaters to do Carmella &
King Kong in the basement. We have nerve to knock egos with R&B
supper club legend Arthur Prysock. His people get mad at us for
taking up too much dressing room space. In the hallway we run lines
as the guests arrive. Suited-up black folks from the upstairs, up-class
Sweetwaters come watch our show, along with our dread and Lycra
friends from downtown. The Uptowns snicker and squirm. But we
are hardly studying them; this is for us. After the show Prysock's
henchmen ban us from the dressing room, so we gather instead in the
tiny ladies john. Wasn't Sandye's eye rolling absolutely brilliant?
How did Candace manage to give La Josephine and valley girl all at*

once? We are the most beautiful women in the world. Art, says Nan Goldin, is about leaving a record no one can revise. We are not thinking of hereafters. Art is how we love ourselves now.

In the summer of 1985 I took a trip with my sister Kellie to the Virgin Islands, where we had some meaningful exchanges with local gigolos on the beach. My sister's a curator and art historian and she suggested I write a piece based on our encounters, a performance work to go along with the latest exhibition she was organizing, this one at an old schoolhouse turned alternative art space in the Bronx. The exhibition, "In the Tropics," was to examine the Caribbean's image as playpen of the Americas for some, and as hometown for others. At the time "my writing" consisted of a few record reviews and a short story published under a pseudonym in a college literary magazine. Kellie kept insisting I had that elusive thing called a "voice" that would lend itself to more ambitious work. I doubted this, though I took her invitation anyway, and came up with something that didn't quite fit the bill, but was what I had on my mind at the time. *Carmella & King Kong,* billed as "an act of jungle love," is the story of pagan goddess Carmella who falls in love with Sepia dawg Kong and loses, among other things, her mind.

Carmella became a performance piece, whatever that means, a play with photographs, shown as slides projected on a screen above the stage. The stage in this case happened to be the hallway of the old schoolhouse. I got together some actresses and singers I knew, or really young women aching to be, and put the thing on, which meant directed, carted props, cleaned up, and played financier on my two-cents-above-minimum-wage salary as a copy editor. The exchange of energy and kinship had to continue, so us young women aching to be proclaimed ourselves a group and kept going.

For such a grand name, Rodeo Caldonia High-Fidelity Performance Theater, we had a small repertoire: two theater pieces written by me, *Carmella & King Kong* and *Combination Skin,* and one poetry revue, *Welcome to the Black Aesthetic,* that never made it to the stage, though was quite the out-of-body spiritual experience to rehearse. Probably our most significant contribution to the world of performing arts was us roaming the streets as a pack, showing up at parties, and talking race, sex, and hair into the night over Celina's barbecue wings and Donna's guacamole. A kind of traveling conceptual art piece on black female representation, in which Diana Ross's whine matters as much as Mary McLeod Bethune's institution building. We kept the Rodeo together for two years, from 1986 to 1988, then hit the road alone.

With my body on fire. We are now booked at Sweetwaters' basement for the entire month of August. Tonight is my birthday. The Caldonias bring out a plastic gag cake and the whole basement sings. Look at me, smiling and sweating; me, ravenously horny with cheeks flush red. We hide our props in a utility closet hoping no one will notice and trash them. We head downtown. There's a surprise party at Mom's. The gold earrings from Derin mean so much, I know how tight money is these days. We are always going someplace else, with our pedal-pusher pants and naps on display, and our dangling earrings and men's oxfords. Head further downtown. The secret lover has thrown a party at a squatter's loft in my honor. The Caldonias dance together in a circle, laughing loud and showing off. Lover eyes me from a corner where he works the turntables. Can there be another, another, just another night, I say, please.

Presenting, the Caldonias. The empress of 'tude Celina Davis, dancer/writer/director, runs ground control and protects us from wolves in sheep's dreads. Derin Young, singer/songwriter, is 100 percent adrenaline uncut. Our resident coquette, Candace Hamilton, does Marilyn mopped up with a biscuit and a side of collards. Lorna Simpson is simply the most beautiful woman west of Dakar and north of Papeete. Her photographs, with their silences and whispers, inspire us to bring our own secrets to the art. Donna Berwick translates big ideas into costumes with little explanation. A trained actress with a capital T, Sandye Wilson gives us a healthy dose of grief for being laissez-faire about theater form. We adopt sixteen-year-old actress Amber Villenueva as our baby girl. Kellie

Jones, advance squad, cooks a mean fried porgy and spreads the word about the shows. Actress Raye Dowell and her ingenious sense of style (Negress flower child roams the diaspora while reading biographies of Frida Kahlo) are the impetus for many a Caldonia to practice dress-up as daily performance art. (A look Raye made classic: a Black Power button stuck on a floppy, resort-wear hat. The effect: Baps do revolution too.) Our most accomplished craftsperson onstage, Pamala Tyson, gives big sister and class clown. Alva Rogers becomes our mascot. Her haunting indigo beauty is "ancient to the future," like the arias of Art Ensemble of Chicago. Alva's sheer presence and her singing, a blend of opera, jazz, blues, and nursery rhyme, always explain us better than any motto.

We are joined at times by artist Alice Norris, hat designer Suzanne Kelly, and actress Daphne Rubin-Vega, and later by Stephanie and Suzanne Jones, twin turks of parody. But we remain a constant: Smart-ass girls with a sense of entitlement, who avail ourselves of the goods of two continents, delight in our sexual bravura, and live womanism as pleasure, not academic mandate. Ten years earlier, when most Caldonias were just graduating junior high, Shange had told black women to find God in themselves. We are the prodigal daughters come home to roost. Lots of lip and shorter hemlines.

Derin's mom taught her Yoruba songs in their apartment in East New York. Derin went to Stuyvesant, the brainy-kid public high school. She majored in political science like I did. Thought she was gonna be lawyer too, but ended up singing. Vicious Deenie I call her, 'cause she talks as fast as she thinks: subway vibrations as music; hidden messages of cartoon theme songs; a racist master plan coded in Social Security numbers; the splendor of black velvet against brown skin. Ironman calls her the Last African Virgin. It's her eyes. The eyes of a princess sold by her tribe to the slavers. Old eyes.

A cherished keepsake of Rodeo is that it was, without premeditation on our part, a walking tableau of diva complexity. Each eccentric self and artistic point of departure—from the composer of fabulist slow jams (Derin) to the collard Marilyn (Candace)—made possible one's own. We didn't come together around a rigid ideology or fixed notion of black identity. We came simply to break bread and share our yearnings. And in this common space, each found her own voice, her own funk.

Black men had jazz and athletics, places where dignity, auteurship, and creative exploration were possible despite the barbwire elsewhere. Where were such collective spaces for black women? African Americans have a regal history of solitary divas. Pick any number of great artists—Josephine Baker, Billie Holiday, Adrienne Kennedy—they made amazing work in isolation or under the wing of white patronage or in a community of men. And, yes, there were the quilting circles and the club meetings and the antilynching activist groups and Madame C.J's cadre of beauticians. The girl groups of the sixties made their mark (though as a whole, they were more prefab vehicle than acts of woman genius). The literature had its own matrilineage. But where were the women who made mad, reckless, and twisted music, dance, and theater together? Who told of longings other than the arrival and departure of characters called "my man"? Or invested these arrivals and departures with a deeper echo?

Later on we found out about the International Sweethearts of Rhythm, *dames de couleur* in a blazing swing band from the forties; and the social protest folk of Sweet Honey and the Rock born in the seventies; and the poetry-theater jam sessions of Jessica Hagedorn, Thulani Davis, and Ntozake Shange in the early eighties; and found contemporaries, like choreographer Jawole Willa Jo Zollar and her company Urban Bush Women, who slam-dance to the squeaky dream songs of writer/performer Laurie Carlos. So "we the wild girls," as Alva Rogers called us in her swan song to Rodeo written in 1989, were not alone after all.

Critics were convinced that women responded to *For Colored Girls* only because it spoke loud about black male sexism and ended with a man throwing his children out the window, which said critics read as a declaration of war against all black men. But the real thrill, the visceral thrill of *For Colored Girls*, was those seven women characters, in their matching dresses, each in a color of her own, carrying on in their girl language in their all-girl space. Have you ever stomped with a drill team? Played jacks? Jumped double dutch? Or been grateful enough just to turn the double-dutch rope? Put on makeup in a bathroom crowded with Kabuki dolls? Out-switched and out-sang the Supremes, the Ronettes, or the Vandellas, casting yourself as Diana and your two best girlfriends as Flo and Mary? If not, you just haven't lived. Men end up by default of imagination being the justification for these acts of bliss. Like they say in jazz, "He thought it was about him." And he was wrong.

Donna and Lorna together. Friends for ages from Queens who found their way to the Rodeo. Their sign language is all raised eyebrows and pursed lips. They converse in an intricate syncretic dialect of Queens b-girl, art criticism, and haute couture–speak known only to sets of Silent Twins. Them giggling and leaning against each other expresses all that I love about being a colored girl. They are always in conspiracy; a whisper, a poke, then Lorna's belly laugh and Donna's tee-hees. Lorna's skin is seamless brown silk, Donna's all cream. Their difference in color is minus the familiar divide of privilege and shame and seems to exist just for our looking pleasure. They must know how beautiful they are side by side; they cannot contain their good fortune to be, as Nel longs for Sula, girls together. Thick as thieves, rushing boys' hearts with a glance. If we all could be like Donna and Lorna, girls together.

With Rodeo I was able to dig out that voice Kellie was so certain I had. It surprised me when I did find it. It is a laughing voice, impudent, at times even sinister. Not at all, some say when they meet me, like me, a short girl who is polite to old people and painfully shy. In the company of the Caldonias I become a rogue. Our call and response is lusty and loud. I begin to write thinking of Rodeo as my audience, not, as I had done before, the gray bosses at work, gray professors at university, gray poets of the textbooks. This frees me, I feel at the time, to say and do anything.

Talk about blue lights in the basement. We were witnesses tonight. Saw this power hovering above, we actually saw it. A blue magnetic field. Freaky-deaky. A visit from ancestresses or something. Alva, as Carmella, and Sandye, as Torch Singer, took the spirit and rocked. Had a table reserved for Gramma and Aunt Cora. They got stuck in Jersey traffic and missed the show. Sweetwaters agreed to let us do the entire thing all over again just for Gramma. Must've been her silver Afro and the way she strut into the joint like it was a meeting of the Phillis Wheatley Literary Society. I did hide behind the bar while Derin and Amber, as Beautietta and the Twilights, set up the voodoo pyre with those diaphragms next to that Alice Walker datebook and those plastic watermelon harmonicas, but Gramma and Aunt Cora laughed for days. Those Sweetwaters people must think we're très weird. Our boyfriends don't comb their hair. Derin's running around calling herself the reincarnation of Lieutenant Uhura. Alva mainly stays to herself munching on blue corn chips and reading Black Women in Nineteenth-Century American Life. *And there's Candace, always trying to sell the bartenders antique jewelry or Jamaican cupcakes, then getting onstage as Princess Pamela the restauranteuse in those polka-dot spike heels, waving plastic pork chops around and talkin' 'bout the affair she's having with Idi Amin.*

Satire was a large part of the voice I found in Rodeo. As I saw it back then, satire made possible both a celebratory and critical dialogue with one's self and the world. I got to disarm the pain and dance away triumphant. I never studied it formally, but found it in steady supply in my Rodeo cronies. Pamala Tyson's *Soul Train* locker-dancer interpretations told a minihistory of black gesture and dance, of coonery in bed with racial pride, of elegance and the persecution of those who measured uncool. Alva Rogers's nursery rhymes were either theme songs of horror films or vestiges of a "Brady Bunch" childhood in the South Bronx or more likely both.

The Rodeo got taken to task for our humor and enjoyment of it. One memorable occasion was on a late-night talk-radio show. How dare we, the host was anxious to know, call a black male character King Kong? Had we forgotten how scorned black men were in America? How could we, as we did in the slides that accompanied *Carmella & King Kong,* show photos of bare black breasts alongside Fannie Lou Hamer trudging through the southern dust? Was Pam Grier worthy of being named in the same breath as Coretta Scott King? There was this assumption that being black and a woman carried with it a responsibility to be dire and remorseful. Or mystical and abandoned. Or issuing proverbs from the rocking chair. You-all are having too good a time, said the stares we got from the host, you don't want folks to think you girls are hoes. As if there was no identity between that of the girl who wanted the bluest eyes and that of the grandmother who had learned to love her brown ones, except that of a ho.

He tells me the play is all wisecracks, one-liners. Not as smart as the first one. Midnight somewhere downtown, on a side street empty except for cabs shooting from the dark like comets. I sit on a stoop and stare at my hands. Then get tough, shake a finger in his face, throw a punch. Finally I cry. So it had mattered what he thought. Rain falls and I go on crying like the movies. Unlike the movies, he stands there guilty, twenty-eight years old and still unable to put his arms around a woman in public. Years later he tells me I was postmodern without reading up. Way ahead of my time. That good. After all.

Growing up, the Caldonias inhaled the parody so evident in blaxploitation flicks and saw, through the rose-colored glass of childhood, the Black Arts movement's celebration of everything Afroed and black. The renaissance of fiction by black women that dawned in the seventies, we caught that too. These books made us feel less invisible, though their stories were far from our own lives as big-city girls; girls who took ballet and were carted off to Planned Parenthood in high school so as not to risk that baby that Mom, not Mama, warned would have "ruined our lives." College was expected. The southern ghosts of popular black women's fiction, the hardships and abuse worn like purple hearts, the clipped wings were not ours. We had burdens of our own. Glass ceilings at the office and in the art world, media and beauty industries that saw us as substandard, the color and hair wars that continued to sap our energy. We wanted to hear about these.

I travel to New Orleans. For sale, for sale, get your mammie figurines, for sale. Stout blackened women with red bubbles for lips and starched white aprons. No resemblance to my grandmother or great aunt. Women with width, but women whose mothers made sure their baby girls never had to step foot in the big house with a rag and Murphy's Oil Soap ever again. CONTEMPORARY REPLICAS OF A BELOVED AMERICAN CLASSIC, *says the sign in the curio shop. I buy two. Back home I chop off their heads and put the torso mammies in a performance piece.*

There was talk in 1986 of the arrival of a new way of looking at the world by young black artists. The new black aesthetic it was called by those who christened it, namely Trey Ellis and Greg Tate, and those who spread the word such as Michele Wallace and Henry Louis Gates, Jr. This aesthetic was described as being wide enough to contain everything from Spike Lee's Hollywood-financed dramedies, to Lorna Simpson's photo-text and its landscape of female symbols, to the revamping of the classics by Armani-clad jazzbos who had no use for the avant-garde, to hip-hop's deification of Malcolm. It was said to embrace, among other things, irreverence, profit-making, an elastic view of "black" art, ideas of integration and nationalism, a yen for tradition (or at least the apparel), and the usual questions about who we are and where is our home. Rodeo was named as one of upstarts of this aesthetic. Such a lofty goal was the furthest thing from our minds back then, I can testify. Though reflecting on those performances of ours—really rites of self-discovery staged in supper-club basements, church sanctuaries, and bars —it's clear to me that our take on blackness and femaleness did trumpet the cultural explosion that followed.

Two photographs of Rodeo, one that appeared in *High Performance,* a magazine covering performance art, and one in *Interview,* scorched through the available portraits of black women and caused a stir at the time, this being 1986. In the *Interview* photo we pose in party dresses from the fifties and African-print lapas. Alva holds a flower. Lorna wears glasses. We are not selling sex or pain, but we are sensual. Our skin color variations make a lush fresco, and our jumble of hair textures and styles is throwing curveballs at correctness. There we are, breathing intelligence, mischievousness, and triumph (that word again). There's also something pampered about us and fancy-free. We're not career girls or call girls or Bess or Beulah. We seem to be urban intellectual bohemians or art school grads or some such diva. Miles from naturalistic. In 1986 this was still a brand-new image. Had young black women been presented this way before in the mainstream? Apparently not.

Julie Dash called. She was in preproduction for a film called *Daughters of the Dust* and wanted Alva Rogers as her lead. Cinematographer Arthur Jaffa was equally spellbound. There were calls from Hollywood agents and production companies. Letters from young bohemians from Iowa to Teaneck. We became a metaphor for a new generation by standing in front of a camera and being ourselves, with a little stardust courtesy rags from Donna's bottomless closet. In the *Interview* photo, I am wearing a red silk bathrobe. A white baby doll is pinned to my temple like of one of Billie's gardenias. (Who knows what look I was going for—Lady Day reincarnated as a womanist kitchen-table surrealist playwright?) I remember the day well. After the photo session the Caldonias walked around downtown, where we continued to act out and take photos of ourselves. Look at us, we were saying, acknowledge us, commit us to memory.

Nellie throws a fundraiser for us in his new brownstone duplex in Fort Greene. Filmmakers and cartoonists and hip-hop enfant terribles show. Everyone takes their shoes off at the door so as not to mess up Nellie's polished wood floor. This reminds me of the old days when Papa B. was a Moslem, no shoes in the house and no bacon. The Caldonias cook trays and trays of chicken. We stand beautiful and strong and explain our mission: to carry Hansberry's legacy to the twenty-first century. The men compliment us on our chicken.

Everyone was forming tribes. The Black Rock Coalition. Forty Acres and a Mule Filmworks. The nations of hip-hop. The Hudlin Brothers. George C. Wolfe assembled a team of collaborators that would eventually bum rush the American theater. At Irving Place, a club in Manhattan, some Caldonias and our lovers saw for the first time a band called Fishbone that manages to set our racial angst as black-teens-in-the-buttermilk to giggling power chords. The Caldonias held a benefit for *Diva DeKooning,* a magazine we planned to publish on the subject of black women's style as high art. (Our funders pulled out at the last minute, but the magazine remains a provocative idea.) At the benefit Robbie McCauley, Laurie Carlos, and Jessica Hagedorn debuted their new performance collective, Thought Music. Comedian Phyllis Stickney declined our invite; Hollywood beckoned. There was this feeling that we were living a movement marked by particular hairstyles, catchphrases, and T-shirts. The (white) American imagination had shifted. To be alive, young, and this new thing called African American suddenly made one relevant and commercially viable. Folk art, be gone. And so entered the vultures of commerce.

We help Derin move the rest of her stuff from her mom's place in Brooklyn to her new studio in Sugar Hill. She swears to us she lives underneath Butterfly McQueen, who may be mad and may zoom around her apartment all day on roller skates. Her man is up in the loft bed writing songs on acoustic guitar. Derin and I go stand in line for fish sandwiches. Fish "sangwiches" remind me of fried whiting in Newark. "Fried whitey," as it was called, which you ate with ice-cold watermelon. While Rodeo rehearses, sometimes I think of Papa B. Of Sterling Street, Spirit House, and the Spirit House Movers; of Papa B. rehearsing plays in the theater on the first floor of his house, Spirit House. How a dozen of us, adults and children, piled into a broom closet one night to record sound effects for Slaveship. *Recreating the entire Middle Passage in a broom closet. I was not more than seven, but I remember women crying and men moaning and someone holding me very tight, as if the ship and the water that Papa B. had told us to imagine were right there. I remember a flood of terror. The shackles and chains. The heave of the ship. The rocking.*

One night at Sweetwaters Sandye Wilson, who played Torch Singer in *Carmella & King Kong*, thanked Greg Tate for hanging. He had not come to lift props or lend some cliché version of emotional support; he was there to dig the art. Tate came every weekend of our run, along with other male artists-in-arms. It meant a great deal to have black men respond to the work. I was excited by the possibility of belonging to a community of artists where women and men could engage each other's minds with candor and the assumption of equality. Given the hostile divide in black literary circles, stoked to boiling point by the media, such an alliance seemed all the more meaningful. Though Rodeo and the male artists we moved with never did realize this community in any organized way, there was definitely an exchange of ideas going on, and a potent one.

Rodeo connected with black men who knew our art was woman-centered and were drawn to it for just that reason. Marc Brown, our makeup artist, lavished the work with the drama of opera and enthusiasm of a chocolate fiend in Nestlé heaven. (Marc's death from AIDS in 1988 was the loss of a true friend and a collaborator who I had hoped to work with for eons.) Steve Williams designed our flyers and was a loyal fan. Al Blue spread the word and helped on the technical end. Lewis "Flip" Barnes was a familiar beaming face in the crowd. Vernon Reid took part in an early workshop of *Combination Skin.* Brothers, all.

We carry crates of records to Harlem as the sun comes up, then make love all morning on a bare mattress on the floor. He tells me stories about Indian reservations in Florida and bars in Brooklyn called Dirty Bud's Recovery Room. He calls my clit a little old woman in a boat. At four in the afternoon we surface finally, but then only to take photographs of signs: WHITE HOUSE OF BEAUTY. MUSEUM OF COLORED GLASS AND LIGHT. SPACE ANGLES MYSTERY SOLVED.

The Caldonias were in relationships with men who were anything but "sitcom brothers." Young schemers like us, they were conversant in black politics and culture and had passed on job security for creative freedom. They too were exploring "out" texts of blackness—from minstrelsy to the dread hardcore of Bad Brains. Though I chose women as my primary subject, these brothers hit me with a challenge to make art that could also upend stock effigies of black men. Arguing, busting up, chowing down, and partying with these guys, I often felt during those days that the brother-sister thang glorified in black folk talk was a genuine, nourishing part of my life. It strikes me now how only one of those relationships survived the ain't-nothing-going-on-but-the-rent eighties; and how the men and women artists I knew from that period had wild-monkey passion but rarely ended up together; and how the men went on to marry women who were supportive, but not artists, while the women were still searching for love from a like mind.

I squint at the mirror. All my life I felt I was too big down there. I always covered up. Now I have calf muscles from climbing flights of stairs to the train, to my apartment on the fifth floor, to work, carrying props, journals, cameras, but still hips and still ass. Show that butt, wear tighter clothes, flaunt those hips, Donna says. It's Donna who dresses us and tells us how fab we look. Alva does our hair.

These two roommates know all the beauty secrets for black girls. Use this. Don't use that. Their elaborate rituals at the quest of beauty amaze us. They take this very seriously. Like Madame C.J. inventing a wider tooth hot comb. You will love yourselves by any means necessary.

The portrayal of feminism as some sort of game sport of man hating or pulpit of crunchy-granola correctness has always read to me like some impossibly cartoonish send-up. It remains so far from the feminism that I have lived, particularly the one I knew in Rodeo. I'd count Rodeo as my defining feminist experience, even though I've been calling myself the f-word since high school. In Rodeo I learned that feminism was to me, stripped to its intimate essentials, a passion for the creative culture of women and a belief that communion with other women was a bread-and-water necessity. Outside of debates on employment rights, abortion, child care, and whether feminism serves women of color—and the other big politics of the movement—what has kept me interested in feminism and *identifying* is the pleasure. The pleasure in women's voices, our dozens, our ways of caring and getting mad, and above all, in the way we love deeply. As some call it, *hard.*

Give me a girl gang, a crew. A zillion sisters ain't enough. To be a girl among girls, I feel as if I am at the height of courage and creativity. As an adult I am continually trying to re-create these spaces of safety and unconditional love. Like my grandmother's house, where Gramma, Aunt Cora, and Mom addressed the world's ills with a little Johnnie Walker Red and a clean dishrag. Like Mom taking her daughters out of the city in her geriatric car, us three singing love songs from the forties like belles of the ball. Like the We Waz Girls Together Off-Campus Collective at Renee, Myra, and Maria's, where we took character names from black women's fiction and imagined ourselves divas of myth. Renee was Willy Chilly, after the Wild Child of *Meridian;* let Desdemona keep stepping. Like Rodeo.

Lorna's photographs are in museums across the country now.

Amber is a rap star. Pam was an Ikette in *What's Love Got to Do With It?* The Jones Twins' crossbreed of theater and music, "be-bop muzak," can be seen around New York. Derin just got back from Japan, touring with French pop star Vanessa Paradis. She's gigging now with her own band in Parisian nightclubs. Alva is workshopping her play with music, *The Bride Who Became Frightened When She Saw Life Open,* and studying toward a masters in musical theater. Raye's living and working in L.A. Donna designs costumes for film. Celina's still directing. Kellie's exhibition, "Malcolm X: Man, Ideal, Icon," is touring the country. Candace, the relentless romantic, found love, made a baby, and now runs a small press with her husband. We never officially disbanded, just moved on. I went off to film school, a trade mill that frowned on the word "art", a drastic change from the feel-it, do-it aesthetic of Rodeo. The trade mill succeeded in convincing me not to trust that voice of my own, so recently found. Eventually I did get her back and I don't plan on letting her go any time soon.

There are times when I mourn Rodeo's passing on. Our grand schemes still beg to be realized. Imagine if we had launched, as we dreamed, an institution or two: a center to finance and stage work by black women in the theater arts regardless of waves of commercial interest, a multimedia production complex devoted to collaborations between African-American women across disciplines. Or think of what we could have done just as a theater collective, touring the country as ambassadors of kitchen-table surrealism, hauling our conceptual art piece on black female representation around the world. If we had gone national, Greg Tate is sure we could have done for womanism what Public Enemy did for black nationalism—made it pop. The next generation of Caldonias will have to take up that flag. Perhaps the young women of hip-hop, groups like T.L.C., have already begun.

Tonight's our reunion. We sit around 'til late (not so late this time) talking about days present and past, over Donna's guacamole and Celina's wings. Everyone's radiant and full of gossip. I ask for old

Rodeo stories. Celina, C. as we call her, goes first. Hers is about our gig at Blackbyrds, a little bar downtown that's long gone. Some young white gentlemen were using the stage as a chaise lounge. Our show was going up in an hour, but they weren't moving. I had arrived first and they flat ignored me. C. came next; they weren't having her either. The two of us sat there all frustrated with these white gentlemen. But soon the other Caldonias floated in. Just these women setting up slide projectors, throwing clothes, fixing hair, talking about last night's date and who would come to the show let loose a stream of energy that swept the white gentlemen off the stage; which is what spirit bound together should do, move mountains or, as here, molehills. After C.'s account, there's silence around the table. C. lets the silence lie. After a while she says, "That's my story."

My dowry: a motorcycle jacket and a mammie doll missing its head. Plastic pork chops and New Orleans amulets. Diana's whine, Josephine's wiggle, the roll of Nina Mae's eyes, Fredi's demons, Bessie's stomp, Billie's fruit, Adrienne's ghosts, Julia's wig box, Pam Grier's gun, Shange's God. A Caldonia girl. Swollen with dreams, fearless and fine. I came with the Rodeo.

1993

three

the blackest market

1-800-wasp

If you dropped dead tonight and were reborn in a mail order catalog, you'd say, "Please Lord, let it be J. Crew." So even in the next life, you could be seen, says the new fall catalog, "placing bids at Christie's" or "huddled in the stands at the Army-Navy game." Nouvelle prep, it is. Roll-neck sweaters dyed java ("the new black"), flannel blazers in basil or dijon. Working in the city, though bound for Cos Cob. Not as straitlaced Yankee as L.L. Bean, but urbanely WASP (more a state of dress, a wallet size, than a rigid racial criterion). Even Afrocentric iconoclast-bohème-girl writers hunger for some version of it. We mix the felt bowlers and peg-leg wool pants with kente knapsacks and MAKE BLACK FILM T-shirts. It's a look we can't resist: Zora Neale Hurston meets George Sand and Jessie Fauset at Emily Dickinson's cabin in Amherst. Our kind of weekend.

Catalogs are mighty image banks these days. The top trendies —Lands' End, Tweeds, and J. Crew—together mail millions of books each year to potential customers in fifty states. One quarter of J. Crew buyers are college students. (The catalogs are dropped in dorms by the pound.) Like MTV, these designer advert-zines arrived in the eighties; they seemed to enter our lives in a new way (in the mail and largely unsolicited) and they fed our national lore. We look for ourselves in their cultural display cases. When people of color are missing as models—and they are for the most part— they're "disappeared" as ideal consumers, as sample citizens.

J. Crew, born in 1983, is not really a catalog at all, but a lifestyle guide with full-page photos and commentary (low boots to take you from "Park Ave. to Patagonia"). Stores and magazines have lost their point of view, gloats company creative director Jim Nevins, but not J. Crew. What that p.o.v. is is not too hard to suss out: Class. The name's a dead giveaway: "Crew" for the Ivy League trademark sport. And "J.": possibly borrowed from J. G. Hook, which packages "well-bred, classical apparel for women with an upscale lifestyle," recites a company spokesperson. One of J. Crew's retail stores arrived in New York City two years ago at, where else, that yuppie theme park, South Street Seaport.

J. Crew sells its WASP fantasies not from a converted farmhouse in Greenwich, but from Manhattan, a few blocks above Fourteenth Street. (Their warehouse, in Lynchburg, Virginia, has a prefab elite address: One Ivy Crescent.) Perhaps it's a small irony, but Crew's customers are 60 percent urban, and California is one of their strongest market bases. Being a WASP these days may carry some modest stigma in name, though not in name brand. Everyone, so it seems, wants to wear WASP clothes. Or, more to the point, fill their shoes, confiscate their myth and power.

Flipping through J. Crew's aisles this fall, you'll notice more black models peppered throughout. More, but not many: four—three women and one man—out of more than fifty total. (One black model per catalog had been their running standard.) September's male model has an eerie resemblance to actor Courtney Vance in John Guare's *Six Degrees of Separation.* (The play's based on the true story of a young black man who—armed with nothing but an oxford shirt—ran a con game on rich whites.) With so much banking on image, since the consumer can't touch or try on, every choice designers make is carefully considered. The decision to use black models, especially in a catalog like J. Crew that oozes Anglo out of every 100 percent cotton pore, must be no exception. Were J. Crew's black models a nod to the racial rainbow seen in fashion mags or liberal window dressing? Or, better yet, a conscious effort to attract African Americans in what may be the waning days of the catalog boom? With annual postal rate hikes, catalogers can't afford to prospect randomly for new customers, why not target blacks?

"We don't do race-oriented marketing," said Adrienne Perkov, J. Crew's director of new market development. "We try to make the product available to everyone." That's an old standby: We don't market to a particular racial/ethnic group (i.e., whites, when we use all-white models), we sell a life-style. As if whites are "everyone," because it's assumed they have no race, and blacks can't signify this "everyone," because we do have one. "We always use a few," offered creative director Nevins, but he didn't have a clue why there would be more black models this fall. Although the company did a customer survey last year, according to Rae Slyper, director of marketing, race wasn't queried. "We wouldn't think of asking anything like that," Slyper yelped, nearly horror-struck. "Is this article about MINORITIES?!?"

"Invisible People" is the title of a new study of "minorities" (whatever that means in these times of shifting demographics) in magazine ads and mail-order catalog, compiled by New York City's Department of Consumer Affairs. The meager representation of nonwhites is supported by two industry myths: that blacks in particular don't have disposable income (black consumer spending, the study says, will max out at four hundred billion dollars this year); and that when blacks appear in ads, companies experience "white flight" (a falsehood disproven by market studies since the sixties. If anything, putting black models in ads increases sales because blacks identify with them and buy more). Of the 157 catalogs reviewed, blacks made up less than 5 percent of 22,685 models pictured, despite the fact that blacks buy from catalogs at nearly the same rate as whites. (And a disproportionate number of the black models used were juveniles or light-complexion adults.) Several high-circulation catalogs, such as L.L. Bean and Laura Ashley, were whites-only.

Courting black consumers could mean better business for a catalog like J. Crew than the company might realize or be willing to acknowledge. Black people spend a good deal of their disposable income, says African-American consumer-market specialist Persephone Miller, on "image-enhancement" products, which include designer-label clothing from "upscale retailers." We tend to have poor images of ourselves, and through these products we seek to belong, to be accepted.

For those of us who don't "belong" in stores, the idea of shopping in the privacy of our own homes has a double meaning. Mail-order catalogs—toll-free, twenty-four-hour hotlines—are a racially stress-free shopping encounter, no more hassles, no more watchful eyes. All you need is a major credit card (which you might not have, since a lower percentage of black folks have them), and you're guaranteed unconditional acceptance. No one has to know your race, just buy. Or as some might say, buy in.

1991

a doll
is born

This is my doll story (because every black journalist who writes about race gets around to it sometime). Back when I started playing with Barbies, there was no Christie (Barbie's black friend, born in 1968) or black Barbie (born in 1980, brown plastic poured into blonde Barbie's mold). I had two blondes, which I bought from girls at school with my Christmas money.

I cut off their hair and dressed them in African-print fabric. They lived together, happily polygamous, with a black G.I. Joe bartered from the Shepp boys, my downstairs neighbors. After an incident at school, where all of the girls looked like Barbie and none of them looked like me, I galloped down our stairs with one Barbie, her blonde head hitting each spoke of the banister, thud, thud, thud. And galloped up the stairs, thud, thud, thud, until her head popped off, lost to the graveyard behind the stairwell. Then I tore off each limb and sat on the stairs for a long time twirling the torso like a baton.

Do little black girls still grow up slaughtering or idolizing pink-fleshed, blue-eyed doll babies? Even after two cultural nationalist movements, four black Miss Americas, and integrated shelves at Kiddie City and Toys 'R' Us? In 1987 Dr. Darlene Powell-Hopson, a clinical psychologist, replicated a landmark study done by a team of black therapists in the forties; a study that was later used to argue *Brown v. Board of Education.* When asked which doll is the good doll, which doll is the right color, a large percentage of children, black and white, still chose the white doll. Powell-Hopson's twist was intervention. Before kids were asked to choose, they were told stories about the black dolls, stories that presented them as great beauties, as heroines. The percentages reversed.

Powell-Hopson got a call last summer. Some folks at Mattel toys had read her book, *Different and Wonderful: Raising Black Children in a Race Conscious Society.* Would she be interested in consulting them on a new product, a line of African-American fashion dolls to be introduced in fall of 1991? A number of black women were involved: There was Mattel product manager Deborah Mitchell and the principal designer for Mattel's fashion doll group, Kitty Black-Perkins (who outfitted the first black Barbie eleven years ago). And Alberta Rhodes and her partners at Morgan Orchid Rhodes running the PR train. Powell-Hopson did a little research on Mattel. Her main criticism: Like many large toy companies, Mattel had put few marketing dollars behind their black dolls. "Christie was always in the background in group ads," Powell-Hopson remembers, "and kids pick up those messages." But eventually she did sign on.

These women midwifed "Shani," whose name according to Mattel means "marvelous" in Swahili. (My Oxford University Press Swahili-English dictionary says "startling, a wonder, a novelty.") Shani's being touted as the first "realistically sculpted" black fashion doll, though small black-owned companies have been making fashion dolls for years. (And black-owned doll companies have been around even longer, perhaps even before Marcus Garvey's Negro Doll Factory run by the United Negro Improvement Association). Shani's debut at the American International Toy fair last month was an extravaganza fit for a bap in miniature. Mattel threw a party in her honor, complete with En Vogue singing the Negro national anthem.

Mattel calls Shani "tomorrow's African American woman" (one-upping *Essence*'s "Today's Black Woman"). She has a new body ("Rounder, more athletic," Mitchell giggles into the phone. "Her hips are broader, but she still can fit Barbie's clothes"); a new face (fuller lips and broader nose); and new clothes ("Spice tones, ethnic fabrics," glows Black-Perkins. "Not fantasy colors like pink or lavender"). And her new skin alludes to the range among African Americans: Shani, the lead doll, is berry-brown; Nichelle, deep mahogany, and Asha, honey, are her two friends.

I carry around a photograph of Shani and her playmates to show the girlfriends, who are single and childless and have no idea of the hard time black parents have tracking down culturally affirming toys, as do Powell-Hopson and Black-Perkins, mothers both. Not so fast, the girlfriends snap. "Why can't they make one with dreads?" whines Susan, who wears extensions and works for the U.S. Attorney's office. "They must be from D.C.," observes honorary girlfriend Alejandro, eyeing their loud costumes and sculpted hair. "That light one, Asha, is gonna sell out and leave poor Shani and Nichelle on the shelf," comes the usual grunt from the ever color-struck Tamu. Deandra is most upset: "It's the hair."

All three dolls have hair past shoulder length. Powell-Hopson had hopes that one of the dolls would have shorter hair, "an Afro, an asymmetrical cut, something." Mitchell admits that Mattel heard similar concerns in the focus groups: "To be truly realistic, one should have shorter hair. But little girls of all races love hair play. We added more texture. But we can't change the fact that long, combable hair is still a key seller." (When I relay this to Deandra, she sucks teeth: "More chicken-before-the-egg theories.") Fantasy hair or not, Powell-Hopson holds that the Shani doll shows "social consciousness on Mattel's part."

More like marketing savvy dressed up, nineties style, as social consciousness. Mattel knows that African Americans will make up nearly 20 percent of the population by the next century and that we have more disposable income than ever before. Sales of black Barbie doubled last year, following an ad campaign in black print media. Mattel decided to advertise after research showed most black consumers didn't know the doll existed. Black Barbie had been around for ten years (twenty-one years after Mattel introduced what it calls the "traditional, blonde, blue-eyed Barbie"), yet Mattel had never given her a major marketing push. The doll had only appeared, as part of a group of other Barbies, in a few adult-directed TV spots; kids had never seen her on the tube on Saturday mornings.

Fashion dolls aren't born every day. At least not at Mattel. There's Barbie, her friends, boyfriend Ken, and a few celebrity dolls now and then. Shani is Mattel's first "non-Barbie fashion doll." The women behind Shani, like Mitchell and Powell-Hopson, want her to be more than just a Barbie in blackface. Shani's "character sketch" (the doll's publicity fact sheet) matches her, dare we say, ethnically correct physique. ("She's not just a pretty face . . . she's very conscious of her culture.") In 1992 Shani gets a boyfriend. What about a play set? How about "Community Center," where Shani can teach black history to inner-city youth? Or "Corporate America," where Nichelle can argue with her boss about whether her braided hair is really appropriate in the boardroom?

1991

faded
attraction

I've got some crazy friends, I'm telling you. Now, Tamu is big humor. Tamu's thing is skin color. My girl is as high-yella as they come, or "light, bright, and damn near white," as goes another expression from the archives. Yet if a Negro is not pushing blue-black—complexion and politics—she won't give him the time of day. You've heard of reverse discrimination, well, she's reverse color struck. But don't blame Tamu, she's just a Black Power baby. In junior high in the early seventies she heard tapes of Malcolm X lamenting how the rape of black women during slavery deprived him of his rightful pigmentation. Well, she pitched her tent right there and hasn't changed camps since.

If poor Tamu had been in *The Wizard of Oz* she'd be the one singing, "If I only had some melanin." Naturally, anything folks do to lighten their skin gives her the heebie-jeebies. Mention Michael Jackson, she screams genocide. Skin peels and nose jobs are acts of treason. Her latest pet peeve: fade cream, also known as skin-tone cream, bleaching cream, skin whitener. Check *Ebony, Jet,* or *Essence* for the advertisements.

To remind me of the pain, the wounds, the subtext that these products carry with them, Tamu carts me off to the Schomburg Center for Research in Black Culture ("in Harlem, U.S.A.," as she would say) to scan back issues of *Ebony* and *Sepia* for fade-cream ads. Alongside ads for Sweet Georgia Brown Hair Dressing Pomade and Alaga Syrup, we find some beauties:

Nadinola Bleaching Cream (1952): "Few men can resist the charm of a honey-light complexion," says a fair-skinned model with a wink. Palmer's Skin Success Cream (1956): "Works to help your skin look clearer, fairer even when neglect and the sun of passing summers have made it hopelessly dark." Black and White Bleaching Cream (1949): "Those moments when he tenderly draws you closer for your triumph before his admiring eyes, that's when shades lighter skin becomes a priceless treasure."

The marketing and product identity of fade creams have kept up with the times: A 1966 ad for Nadinola, a skin-lightening cream first manufactured in 1899, reinvents it as a cosmetic that "brightens away skin discolorations." Fade creams kind of laid low in the seventies (in *Jet* they were replaced by ads for Raveen and Duke grooming aids for Afros). They made a comeback in the eighties, which saw a return to "lighter, brighter" standards of African-American beauty. (Dark and Lovely, a line of hair products born in the black-is-beautiful seventies, proclaimed in 1986: "Dark and Lovely Lightens!") Some of the recent print ads Tamu loves to hate:

Porcelana Medicated Fade Cream's 1989 campaign featured an early period Lisa Bonet look-alike, giving second-generation Spelman or Smith bap attitude. The kicker: "The faded beauty of Marlénne Kingsland." (This made Tamu's blood boil. How dare a product with such a dark—I mean, white—past try to be so damn upscale?) Ultra Glow Skin Tone Cream made it to the Afrocentric nineties this way: In African-print headwraps, models representing three shades of black beauty stare ahead defiantly. Ultra Glow, the ad boasts, keeps "women of color radiantly beautiful."

Tamu and I hop over to a department store down the street from the Schomburg to examine their fade-cream collection. A salesclerk named Verona, who's worked there three years, tells us that Dr. Fred Palmer's Skin Whitener is the most popular cream ("People come in and try to buy up the whole supply; we need to order more"). Verona reports that customers use the creams to fade dark marks left by blemishes. She herself stays clear of them: "I tried to use a fade cream once, but it changed my face different colors." What kind of different colors? "Dark black and blue." Blue? *Blue?* Tamu's on a mission.

Back home Tamu calls Dr. Claudette Troyer, a dermatologist at Harlem Hospital. The active ingredient in over-the-counter bleaching creams is hydroquinone, Troyer says, "a melanin-inhibiting" agent. Doctors prescribe it to even out skin color after pregnancy (hormonal changes can cause spotting) or to lighten dark scars after injury. Maybe two times a year Troyer gets women who want to be prescribed hydroquinone to bleach their skin a lighter shade, but most are out to get rid of dark spots. Is this stuff harmful? Even the over-the-counter products (which by law contain only 2 percent hydroquinone) can cause adverse reactions. When used too often, Troyer warns, dark blotches can appear on the skin.

Tamu discovers that the Food and Drug Administration (FDA) is reviewing O.T.C. bleaching creams, though the review (a general review that includes many other O.T.C. products) is a very slow process that has been underway since the seventies. In 1982 the FDA banned all bleaching products containing mercury. Until the review proves otherwise, those with hydroquinone are still considered safe. The American Academy of Dermatology faxes Tamu some articles published in medical journals in the late eighties that document cases where skin developed dark spots or was discolored

blue-gray after prolonged use of bleaching creams with hydroquinone.

Then Tamu happens upon the most amazing fact of the day. The
Dermatological Society of South Africa has documented thousands
of cases of black women who were disfigured by hydroquinone-
based skin lighteners. Last December the government banned the
products altogether. South African anthropologists believe one reason skin lighteners have been so popular with black women is that
beauty standards in the country are influenced by notions of racial
superiority. (*"I* could've told you that," snorts Tamu.)

To report the horrors, Tamu immediately gets on the phone
with another friend, a Puerto Rican doctor who also dates only
blue-black. "Yes, child," says Alejandro, "I remember Miss Skin
Success Cream [referring to a man he used to live with]. Miss Thing
had about six jars of it; I thought it was on sale. But no, girl, that was
about self-*hatred*, yes! My college friends came over once and liberated the stuff out of the medicine cabinet. Didn't they read him,
girl? "Miss Thing, you better get to the Clorox, 'cause it's not gonna
work!"

1991

make self-love

A young woman we know writes:

Lately in the mirror I am visited by an extraterrestrial with a Brillo pad for hair, a butt bigger than the land mass of North America, and toothpicks for legs. Has there ever been an uglier black child? Am I suffering from "self-hatred," that infamous and slippery condition pinned to black folks, or have I been in the Midwest too long? And what is this self-hatred stuff, anyway? Is it an accurate description of how Eurocentricity makes folks feel about their bodies, skin, hair, intellect? Doesn't it sound a bit severe? I mean, I don't *really* hate myself, do I?

Can we talk self-hatred? Maybe I know a lot of confident, in-the-positive black folks, but this idea of *hate* just rubs me wrong. The cultural renaissance and kente-youth movement aside, I've been all over the country and to Canada this year and have witnessed plenty of African Americans loving themselves (sometimes to sheer abandon!). You can see it in their pride, style options, right on down to the way they walk. And what about whites emulating us? Yesterday on the bus in Minneapolis I noticed five, count 'em, five white guys with dreadlocks. X-tension Generation, a hair salon in town, does nothing but dreadlocks and African-inspired braids for Caucasians. Does anyone talk about whites hating themselves when they do cross-cultural bonding, borrowing, or highway robbery? Of course not.

Before we buy the concept wholesale, seems to me black folks could benefit from a vigorous discussion of self-hatred on all fronts —in academia, media, the mental health community, at house parties. And, for once, can we put aside positive/negative image arguments, and what's black and what ain't arguments, and listen to what living, breathing people have to say about their choices and cultural balancing acts? Thank you very much.

You're not the only one all caught up with this self-hatred question. I've been devouring bell hooks's new essay collection, *Black Looks: Race and Representation*. You know hooks is my girl; she always gives a most fierce reading of race/sex conundrums. In "Loving Blackness as Political Resistance," hooks tells us that obsession with self-hate eclipses dialogue around loving blackness. The question she asks is not as obvious as it might seem: What would it mean to replace the discourse of self-hatred—rooted in victimization— with one based on loving, as the Batson Brothers say, "the Africa in you"? I'm right there with hooks. Thing is, hooks never challenges the notion that there are masses of folks out there hating themselves. I don't think there are myself, not exactly, at least. Then again, I live in the nation of Brooklyn, where switching butt, hair freestyling, dress-up, noses in the air, and black folks enjoying each other's bodies are national pastimes, so maybe I'm biased.

A couple of years back I clipped an article from *Essence*'s twentieth anniversary issue. I saved that thing in plastic, carry it with me everywhere. Audre Lorde, Octavia Butler, and other literary foremamas talk about surviving the last two decades. One piece came from Louise Meriwether, author of *Daddy Was a Number Runner* (which, along with *The Soul Brothers and Sister Lou* and *The Street*, were this girl's *Catcher in the Rye*). Meriwether says this: "I dislike the term 'self-hate,' which often is untrue. Disliking certain aspects of yourself is not the same as hatred. I prefer to describe the condition as a lack of self-love. I emphasize love, because whatever we focus on expands." The Meriwether approach speaks to me, okay? Let's contemplate and learn from how we got ovah, instead of dwelling on how we stay under. Can I get a witness?

But I know. It ain't as simple as all that. The lack of love for and devaluation of black bodies, black selves, is all too close. Just the other day, this woman pushing thirty comes up to me at a party talking about what "good hair" I have. I wanted to smack some sense into that child. Problem was, girlfriend had blue contacts on and I would've risked dislodging her retina. Then this friend, Jewish, who has a niece, Afro-Brazilian, told me about taking the eight-year-old to an exhibit at the Smithsonian on sixties fashion. In front of the Afro wigs, dashikis, and Black Power buttons, black niece asks white aunt: "Is black still beautiful?" Black is always beautiful, my friend coughed up between tears. She questioned later how many others could be counted on to give her niece this message, including the little girl's own mother, who is black. In *Black Looks*, hooks asks that we take a hard look at black children before engaging in "some new-age denial" of self-hatred.

Self-hate or not self-hate? I took the question to some mental health professionals, you know, black headshrinker types. The consensus was that the term wasn't appropriate or exact enough, although the "symptoms" are prevalent and exist across class. Psychologist Darlene Powell-Hopson prefers the term "low racial self-esteem." Often, she says, people, particularly children, "compartmentalize": They have race-based animosity toward other blacks, yet feel they're fine.

Psychiatrist Joseph Brewster, in private practice in Manhattan, tells me that what constitutes the "self" is the biggest debate in his profession, so "self-hate" is amorphous when it comes to any cultural group. Arguing race politics off the time clock, however, Brewster does use the term because it's familiar. More often than not, he says, black people, not the white power structure, are one's first channel of self-hating impulses. Brewster recalls some precious dirt he heard on an entertainment exposé show. Apparently it wasn't crossover success that drove Michael Jackson to a nose job, but taunts from his siblings about the width of his schnoz. The most cleverly disguised form of "self-hatred," according to Brewster, is the blame-whitey-hate-all-whiteys syndrome, which offers a false sense of comfort and superiority. Like a professor of Pan-African studies who told him as a college student that the white man was the devil, though not to bother majoring in math because "we didn't do well in it."

Of the dozen folks, young and old, that I got nosey with on the subject, all were vehement that they did not "hate" themselves, past or present. They did describe, at one time in their lives, disliking shape of nose, skin color, booty size, or hair texture. Denial, semantics, or evidence of the complexity of the issue, you choose. The only person who actually admitted to feelings of self-hatred was a very dynamic sister named Nora Hall. In her work as an organizational consultant Hall repackages the idea of self-hatred as shame. She says most people find ideas like psychological oppression, racism, and other "isms" so depressing they'd rather not deal with them at all. Shame makes it more intimate—and surmountable. Though whatever wordsmithing we do to dress up or dress down the matter, it's near impossible to grow up black in America without running smack into it.

I don't know if any of this is of use, but to hear hooks and others tell it, awareness is crucial. There's a body of evidence that speaks to our subjugation and one that speaks to our triumph. It's your choice which cloak you wear. In "Loving Blackness," hooks begins with Malcolm: "We have to see each other with new eyes." Girl, what can I say? Find yourself a new pair of eyes.

And would you please, in the jargon of self-help lit, stop awful-izing? You don't hate yourself, you've probably just come down with a bout of *Eurocentricity Blues*. Try dancing naked in front of a mirror to Sir Mix-A-Lot's "Baby Got Back" or Labelle's "Going Down Makes Me Shiver." Marvel at the magnificent soft sculpture of your cheeks. The fruit, the flower, of it all. Ask yourself, can a butt be too big? Then repeat after our patron saint of desire, Shange: "I found God in myself . . . and I loved her fiercely." If all that don't work, call me in the morning.

1992

profiling

Before Madonna discovered vogueing—and gay men gave birth to it in Harlem Elk lodges—there was profiling. Profiling is about being the high priestess of the moment. The feature presentation. It's about walking into a room, anywhere, anytime, and owning it. People of African descent are the kings and queens of it. Like my friend Alejandro, the doctor, who sashays into my apartment without a hello, sits at the table (as if waiting for the maid to wipe up the crumbs), crosses his legs, gives a half glance my way, and says, deadpan as hell, without missing a beat, "Here it is, Miss Two, just for you."

Profiling has a zillion and one meanings: To

know you look good or *think* you look good; to dress or behave in a way that attracts attention. Depending on the speaker's tone and delivery, it could be cut or compliment. My friend Percidia remembers the word from her high school days in Virginia in the late sixties: "There were two all-black schools in Richmond—Armstrong and Maggie Walker. And when these two played each other in football, nobody would be in their seats, everybody would be profiling *down*. People would walk from end line to end line and back, showing off their outfits, their hairdos, and talkin' 'bout other folks and their outfits and hairdos. Didn't see a play on the field."

Lately, profiling has been on my mind, and not just because of *Paris Is Burning*. (Do the dispossessed make mockery of the affluent when they master the pose, or do they reaffirm the vise grip the pose has on their psyches?) A few Saturdays ago I took part in a bare-bones spectacle of profiling. I haven't indulged in such shameless profiling since girlfriend Kim and I dressed in matching camel-color pantsuits to see the Commodores sing "Brick House" at the Garden. Because we were sitting in the boonies—second to last row—we felt obliged to sing, at the top of our lungs, along with every word out of Lionel Richie's mouth.

I'm here to confess.

Desperately in search of Negroes, my friends the Twins dragged me to a house party the Brownstone Underground was hosting at a Manhattan loft. The BU is a group of cousins in their twenties—the Jellerettes and the Griffiths—who work in media. They went to white Ivies (Cornell, Brown) and black Ivies (Morgan, Howard) and among the four of them they know just about every on-the-verge young specimen in the city—filmmakers, lawyers, writers, investment bankers, TV producers.

We rode by in a rusty sedan from El Barrio Cab Service, but had the driver drop us off one block west, so as not to be seen ducking out of such a skanky ride. Then we joined the mass of well coiffed, color coordinated, and casually upscale inching their way into the building. Even celebs were doing time outside (anchorwoman Rolanda Watts, with new long, blondish tresses, exchanged pleasantries with actor Kadeem Hardison). After an hour and a half on a line that wasn't moving, the Twins and I started acting out: the verbal component of profiling, engaging in loud and bodacious commentary to call attention to ourselves. Can you blame us? How could we justify waiting on line to get into a house party? Don't we have more juice than that?

Okay, so I led the pack by obsessing on the anchorwoman's supernatural hair color. But like all successful profilers, a scene began around us. Conversations flourished, most involving our favorite topics, race and sexual politics. "If black folks really want to control our culture, we're gonna have to come out our pockets," said a performance artist with corkscrew dreads. "To be perfectly honest," whispered a woman in a Ralph Lauren shirt, "I go home every night and play with myself, what do I need a man for?"

Our group left the herd pushing to get in and leaned against cars. At three in the morning newcomers were still arriving, and they had to decide whether to queue up with the desperados or lounge with us. Somebody rolled down a car window and turned on an AM-only radio. ("Oooh," one Twin moaned, "that's so ghetto, I love it!") The other Twin said she felt like pulling up a lawn chair and downing a cooler. She reminisced about the good old days at Howard, when Negroes would cruise the cul-de-sac facing the student center, all slow, showing off their rides. Once a guy drove by in a car, hitched to, yes, a boat.

The profiling high point, I must admit, did not originate with our group. You-know-who, an outside linebacker for a New York team, allegedly the most dominant defense player in football, arrived in a white limo. No, let me restate that: The folks driving the gentleman's limo backed it onto the sidewalk. Well, out comes the Hulk and, what, he can't get in. Even *he* doesn't have enough juice. (Or he hadn't profiled it successfully.)

An act of profiling justice arrived in the form of Ray Hands. A hatmaker who gives rent parties in his Bed-Stuy loft, Hands is no millionaire, unlike the Hulk. But, so says Miss Roj in George C. Wolfe's *The Colored Museum*, "God created black people and black people created style." And Hands is one of those folks God put on earth to throw together some style. Well, didn't Ray Hands pull up in his own white limo. (I saw those "Z" plates, Ray, don't lie, a friend must've cut you a deal for the night.) And didn't he emerge wearing a plaid Nehru jacket with matching shorts and, get this, the largest applejack I ever saw in my life. (Move over Lawrence-Hilton Jacobs.) Don't ask if the hat matched, you know it did. That damn hat was so big, one Twin dubbed it an "actual-size" applejack. Need we say, Ray got in. Swiftly.

1991

color therapy
by deandra

Love, peace, and hair grease, this is Deandra, coming to you live from Minnesota. What do you mean you don't know where Minnesota is? Get out your map, I'm talking Midwest and then some. Malls, snowblowers, jumbo thruways, a Lutheran church on every corner. Don't talk to me about sixty-below wind chill factors and hail the size of deer turds. I will tell you one thing. Hell is *not* about fire.

You know my best friend, Miss Columnist? She's here for nine months to explore the kinder, gentler America, where they don't run folks out of the neighborhood with baseball bats, they just burn a cross on your lawn—

your private property—and call it free speech. Girlfriend asked me to do the column this month, being that she's wrapped up in a severe case of culture shock. It started on the plane with the announcement of connecting flights to Dubuque (where they burn lots of crosses) and Milwaukee (where they eat lots of blacks). Never mind she was on her way to that happening, politically progressive town, Minneapolis, home of the Save the Earth movement and the purple Prince. What if she wandered into some Aryan Nation booby trap? What if Nazi yuppies chanting WELFARE SCUM! ate her for lunch? Poor diva hasn't left the house in two weeks and I'm nothing but an errand girl: Buy me Tampax, buy me blue corn chips, buy me *Essence* magazine.

Now girlfriend is picking up creepy vibes from the wheat field–theme Contact paper in the kitchen, the liver-colored tile in the john, the gerbil-beige carpet in the living room. The color scheme, she's convinced, is sending her subliminal white-supremacist messages. She yells, why didn't I pack her Nelson Mandela and Frida Kahlo T-shirts? She threatens to hang herself with the shower curtain if she doesn't see someone wearing faux kente cloth in the next forty-eight hours. Get to the couch, I tell girlfriend, it's time for color therapy by Deandra.

We begin slowly. I have her read aloud passages from Jean E. Patton's *Color to Color: The Black Woman's Guide to a Rainbow of Fashion and Beauty,* published this year. *Color to Color* is "Afrocentric color analysis" that brings racial uplift work to the closet and makeup counter. Patton claims Charleszine Wood Spears and Ella Mae Washington as godmamas in the struggle. Spears and Washington were African-American home economists who, as early as the 1940s, self-published manuals on selecting colors for skin-tone enhancement. Like "bad hair," Patton preaches, there is no such animal as "bad color." Purge your psyche of old race tales about hussy red and other "loud" hues that call attention to lusciously endowed Negro bodies. Don't take refuge from the hard eye of status quo aesthetics in muddy colors that "recede" you into the background.

Too hip for the "four seasons" approach, Patton arranges black folks in four "palettes" drawn from the diaspora and ancestral cradle. (Miss Columnist, you take the "spice" palette, which makes your celebrity models Tina Turner and Malcolm X.) Skin color variations are christened with references to sensual fabrics and high-caloric foods. And that enduring affliction of being "color struck," the preference for or hatred of complexions dark or light? Patton gives it joyous, new meaning just in time for Kwanzaa. Revel in the rainbow, *struck by color*, praise the Lord! Ssshh! says girlfriend, can't you hear the wallpaper whisper, "white power"?

I try the historical approach. We discuss culture and color research. The "color revolution" of the 1960s (psychedelics, anything-goes brights, the sophistication of monotone black or white) wasn't spontaneous generation but the by-product of nothing less than global political upheaval—the surge of youth culture, feminism, African independence. Before this, the Euro-American tableau had shunned colors associated with darker-skinned peoples (the African indigos, the hot Spanish reds), with a few departures, except as costumes. The enduring symbolism of evil, menacing "black" and innocent, clean "white" has its roots in nineteenth-century Europe's scientific racism. The "blackness" of Africans was seen as a disturbance of nature. (Were babies born black, French anthropologists who traveled to West Africa in the early nineteenth century wanted to know, or did they turn that color from too much sun or being kept in smoky huts?)

Color theorists in the seventies were quick to conclude that using "black" as a racial identifier would only hinder the social acceptance of people of African descent. Patton jumps on this in *Color to Color*, asking, what makes black-as-negative so fixed when the "values" of color change? Black, featured boldly in many flags of Africa and revered there as a symbol of power, health, and strength, has been in transition on Euro-American turf since the color revolution. By the eighties, Real Men Wore Black: It was out of mourning, it was "daytime." And though in clothing and design "all-black" is getting kinda tired, what's it being replaced by? High-energy color. Diaspora color! Girlfriend's still distracted. She throws every white towel, every curtain, every sheet into the middle of the room and yells, WESTERN, CHRISTIAN VALUES; EUROPEAN HERITAGE!

I walk girlfriend back to a chair and dump a pile of magazines and CDs on her lap. Look, I tell her. As they dominate the pop eye, isn't it arresting, inspiring, titillating to see young African Americans shake up colors—their iconography, their appeal? How these musicians, actors, and models saturate the cultural canvas with a prism of skin tones and the way they wear and present colors— Queen Latifah in warm pumpkin crowns, Arsenio in cobalt-blue suits, Living Colour, the band, throwing paint like Pollock, its Brit spelling shouting out to diaspora blacks: We are living, we are everywhere, we look good in fuchsia.

Girlfriend throws the magazines on the floor. She misses Brooklyn. She misses sisters in tangerine lipstick, stoops in Park Slope painted red, black, and green, nose rings, Isaac's purple high tops, faux kente shoulder bags, baby jumpers, evening wear, and place mats.

I give her a new box of Crayola crayons. Listen to this: In the eighty-eight-year history of Crayola, only two colors have ever had their names changed. One was "flesh," which became "peach" in 1962, "a result of the civil rights movement," says the official company fact sheet. (The color "indian red," lowercase to keep it consistent with other crayon names, still remains in the line.) Crayola has been spurred on by American teachers to test-market a "Skin Tones of the World" collection. You'll love the sticker on the pack: "A multicultural assortment . . . plus black and white for blending." Go ahead, I tell girlfriend, draw Brooklyn. She pouts.

Come on, you need a walk. We battle snow in search of cappuccino. We pass buses, billboards. Hey, isn't this a trip, we're in a state with a tiny, 6 percent population "of color," but all the outdoor ads we've seen feature black people: The Virginia Slims Afro-chic model in electric-blue kufi, Oprah in a different color low-cut sweater for each day her show airs, Joey Browner of the Minnesota Vikings in an ad for Zubaz workout wear uses a globe for a footrest. What does it mean? I'll tell you what it means, girlfriend snarls, they don't lynch Negroes here, they just put our faces on pancake mix. Obviously, I tell her, this color therapy stuff isn't doing you any good, maybe you're just PMSing. She sucks teeth: You have twenty-four hours to find faux kente.

In the coffee shop we meet a young man who says things like "my beautiful Nubian princess" and has, thank God, his very own faux-kente kufi. Walking home, Miss Columnist buys the latest *Ebony Man* with chocolate cover boy Wesley Snipes in, all at once, magenta pants, a goldenrod-and-hot-pink vest, and persimmon blazer. She tacks it above her computer.

I think she's gonna make it after all.

1991

dirt and overness

This is Brooklyn, there *are* no secrets. And if you can't take the heat, Miss Nine Months in the Midwest, call U-Haul to carry your wide-load receiver back to the cornfields, and don't expect me to visit." That's Deandra, of course, ever demure, ever tactful, ever too fabulous for her paycheck. Her advice: Give up hope for a private life now that I'm back in the borough. But didn't we all move from trigger-happy Sugar Hill and the overhip Lower E. to the maple groves of Fort Greene and Prospect Heights for sanctuary? So that no one we know or care about would see us in raggedy plaits pushing ten tons of dirty panties and humming our favorite laundry song, Phyllis Hyman's "Don't Wanna Change the World (I Just Want To Be Your Girl)"?

Well, I hate to break it to you, as Deandra broke it to me, but brush those teeth, take off those mammy-for-a-weekend headrags. You're being *watched* and your outfits are being *rated!* Didn't we find out that Miss Brooklyn is the most fabulous Negress of all? So fabulous, she makes a Pedro Almodóvar movie look like *The Muppets Go to Ibiza.* Know why? 'Cause we're all here! So and so, the songwriter-producer, and so-and-so, the model-actress turned cosmetic saleswoman, and we all live within five blocks of each other. You know what that means, don't you? What those polite little *New York Times* profiles on black, artsy Fort Greene won't tell you. Dirt! Dirt for days, years, centuries. Who's boning whom (or whatever the hype word of the week is), who left whom, who should've left whom, and who is "in euphemism" with whom, as in, "seeing," "friends with," or the least subtle, "talking to."

And overness? Self-absorbed, self-conscious, self-righteous, that's us. *Over*come with ourselves. We're too grand, aren't we, with our mud-cloth top hats and kente parasols? (Accessories really help us strike that balance between African and American, don't they?) And too fabulous, with our three-picture deals, European subsidiary rights, and our jazz-pop albums stretched out on the R&B tip, platinum-bound, no question. Johnny Kemp was a sage, wasn't he? It's about getting paid, because after all, getting paid *is* a black issue, isn't it? Naturally, there's concern that so-and-so is getting paid more for being black and fabulous than we are, but there's enough to go around—isn't there?

So when Deandra called last night to say meet me at Two Steps Down, one of those Fort Greene hangouts where the dirt flies fast and furious, I wasn't exactly rushing the door. Nothing against Two Steps, fine establishment, good food, but truth is, I wasn't ready to make my Brooklyn debut. I was two paychecks away from that kind of wardrobe. But Deandra has this way of twisting your arm, leg, and upper thigh, so I found myself on the D train, DeKalb bound. Along for the ride was a white woman in violet lip gloss holding a kitten and a black man in shades holding a fat, oily snake. They seemed to have just met, by chance, on this train car. Another woman was dressed head to toe in gold, to match a fifteen-inch gold beehive and nails, twenty-four-karat plated. Sitting next to the Flo-Jo lady was a young black guy with jeans way past his butt, a Mötley Crüe scarf tied on his head like the rock boys do, and his nose deep in the Holy Koran. I felt very much at home.

Two Steps, on the other hand, was full of mannequins from the Armani A/X sample sale. Deandra's friend, the young jazz-hybrid singer Gordon Chambers, was gospelizing his precious heart and soul out, yet the Fabs, having to choose between catching the spirit or striking the pose, chose the pose. Sucking down Kir Royales at a table front and center were Deandra and her crew, their heads bent together in weighty cultural exchange.

"I want to make it with Chris Rock, Wesley of course, fine Kevin Jackson last seen in *Caucasian Chalk Circle,* Sinbad but only on the cover of *Essence,* Cynda Williams's in need of a comb in *One False Move,* but did you get an invitation to the Jean Michel Basquiat opening, I did, it's a shame that *Vanity Fair* article tries to discredit Basquiat's work, white jealousy if you ask me, and by the way, should I name my dog Richard Wright or Wilfredo Lam?" said Deandra.

"Wilfredo Lam. Lam was a race man too, but he was an absolutely more sexy one than Wright 'cause he was a surrealist, and if you name your dog after him, more people will appreciate him, but really, I've got to figure out a title for my new book, obviously I need something womanist, something colored, and something to express my hybridity, but before that, I must talk for a moment about how guilty I feel sitting here drinking five-dollar champagne coolers when Fort Greene has the highest infant mortality rate in the city, and babies in the Walt Whitman projects two blocks away are being raised on a strict diet of Hawaiian Punch and Devil Dogs, and fine young men in Bed-Stuy shoot each other for recreation, but honestly the only bad thing about being a notorious black woman writer is that the current side pieces of all my ex-Negroes come up to me at literary events and try to run these weird power moves by announcing, in front of as many innocent bystanders as possible, that they are now screwing my ex-Negroes, then they look at me solemnly like I should care," said another dear friend, Tamu.

I used to care (about middle-class negritude and identity angst, that is), though lately I've been questioning my market niche. A job at *PC Magazine* is sounding real good. I met some nice guys at Cables & Chips the other day. I bet they could teach me a thing or two about ports and circuits. When I left Two Steps Down, Tamu and Deandra had their arms above their heads playing freeze tag. Deandra explained later that indeed they were not playing freeze tag, but attempting to be more colored, more fabulous, and more paid than anyone else in the room. And the only way to do this was to assume Diana Ross's I-Am-the-World pose, so vividly preserved on celluloid in *Mahogany*. But why were they doing this? Because Deandra's new Negro's ex-ex had just walked into the room and someone had to throw shade first. I headed straight for the pay phone downstairs. Forget the D train, get me a gypsy cab. Is this Black Pearl? Take me to Manhattan quick, Brooklyn is just two steps *over*.

1992

school
clothes

The white children on the back of the White Pages are smiling. They all have freckles and warm flannel shirts. "Can You Find the Drug Pusher In This Picture?" the caption asks, since this is an ad for the Partnership for a Drug-Free America. Read on, and in small type you'll be assured that none of these cherubs sell crack because, after all, "We all know what drug pushers look like. We've seen them often enough on television." The pushers are the guys in the baggy jeans with their baseball caps turned around, right? But wait, not *those* guys in the caps; the *black* and *brown* guys! Shucks, under those caps these days it's so hard to tell.

Our favorite storybook of the supernatural, surreal, and painfully real, *Jet* magazine, recently sampled black educators on the value of dress codes at inner-city public schools. All saw codes and uniforms as bait to get poverty-cycle kids to focus on academics and as an effective deterrent to school violence. Sobering tales were told of kids getting shot for wearing the wrong color or the right Nikes. And even of a rash of homicides in Chicago called the Starter Jacket Murders after the to-kill-for sports-logo jackets. Oddly enough, or not so for *Jet,* there was an item in the same issue on the rap duo Kris Kross and their oversize sports-logo clothes worn backward—a form of "Kross" dressing *Jet* found inventive and charming.

There's something sadly ironic about endorsing dress codes in city schools to curb violence, while Madison Avenue, Hollywood, and Afro-chic entrepreneurs ride the jock of young black male style straight to the bank. A recent sighting guaranteed to induce nausea is Mattel's "Rappin' Rockin' " Barbie and Ken, Vanilla Ice clones who come with thick gold chains and a boom box: Hip-hop style repackaged and safely distanced from the black subject/suspect. So we see: It's not the gold chains, the Starter jackets, or the Nike high tops that are inherently criminal, it's what George Bush likes to call "the little brown ones" wearing them.

Though you could argue that policing style is just another form of policing those doing the stylin', some parents and folks who run schools in New York City would disagree. They see it as a means of protecting kids in war zones. As of last year, close to twenty city public schools, backed by parent-teacher associations and district offices, have instituted voluntary dress codes.

Parents say they favor the codes primarily to cuts costs. (Most codes call for a white shirt and simple black skirt or pants.) In the age of BabyGap, GapKids, Nike baby shoes, and so on, it's no small expense keeping the young ones up-to-date in the hype gear. (With 40 percent of black children living below the poverty line in families headed for the most part by single women, it's more like a serious hardship). Parents also agree with *Jet* that school codes help stop the theft of high-status clothing that they say happens in and around their neighborhood schools.

Teacher and mother Isabel Cacho leads a class of bilingual fifth graders at a school in Bedford-Stuyvesant that adopted a dress code this year. To Cacho, "right" and "wrong" clothes are a source of unhealthy anxiety for her students, even at eleven years old. She describes how painful it is to see children in threadbare pants sitting next to others decked out in Ralph Lauren Polo. Though not Catholic, Cacho says she sent two of her own children to a Catholic school in the eighties to cut down on clothing costs and steer them clear of the "deadly" sneaker and leather wars. She's glad her younger son, O'Neil, eleven, is able to attend a dress-code elementary school, P.S. 308. O'Neil, who can tell you anything you want to know about Cross Colours and Marco Polo pants though he doesn't own any, says the dress code instituted at his school last year makes kids "prouder to be from our school." Still, sometimes, he feels, "you want to make a look that's you, but the principal is saying be somebody else."

At his comical and patronizing best, Ed Koch unveiled in 1988 a plan to improve the quality of public education in the city: dress codes. The mayor made a deal with a manufacturer to donate uniforms to one Harlem school. That's as far as he took this educational initiative. Board of Education official policy on the codes is that they must be voluntary, as the federal Department of Education has suggested that restricting dress could be a violation of the First Amendment. The surge of interest in codes began a few years back. Principal Carole Foster of P.S. 175 in Central Harlem claims uniforms tripled enrollment and upped reading scores there. With over one thousand public schools spread throughout five boroughs, it's doubtful that codes will ever be a citywide movement, yet more schools are opting for them, including, this fall, Brooklyn's J.H.S. 265 in Fort Greene.

You'll find Susan Smith McKinney Junior High underneath the long arm of the elevated Brooklyn-Queens Expressway. Boxed in between the Brooklyn Navy Yard and the Walt Whitman projects, it's a modern prison of white brick and wired-in windows. The school has been getting press of late due to its new principal/ crusader. Henry Pankey is out to turn one of the city's most infamous war-zone schools into a photo-perfect model of inner-city pride. A former actor, the fifteen-year vet of the public school system thinks educators could stand to learn something from theater and advertising.

Armed with nothing but high ambitions and a deep voice, Pankey has refinished 265 with the title of "prep school," complete with academic goals and uniforms to reflect "Wall Street–style success." The seventy-three-dollar outfits combine a preppy blazer with a vest or tie of an African-inspired print. Pankey resents that articles on the school have focused on the uniforms; they're just the first step in his plan to raise up a school once known for absenteeism and assaults on teachers.

With portraits of Mayor Dinkins and Malcolm X holding vigil, eight McKinney preps file into Pankey's office to discuss the uniforms. These are young adults not likely to be cowed by the conformity that school uniforms represent. They have other questions for Pankey: What if the kids from the shelters can't come up with the money? Why should seniors pay for uniforms? Isn't the African print "kind of played"?

When I tell certain colleague friends about my trip to 265, they aren't as romanced as I was by the African-print vests. Cultural critic/hip-hop observer Tricia Rose likens dress codes to airlifting swimsuits to Somalia, but no food. "What about more counselors, a lecture series, a book reading drive?" Rose reminds me. "Can't we do anything besides tell kids if you look like the white middle class everything will be okay?"

In the lobby of J.H.S. 265, there's a sign: NO WEAPONS, NO BEEPERS, NO RADIOS. The eight kids in Pankey's office voiced real fears about the violence around them. Tyrone wanted to know why the girl on his block who got killed over a pair of earrings didn't make the six o'clock news. Lisa swears that Pankey is the only principal she's met brave enough to wait with his students at the bus stop. These kids know their immediate predator isn't the amorphous white system chipping away at their civil liberties, it's the little knucklehead next door with the semiautomatic.

On the train at DeKalb Avenue, the closest stop to 265, there's a public service ad that kindly reprints Emily Dickinson's poem, "Hope is the Thing with Feathers." Someone has crossed it out and written: "Hope is making it off this fucken train and not gettin kill [*sic*]."

1992

mandela diary

They said he was tired. They said he spent twenty-seven years of a life sentence in jail for treason (a fancy way of saying he fought for the right to vote in the country he was born in; a right, it was said, over and over again, he still doesn't have). They also said the man who had the sense to release him from prison should be rewarded for his foresight.

They said the man who had been in prison would visit eight cities in America, the land of the free, and that the first city would be New York, the city of opportunity, where most of the people in prison are black, and most of the people who run the prisons are white. Others said for a country like America to welcome this man with open arms (so much so that he would declare during his visit, "I am a Yankee") was the biggest hypocrisy of all. Because back in 1962, the Central Intelligence Agency, an organization, some people say, America uses to spy on and even kill people who live in other countries, may or may not have had a hand in putting the freedom fighter behind bars.

Yet he came anyway, the freedom fighter (which is easier to say or has fewer complicated implications than deputy president of the African National Congress). At the airport he was met by the governors of three American states. And the flag of the once banned African National Congress, not the "official" flag of South Africa, was flown next to the American flag (which is so sacred, it soon may be legally protected from fire).

Some people, many of them black, thought the high points of freedom fighter's visit were his pilgrimages to Brooklyn and Harlem. Others weren't satisfied; they said he spent too much time nuzzling with the mayor and affluent New Yorkers than communing with those people in New York, many of them black, who had supported his cause all along. But in Brooklyn and Harlem, most people who greeted the freedom fighter and his wife, also a freedom fighter, opened their arms without question.

At times their visit felt like the most joyous and historic reunion in years; a time akin to the early sixties, when the newly independent nations of Africa led black Americans to rethink their culture and politics in relation to the continent. The visit of the freedom fighter positioned us, for a minute, at the center of world politics. It made us the First Family. It gave us, once again (and perhaps for longer than a minute), an accessible past, so that the African part of the equation suddenly made a lot more sense. And we bought, the T-shirts to prove it.

What becomes a legend most? Nelson Mandela.

Day One: Bedford-Stuyvesant, Brooklyn. Where this morning, and it's not even eight o'clock yet, you wake up to African drums. Police barricades and vendors hawking T-shirts line Fulton Street as far south as you can see. Families pack into the athletic field of Boys and Girls High School (which bans students from wearing gold jewelry, shearling coats, and miniskirts). There's no shade in the field at all, and in the middle, surrounded by more blue sawhorses, is a small, open-faced trailer draped with the banner BOYS AND GIRLS HIGH WELCOMES NELSON MANDELA. Not counting the airport, this will be Mandela's first stop on American soil. An hour earlier, 1010 WINS news radio said he was tired, that he'd scrap the trip to Boys and Girls in Bed-Stuy, dubbed the "Soweto of New York," and proceed directly to Manhattan and ticker tape. Still, the assembly at Boys and Girls, which is mostly black and under twenty-one, is confident.

Homages to sixties nationalism beam from every corner. Important young men in Malcolm X glasses and important young women in African-fabric headwraps scurry back and forth. These are students from Boys and Girls and the Central Brooklyn Youth Coalition who planned the program. An ANC youth leader, who will later have the honor of introducing Mandela himself, arrives on the trailer's makeshift stage to "share with [you] a few of our slogans." "All the power," he calls, and the congregation answers the usual, "To the people!" Next, a man who doesn't identify himself goes on mike to "thank the sisters for their support of the warriors up here."

Television crews scout photo ops amid the sea of brown children. NBC approaches a seven-year-old boy with a headful of dreads as he straddles a police barricade. The blonde newswoman taps the kid on the shoulder with a pencil to get him to face the camera. He does, but refuses to smile. Elders wait patiently in the hot sun. Anna Nicholson, eighty, who worked for twenty-five years in the garment district, says she's here to see Mandela because, "They didn't break his spirit. My grandfather was a slave, and he used to say, 'If you got an education, they can take everything, but they can't get it out of your head.' "

11:35 a.m.: It's CNN's point man in Bed-Stuy, natch, who breaks the news: Mandela's plane has touched down. But is he coming to Boys and Girls? Day-Glo yellow FREE SOUTH AFRICA signs are distributed to the crowd, which has doubled. Police helicopters begin flying over the field every ten minutes.

Two hours later than expected, two hours of hot sun later, the motorcade graces Bed-Stuy. Though sweaty and thirsty, the crowd is still good for a rock-star's welcome, complete with catcalling and tears. An elevated subway line looms above Boys and Girls's field, and a train passes just as Mandela appears at the rickety podium, its sound drowned out by the crowd. For three minutes straight they yell for him. Mandela smiles widely and seems so young. His silver Afro frames his face like a halo. A woman says out loud to no one in particular, "Look at him, look at him! He looks just like my grandfather." (This woman, our reporter realizes a few seconds later, is herself.) Winnie glows in traditional purple-and-white dress. This is a truly religious experience, a man back from the land of the dead to lead the living and an authentic African queen. (Winnie is not really a queen, though she was the first black medical social worker certified in South Africa.) Mandela brings the crowd back to earth with comments on the quality of education in the Natal province: "Our education is not controlled by our people, but by whites." The people respond, surprisingly in unison, "Same in Brooklyn."

As the ringside photographers pack their gear, a girl in a long, green satin dress and veil, wanders into the press area selling buttons. She says her name is Adashina, that she's nine years old and a member of the African Islam mission on Bedford Avenue in Brooklyn. She says, "The imam of the mission makes the buttons, and we sell them and give half of the money to him." One button insures that ISLAM IS THE ANSWER. Our reporter buys one with the legend SHE WAITED FOR MANDELA.

The township outside City Hall, 3:20 p.m.: Some 350 people have the privilege of sitting on the dais (including ninety-two-year-old black reparations activist Queen Mother Moore, who in the second row is three seats down from Bella Abzug, but behind Dick Gregory, who is front row right). Most who came to see the FREEDOM MAN (says a button with his picture) claim his key to the city are in the street just beyond City Hall. The "townships" is what a passerby coins the area where folks stand in the street, hoping for a glimpse of Mandela but contained by barricades.

A dozen teenage boys stand on these barricades trying for a better view. For support, they lean on a parked Channel 2 news truck. Correspondent Reggie Harris, who is black, sits atop the truck pecking at his laptop and following the dais on portable monitor. Harris warns the kids to stop leaning on the truck. "Hope your ass falls off," one kid yells back. Before wandering away, the boys, all black, give the truck a good push.

Noise from the sidelines has quieted down a bit, and we hear Dinkins make his proclamations: "Mr. Mandela, I am proud to present to you the people of New York, a gorgeous mosaic of races, religions, national origin, and sexual orientation." A twenty-five-year-old Nigerian man, also in the townships section, holds up a sign as Dinkins speaks. "Criticize black Africa," the sign reads, "as you do apartheid, it's a human rights issue." The Nigerian explains that he's not here to protest, just to let people know that "atrocities going on in black Africa are virtually ignored by the Afro-American elected officials and activists. Why is it okay for black Africa to kill other Africans, and not okay for apartheid to kill black Africa?"

4:30 p.m.: The City Hall ceremony ends, though not too many people in the townships seem to notice right away. Michael McIntyre, director of the Queens Independent Living Center, an advocacy and resource center for disabled New Yorkers, was of the chosen who sat on the dais, and he's suited down for the occasion. As McIntyre talks about how the civil rights movement of people with disabilities is related to the struggles of blacks in South Africa, Jesse Jackson is making his exit. Though many people want an audience with the reverend, Jackson spots McIntyre and hurries over to offer his hand. In the hustle, McIntyre's wheelchair is sent careening down the sidewalk. Jesse rushes off and doesn't seem to notice. "I've been outshined," says McIntyre with a coy smile. He puts his chair on course and continues in a quiet voice discussing "the apartheid of the disabled."

Day Two, Harlem, 2:30 p.m.: The number 2 train stops at the corner of Martin Luther King Jr. Boulevard (125th Street) and Malcolm X Boulevard (Lenox Avenue), one block east of Africa Square. Near the train entrance is a book vendor, a golden-skinned woman with blond dreads who asks first if she is speaking to a "sister" before launching into a tirade about police harassment: "I've been out here since eight in the morning. The cops tried to tell us to move. Meanwhile, you've got some white folks around the corner supposedly selling ANC T-shirts. That money ain't going to no ANC. This is our event, this our community. This is the only time we get to make money."

Nearby another vendor, selling copies of *The Blackman's Guide to Understanding the Blackwoman* by Shahrazad Ali, complains that she's been hassled by the cops all day: "They tried to stop us from selling, but they couldn't because vendors make a program. It's not enough to see an event, you need souvenirs." Another, who calls himself "Watermelon Man," peddles chopped watermelon. "Bensonhurst gave watermelon a bad name," he says, "but basically it's good business."

3:15 p.m.: Smack in the middle of 125th Street, in front of the state office building, an impromptu drumming session is drawing a group of dancers and shouters. "Do that dance, sisters!" urges a man in a construction hat, who later yells at the cops, "Your wickedness can never overpower the goodness here." Cops arrive to break up the dancing. They need the space to park police cars.

In African Square, the same spot where Malcolm X, Adam Clayton Powell, Fidel Castro, and Martin Luther King once addressed Harlem, the masses are gathering for Mandela. The dais is set up in the intersection of African Square itself, while the streets that lead into it serve as holding pens for the crowds. On the south side of ACP Boulevard the horde extends to 123rd Street. On every floor of the former Theresa Hotel people lean out of windows and hang banners. A group sitting on top of a bus shelter waves red, black, and green flags. Spotted in the sea of faces: a man strutting a large gold medallion in the shape of the African continent. In the middle of the continent is a mirror.

Jesse arrives earlier than the Mandela motorcade to get an early piece of Harlem. The dais fills up: Congressman Charles Rangel (in kente strip), sour-faced city pol Denny Farrell, Flavor Flav (with clocks), and Chuck D. (with Raiders cap). A tree that is supposed to be planted in African Square in honor of the children of Soweto is moved by forklift in front of the dais, where it obscures all the profiling happening on the dais platform. Folks are most upset. The call goes up: "Move the tree!"

7:15 p.m.: "We want Mandela," comes the chant from way down on 123rd Street. Some folks say they've been waiting in African Square since eleven in the morning. Fainting people are being carried out left and right. Those in the way back see the motorcade first. The screaming, the cheering, the flag waving ripples to the front. A black Secret Service agent appears on stage with a large object hidden behind a raincoat. Harlem's favorite widow introduces herself as "Mrs. Malcolm X" and, as if on cue, an elderly woman near the stage rises to her feet and waves a white handkerchief. There's a shock of recognition from Winnie, then she embraces widow X, a/k/a Betty Shabazz (an image bite that makes evening news). Winnie, in Western dress tonight, notifies Harlem that "we have no reason to trust Mr. de Klerk yet. . . . We want to know if you're with us when we go back to the bush." "Teach," says Harlem. "Tell it," says Harlem.

Dhoruba Bin Wahad, an American political prisoner for nineteen years, speaks almost intimately to Mandela from the podium: "You were the symbol that helped sustain me." Wahad cautions him that the same people who "helped convict you now want to befriend you." Dinkins shifts in his seat.

Nelson Mandela finally walks, slowly, carefully, downstage to address the "working people of Harlem." He recites the names that have been called so often in the last couple of days: Sojourner

Truth, Paul Robeson, Rosa Parks, Marcus Garvey, Fannie Lou Hamer, Malcolm X. "Harlem symbolizes strength, beauty, and resistance," Mandela caresses. Later, in a firmer voice, he contradicts his wife: "We do not doubt the sincerity of Mr. de Klerk." Not once does he acknowledge Wahad, his empassioned words or his cautions.

After the Mandela motorcade pulls away it's announced that ten thousand dollars was raised by passing the hat; cranky, jaded, underpaid New Yorkers, Harlemites mostly, passing bills from hand to hand, had given the ANC ten grand. As the tired and maybe the spiritually fed make their way home, a man sets up a cardboard box to sell Mandela books and biographies. He shows off a rare photo. "This," he says, "is a picture of Mandela as a baby being washed."

Yankee Stadium, the Afterparty, 11:15 p.m.: The speeches are over. Last act, KRS One and Boogie Down Productions, has steam still to share: "Everything you see is not rosy, it's not happy, and it's not hand clapping. What you see here today is called revolutionary-ism. We, here in America and in South Africa, we have got to get together under one roof and say we are sick and tired of the bullshit!" Not the perfect evening news sample, but the crews are long gone, knowing perhaps KRS would be too saucy for the harmony-fest broadcast news is staging out of the Mandela visit.

"Fifteen to twenty years from now," KRS bellows to a nearly empty Yankee Stadium, "there'll be a totally different story about what went on here tonight. Tell your children the truth! Apartheid ain't over yet." The music kicks off. KRS starts rapping: "Mandela's not free, Mandela's not free." A young white woman in a "Black Pride, Providence College" T-shirt grinds her hips to the beat. "He can't even vote in his own country."

Day Three: Winnie in Brooklyn. Driving over the Brooklyn Bridge, the cab driver, age thirty-five and African American, explains that he "objected to Jewish leaders objecting to Mandela calling the PLO comrades in arms. As far as I'm concerned, Israelis are doing the same thing to the Palestinians that white South Africans are doing to black South Africans." After dropping two black passengers at their destination, the next ride he picks up is an Orthodox Jew.

House of the Lord Church in downtown Brooklyn is the site of a "women's leadership symposium" with guest of honor Winnie Mandela. Distinguished ladies in Sunday church clothes and plumed hats, or African gowns and tucked headdresses, line up on this brilliant spring afternoon outside of the church, which, like everything else in the city, is surrounded by police barricades. Ladies like writer Paula Giddings, Jewel Jackson McCabe, president of 100 Black Women, and Assemblywoman Helen Marshall from Queens. And ladies who usually don't have to line up, like Mother Hale, *Essence* editor Susan Taylor, and the NAACP's Hazel Dukes. So many of them sport the Black Cameo, the cameo for the women of color created by artist Coreen Simpson, it looks like the seal of a new order.

When Winnie Mandela walks into the church, everyone rises. There are many black women journalists covering the event, including the *New York Post*'s Pamela Newkirk, and they and other members of the press rise too. The response is the most heartfelt yet: Women whoop, cry, holler, throw their hands in the air. Anything anyone says at the podium after that gets a "That's right," "Yes!" or "Umm hmm." Betty Shabazz introduces Winnie once again: "This sister's presence in our midst is enough. She shouldn't even have to speak ["That's right" "Uh humm" "Yes"]. To have gone through what she has gone through ["That's right" "Uh humm" "Yes"], and to see her present, so composed! There must be a God. There's got to be a God."

Winnie stands in the pulpit with her fist raised, her upper arm tucked near her temple, in the way she does, turning the Black Power salute into a comfortably feminine gesture. "My sisters, my sister Joyce [Dinkins] over there," Winnie bows her head. "I will not address the gentlemen, they have no business being here." Thunder from the audience. Then not in jest, "If women were at the forefront of our struggle, it would have been won long ago." Mrs. Mandela goes on speak of projects for which the ANC needs to raise money; this is the first concrete example of the ANC's works that we've heard in three days.

After the House of the Lord, we all rush up the block to the Brooklyn Academy of Music to hear more Winnie. BROOKLYN'S AFRI-CAN DIASPORA WELCOMES NELSON AND WINNIE MANDELA, reads a banner outside of the academy. Master of ceremonies Cicely Tyson is full of quips for this audience of mostly black women and their children (Empty baby carriages are left in the lobby). "Oh, the joy," she testifies, "of knowing who you are, what you are, and where you're from." Cicely tells a story: Winnie was detained in 1958 for her involvement in a demonstration against passbooks for African women. She was pregnant at the time and later was banned from the courtroom for wearing traditional dress. Apparently Winnie told the court: "Of the few rights I still have in this country, Mr. Prosecutor, I still have the right to choose my own ward-robe!"

For the ladies here at the academy, Winnie adds a glittering green-and-gold headdress to her outfit. Yes, she did say, "We know you will be there to take up arms with us." And yes, we did say we would. But more moving was her simple reminder that the people who die in South Africa, and die often, are children. There's blood everywhere, and mothers like Winnie are tired of mopping it up. It was something that with all this talk of foreign relations, diplomacy, and merchandise, we had plain forgot.

On the D train back to Manhattan: A young black woman, around eighteen or so, wears a Simpsons family T-shirt with the moto FAMILY BONDING. She has a black eye and bruises on her arm, and stares off into space. Next to her is a young black man, around eighteen or so, sporting a thick gold chain and white leather warm-up suit. He glares at other passengers as if daring them to say something. In the entire car, not a single Nelson Mandela or Win-nie Mandela button or T-shirt in sight.

1990

forty acres and a holiday

There are three legends told of how enslaved Africans in the Texas territory came to know of their freedom, and why the word didn't get to them until two months after the Civil War ended, which was a good two and half years after Lincoln's Emancipation Proclamation. Or, to make it plain, rather late. One legend says the messenger, a black Union soldier, was murdered. Another says he arrived, but had been delayed by mule travel. (A variation on this is that he had stopped to get married.) The third and favored is that the news was withheld by white landowners so they could bleed one last crop from slave labor. What *is* held as fact is that June nineteenth—the day that federal troops rode into Galveston with orders to release those kept as slaves—has been celebrated for 127 years, in Texas and beyond, as Emancipation Day, as Jubilation Day, as Juneteenth. The day the last ones heard.

Juneteenth, the name, is one of those fab African-Americanisms, functional, rhythmic, at once concise and not too concise. It fuses the month of June with the number nineteen, and eludes to the fact that the holiday was held in adjoining states on different days of the month as folks got the word. Early emancipation rituals were not exclusive to Texas (South Carolina and Mississippi's fall in May)—or to the South. What may have been the first emancipation ceremony was held in New York as early as 1808 to mark the legal cessation of the slave trade.

No state comes close to Juneteenth in Texas, the black folks' Fourth of July, with its parades, feasting, pageants, and preachifying. Emancipation day organizations in Texas date back to the turn of the century. The most powerful image from the early days must have been former slaves themselves, who, according to tradition, marched together at the end of parade lines. By the 1950s Juneteenth Day came to be linked with, not freedom from slavery, but segregation. On Juneteenth, Texas's Jim Crow cities would allow blacks to be citizens for twelve hours a year by granting them entry into whites-only parks and zoos. With the passage of civil rights legislation in the sixties, refined black Texans abandoned Juneteenth to their country cousins and took to celebrating Independence Day in July along with their white brethren.

A Juneteenth renaissance has been gathering steam since the mid eighties, spurred by the Afrocentricity crusade. Beyond being a hootenanny for black Texas (the condescending folksy portrait favored by the local press), it's become a holiday eagerly adopted nationwide by African Americans in search of cultural signposts. Not to mention one that offers, as is required these days, a dramatic tube-and-T-shirt–friendly soundbite of black history.

The J-Day momentum is due in large part to the efforts of a man you might call Daddy Juneteenth, state representative Al Edwards from Houston. Edwards sponsored the bill that made Juneteenth an official Texas holiday thirteen years ago, a feat in a state that still closes banks for Confederate Heroes Day. Juneteenth U.S.A., Edwards's organization, tracks J-Day rites across the country and is fundraising for a national educational headquarters. To Edwards the holiday has tremendous secular and sacred promise. He sees it as an economic vehicle for African Americans, as well as a day that should be observed with almost holy remembrance: "The Jews say if they ever forget their history, may their tongues cleave to the roof of their mouth. . . . Let the same happen to us."

You can find Juneteenth rituals in all regions of the country now. States like California, where Texans migrated en masse, have held Juneteenth festivities for decades. The New York area's largest is in Buffalo, tapping into upstate's rich history of antislavery activity. Wisconsin counts at least five, including Milwaukee's, where Juneteenth has been celebrated since 1971 and is the best attended single-day cultural event in the state. Far from being family picnics, these festivals sometimes last for days, made possible by the legwork of community groups, city cooperation, and private sector donations. Juneteenth in Minneapolis, now in its seventh year, is building a rep as one of the most progressive and trendsetting J-Day celebrations in the Texas diaspora. What began as a poetry reading in a church basement is now two weeks of programming, including a film festival and an Underground Railroad reenactment. At these celebrations old world often knocks against new world, when Miss Juneteenth pageants (inherited from towns like Brenham, Texas, which crowns a "Goddess of Liberty") share the stage with Afro-chic street fairs ablaze in faux kente.

There are those who think Juneteenth is an embarrassment. That the holiday tells more of our ignorance and subjugation than of an inheritance that predates slavery in the Americas. Or that it's "too black" because it promotes a separate but not equal Fourth of July, or "not black enough" as it's often funded by white purses. And of course that it's far too symbolic and doesn't solve anything. What does a Juneteenth celebration mean anyway when the Freeman's Bureau never gave us our forty acres and a mule? (Not thrilled about news of the state holiday, one former Texas legislator had this to say: "Dancing up and down the streets, drinking red soda water, eating watermelons. . . . I grew out of that.") But Juneteenth critics haven't put a dent in the holiday's grass-roots popularity.

Folks are hungrier than ever for rituals that enshrine our identity as hyphen Americans. Kwanzaa's metamorphosis in the last few years speaks to this need. And merchandising opportunities are never far behind: Evolving in two short decades from cultural nationalist position paper to mainstream ethnic festival profiled in the *Times*'s Living section, Kwanzaa has spawned its own designer cookbook and Santa surrogate, Father Kwanzaa. Now Juneteenth spreads like spring fever. Also gaining steam are rites of passage ceremonies for young men and women that are based on ancient African models and seek to address modern urban ills. (The National Rites of Passage Organization held its fifth annual conference this year.) And spotted last year in *Sage: A Scholarly Journal on Black Women:* plans for a Middle Passage memorial holiday that would fall near Thanksgiving.

Buried in their shopping ethos, we tend to forget holidays were once holy days that defined us in more profound ways than what Nintendo jumbo pack we got for Christmas. Michael Chaney, an arts activist in Minneapolis, believes that Juneteenth rituals could be more than acts of racial communion; they could have a role in redefining America: "We have to realize our own role as historians. We need to ascribe our treasures and offer them to the world. Juneteenth should be a day for all Americans to get in touch with the Africanism within."

Juneteenth does have great possibilities as a new American holiday. Along with reuniting blood relatives, the families that emancipated slaves made embraced family beyond kin, family as community. In this tradition, modern Juneteenth doesn't circumscribe any Dick-and-Jane paean to the nuclear family. You can be a single parent, gay, from D.C. or Ann Arbor; it's a history that includes you. You can read the Emancipation Proclamation out loud or drink some red soda water if you damn please. Or just take a moment out of your day to think about all the folks that laid down nothing less than their lives so that you could see the twentieth century.

1992

looking for mariah

They came to see the nose. The nose never lies. Even the missing nose of Egypt's great Sphinx tells a story. Legend has it that Napoleon gave the Sphinx a nose job in the eighteenth century during the Battle of the Nile—too Negroid, too strong? An Egyptologist friend of mine told me it wasn't Napoleon after all, but Egyptian pharaohs, who made a practice of smashing noses off the statues of their predecessors so the old kings couldn't "breathe," meaning exert influence from the afterworld. Murphy's Law: You can never find a good racial conspiracy theory when you need one.

The nose in question is Mariah Carey's. The twenty-year-old pop singer with a seven-octave vocal range. Mother sang with the New York City Opera. At six, little Mariah could do *Rigoletto* in Italian. Later she discovered gospel, then rhythm and blues, Aretha, Minnie Riperton, and things have never been quite the same. Just before Thanksgiving, two dozen media types gathered at an invitation-only luncheon to meet Carey. The singer's debut album, released last June on Columbia/CBS, was now double platinum. Two singles, "Vision of Love" and "Love Takes Time," had topped the pop and R&B charts.

At the luncheon, held at Lola's, another vibe cafe hovering just above Fourteenth Street, all the guests save two or three were black. Seated at linen-clad tables were folks like Janine McAdams, *Billboard*'s black-music editor, *City Sun* arts editor Armond White (who said, on record, he came to see the nose), and a writer from a dance music trade publication who admitted that "for once race wasn't an issue," he had come for the food. (Fried chicken was served.) Apparently the guest of honor was most interested in meeting writer Nelson George, who had sized Carey up in *Playboy*. George's comments, having nothing to do with her body, had all to do with her soul, or more specifically, her marketing profile. George had dubbed Carey a "white girl who can sing."

It was all over the press that Columbia/CBS had rolled out hordes of money for the Carey project. One questions whether the company would have made the same investment in a black vocalist of comparable talent working in the soul idiom. Take Carey's labelmate Regina Belle. Critically acclaimed voice. But Columbia had waited for a good response from the R&B sector on Belle's debut record before selling her, second time around and without fanfare, to the pop market. Carey, on the other hand, was put out as pop product from jump.

Columbia certainly didn't, for Belle, scrap a video and shoot a new one, putting the combined cost of both at $450,000, or so an inside source told Rob Tannenbaum for *Rolling Stone*. (This figure was later dismissed by the company as "total bullshit.") Or give Belle, as they gave Carey, a "promotional blitz equal to the push given Bruce Springsteen in 1975," says Tannenbaum, securing her an appearance on "Arsenio" even before the CD was released. ("We don't look at her [Carey] as a dance-pop artist," Columbia prez Don Ienner told *Rolling Stone*. "We look at her as a franchise.")

Did it matter that Regina Belle is a brown-skinned black woman sans weave? Did it matter ultimately, in Columbia's decision to go all out like this for a new artist, that Carey looks the way she does (long blondish hair, pale skin), and that she is what the press had said she is—white? But is she really?

Though at times Carey's voice on her CD is swallowed by a virtual solar system of twinkling synthesizers, it does have its own guttural integrity. Not the life-experience soul power of a Miki Howard, but Carey is young yet. No question, it's a voice with more emotional grip than Lisa Stansfield's, the white Brit, who *Entertainment Weekly* had crowned the new queen of soul. The girl really *could* sing.

And what *about* that nose? In the CD's cover photo, one curly strand of auburn-blonde hair is strewn across Carey's plump nose, casting it in high relief. Shot from another angle, the nose might have been fuller still. Sign of the tar brush? Said a friend, framing the CD box in his large brown hands, "Saw her videos, but honestly, I can't call this one. Don't know if she's dating Negroes or what, but I tell you one thing, if she herself is not a Negro, there's definitely a Negro component up in there." *Maybe she isn't white, or all white, or . . . ? What is she, or what isn't she?* And since Carey's record company hadn't found it worth mentioning, did only her hairdresser know for sure?

Turned out Mariah Carey was ready to answer just this question at the Mariah Carey luncheon. A vision of loveliness in, how apropos, a two-tone cat suit (black from middrift down, white up top), Carey appeared even taller and leaner than on video. She planted herself opposite George and calmly set the record straight. "My father is black and Venezuelan. My mother is Irish and an opera singer. I am me." The *New York Post*'s gossip page added some spice the next day. Below the caption, CAREY: MIXED ANCESTRY, it was reported that "rocker" Carey wanted to "sock" George for calling her a "white girl who can sing." As I was sitting at the next table, I can confirm: Things weren't dramatic as all that.

The *Post* managed to bungle up Carey's mixed-race résumé, calling her half "black-Brazilian" instead of half "black-Venezuelan." *USA Today* carried the story the following week with the caption MARIAH CAREY, MISUNDERSTOOD. Courtesy information supplied by a Columbia publicist, it was noted that the *Post* had "blown out of proportion" Carey's anger at George and that George and Carey were friends. Before leaving Lola's, George did stop to pose for a photo with Carey, but the luncheon was the first time the two had met.

How's this for a racial conspiracy theory?: Had Columbia/CBS been engaging in a little nineties-style "passing" of Carey? Did the company profit, especially in the first few months of the record's release, from having Carey's racial dossier remain under wraps? (White soul singers being more lucrative pop meal tickets than black ones.) And now that Mariah's background was the source of speculation, was the company interested in smoothing out the edges so as not to alienate any market group? Carey conducting her mixed-race confessional at a fried-chicken confab with George, McAdams, and other influential black-music journalists played like a media maneuver of high order. Soon stories embracing Carey and her biracial identity appeared in the black press. And compared to her first music videos, those that aired post-luncheon showcased a decidedly black presence. (Black bit players, missing before, were cast in endearing roles.) Perhaps higher-ups in Columbia marketing had decided it was time to "come out" with the Carey story before the company was charged with running some sort of cover-up.

I had frustrating conversations with two publicity reps in Columbia's pop division and two in black music. (Ever wonder how offices are set up at these record companies? Is there the pop big house, and then, a few flights down, the black music shanties?) All were adamant that no attempt had been made to mask Carey's background. Though not one wanted to address this on the record, and not one would comment on who had organized the shindig at Lola's and why.

Each conversation I had became twisted in the cobwebs of racial semantics. One publicist said the label had never pronounced Carey "one hundred percent white or one hundred percent black"; that "Carey's heritage has nothing to do with her voice." And why should Carey have to "broadcast her racial background"? When asked, Carey "will answer, but she's not gonna bring it up."

Another suggested that the record company wasn't responsible; "It's a personal thing, not a label thing." And that, if Carey's race wasn't as important to her as it was to other people, this was not a political issue, but a testament to her marketing savvy: "All entertainers like to be viewed as universal."

One told me I was the only person in America interested in Carey's race (or lack of one) and the connection between her look and her marketing budget: "Mariah had a number one black single and a number three black album. Obviously, the black population is identifying with this woman. So is the white population. White or not, no one cares what her background is."

All judgments about Carey's race, said yet another publicist, came from the press based on photos. Both the *New York Times* and *Musician* had fawned over Carey as a "white soul singer." Nelson George told the *Post* that he judged Carey white based on information supplied in a press release from Columbia and the CD photo. When *Voice* critic Vince Aletti described Carey as a white singer who could "pass for Whitney Houston," he received the following letter from a reader:

> *Yo! Vince,*
>   *You'd better take another look or get yourself some glasses. Not only can Mariah Carey pass for black, she is black! She's just a lighter Whitney Houston. You can't claim this one.*

Aletti says he came to his conclusion from the "gung-ho marketing" of Carey: "It doesn't happen as often with black artists. Especially coming from a company like Columbia."

Last August Rob Tannenbaum arrived at a rehearsal studio to interview Carey for *Rolling Stone*. Tannenbaum asked the publicist on the scene if Mariah was black, because the "way she's photographed, it's hard to tell what her background is," and in person, he was getting a less ambiguous picture. According to Tannenbaum, the publicist "assured" him that Carey was white. Tannenbaum questions why, when the press started calling Carey "the white Whitney Houston," no one from the company came forward to correct this, to mention that she's half black, if not black period. "If they [Columbia] didn't deliberately create a misimpression," says Tannenbaum, "they didn't go out of their way to clear one up."

As the Carey luncheon was wrapping up, the singer posed with two journalists, deep brown and dashing in black suits. Set against them, the darker hues of her skin seemed all the more prominent, seemed to glow. (I remembered the photo of Carey on her CD's inner sleeve, her ample nose hidden behind song credits.) In person, Carey came across, quite clearly, as a rainbow baby of African descent, skin toasted almond and hair light brown. The ivory-airbrushed, blonde-hair-blowing-at-the-beach fantasy on view in her publicity shots appeared to be entirely a studio creation.

So Carey has declared herself to be a person of color. Whether or not there is a political dimension to that identity in her mind is a different story. Is she, as Nelson George had tagged Renee Tenison, *Playboy*'s 1990 Playmate of the Year, another not so much color-blind, but "race-neutral," mixed-race child? Carey was born in 1970, which means she didn't turn ten years old until 1980. She might well be ignorant of the political importance of affirming a black identity, of the role this has played in the African-American freedom struggle.

Along with her declaration, Carey said this: "It seems that most people don't know much about interracial children." What don't people know? I itched to ask, at this most polite of gatherings. That they exist? That they have options? That they can't be blamed for

America's subtle and not so subtle forms of apartheid? That they are the solution? That they *just want to be me* until America forces them to declare an allegiance?

Several months before the Carey luncheon, an article titled "Who's Black and Who's Not?" appeared in *Ebony*. Penned by Lynn Norment, the piece was illustrated with snapshots of actress Jennifer Beals and singers Paula Abdul, Jody Watley, and Prince. Under each photo, readers were invited to check boxes labeled "black" or "white." *Ebony* and *Jet* are known for their campy coverage of interracial identity (geez Louise, look at those half-white, half-black twins!), but this piece had critical gut: "The issue . . . is not mixed parentage and the increasing number of children from such unions. The issue is the downplaying or a denial of a Black parent or Black heritage for economic, social, or career gain by a descendant of mixed or even unmixed marriage." What makes the current trend so "fascinating and provocative," Norment continues, is that "media and moguls, particularly in the entertainment industry, seem to be encouraging crossoverism, especially by *ethnically ambiguous females*" (emphasis hers).

Walking home from Lola's, the questions piled up: By marketing themselves as anything but black, do light-complexioned entertainers such as Carey become, in the eyes of most Americans, de facto whites? And do Carey and other people of color who feel more at ease representing themselves by their combination ethnic heritages, and not by race (making use of a privilege to remain outside), teach the world how to be "raceless"? Or are they are positioning themselves as a separate class along the lines of South African "coloreds"? And why aren't Carey et al., if they know or care how racism operates, more willing to take a racial stance? Or have we arrived at a point in history when "black" and "white" have become, to quote bell hooks, "definitive no-nos, perpetuating what some folks see as stale and meaningless binary appositions"; a time when such stances/affirmations/commitments serve little purpose?

Ebony's known for trafficking in paradox. Two months after chiding racially ambiguous entertainers for hauling tail to the bank without paying their black dues, the magazine published a piece by the same writer, Lynn Norment, on Paula Abdul. Norment praises Abdul for giving "expanded definition to the term 'multiple,' " for being "multitalented, multifaceted, and multiethnic." "Syrian-Brazilian-Canadian-American" is how the singers describes herself. Norment tells us that Abdul acknowledges African-American culture as her most profound influence and is often mistaken for black and Hispanic (or accused of passing for anything but). Yet the singer refuses to be badgered into declaring for any race, for "she is what she is [Syrian-Brazilian-Canadian-American], and stardom will not change that." This time around, Norment has turned multiculti cheerleader, and she congratulates Abdul for working her hybridity for a bigger market share. Why does racial ambiguity get applause in this case? Apparently, to read *Ebony*, what makes the difference is who orchestrates the sell. If it's people of color, it's about *getting paid*. If it's the entertainment industry, it's a sin of omission. Keep that in mind.

I'm on the other side of the spectrum from race-neutral rainbow babies who claim a multitude of heritages but no race. My older sister and I, born in fifty-nine and sixty-one respectively, never explored an option other than black, never wished to. Blackness has always been this wide and miraculous world of people and places and passions and histories and *stances*. Of course, stances. Honorable stances that gave you dignity, that made you part of a much larger world. By all means, stances.

Race politics, the us versus them of it, were spelled out for us early. Growing up on the ethnic Lower East Side (before it became the fashionable multiculti East Village, and New York the gorgeous mosaic), kids from the Ukrainian school on Sixth Street threw evil looks at us and eventually bottles. To be half white, in my mind, in 1965, meant being half *them*. And why should I claim something that wanted no part of me?

There were the aesthetic and intellectual dimensions as well. After seeing Sly and the Family Stone at the Fillmore East just as puberty hit, who didn't want to be Cynthia Robinson, the funky light-skinned sister on trumpet? Later my idols became "high-yella" race women like Angela Davis, Kathleen Cleaver, and Nikki Giovanni. I joined the post–civil rights generation of collegians who took Afro-American history and lit and fashioned ourselves black leaders on campus. We remembered at least the chorus of "Say It Loud—I'm Black and I'm Proud" and clung to fond memories of African dance classes at the New Afrika Houses of our childhood. These signposts stuck in our minds, even when Bakke struck a match under affirmative action and radio melted rhythm and blues down to urban contemporary. And black became less "political vocation" and more "ethnic option."

What does this have to do with Mariah Carey? To value freedom and liberty is to respect the choices others make in identifying themselves, be it by sexual preference, culture, or race. Yet the Careys of the new world have shown me the weight history lays on my open mind. I can't resist comparing them to bisexuals swinging on the closet door in an America in which an "out" gay identity still means a helluva lot. Perhaps I haven't yet figured out what "I am me" solves more than "I'm black and I'm proud." One thing I'm clear on: If we can't find a way to make *multi*ethnic stand for *anti*racism, then I'll pass on it.

The ironies of racial identity and cultural province in the nineties are making popular culture the best sideshow in town. Cultural mulattos (Prince, Madonna, George Michael, Michael Jackson) rule the marketplace. Rainbow baby girls (Mariah, Sade, Jasmine Guy) rule the mirror. Ethnicity is often presented as an open-invitational participatory sport (Vanilla Ice, New Kids on the Block, white female rapper Tarrie B. from Compton). "Separated from a political and historical context," bell hooks writes, "ethnicity is being reconstituted as the new frontier, accessible to all, no passes or permits necessary." Hence my anger when a publicist told me that Mariah Carey's voice had nothing to do with her heritage. I like to think it does, so that people of African descent might still have some sort of title to black culture. Yet this might be romantic, even retrograde, of me in an age when exchange cross culture, cross race happens at a dizzying pace.

The politics of race somersault all around us: More talented-tenths, middle-class blacks, are coming of age in integrated neighborhoods, being educated at majority-white institutions, and laying down roots outside of African-American communities. Pop culture positions blacks center frame as racially motivated violence chokes urban America; President Bush vetoes civil rights legislation as Miss America 1990, a black woman, passes the crown to Miss America 1991, also a black woman; illiteracy, teen pregnancy, and drug slavery dog the underclass, while a new black conservative lobby gains power by showing little sympathy for poor blacks.

How will the expanding pool of mixed-race people figure into this new world? On one hand, our presence could force all Americans to take a hard look at race as political construction, its utilities and its dead ends. On the other, mixed-race people could remain invisible, our numbers having little impact. The white world invites us to be privy to white privilege. In the black world, specifically in black intellectual communities, we shy away from challenging stereotypes of "the black experience" with our particular histories. These days the race-neutral Mariah Careys seem to be multiplying faster than the heirs of Davis, Cleaver, and Giovanni.

I wonder what message the cautionary tales of the passing novels could send to rainbow babies of the nineties. These novels were written by African Americans in the early part of the century. For all their melodrama, tinny plots, and soapbox politicking, they've always resonated with me. The costs of abandoning black culture and community is one of the genre's central themes, and it's a theme that hits me, as they say, where I live. Though for reasons you might not expect. When my mother married my father, she was deserted by her white family and embraced by his black family. I have always been made to feel, in part because of her stories, that black communities and black cultures are a steady home. A home that is still quick to remind me, in ways material and ethereal, that it keeps the lights on for me. To abandon this home, as my mother's stories whispered, would mean to swim with sharks.

James Weldon Johnson's *Autobiography of An Ex-Coloured Man* (1912) is often called the thinking-colored person's passing novel, as it speaks its truth minus the violins. The closing passage hits deepest. Not because it describes an experience I have lived, but because it tells of one that I ache to believe in, despite how the world around me splinters in ways I don't recognize.

The ex-coloured man goes to hear Booker T. Washington speak at a benefit for Hampton Institute. Though Mark Twain and others share the podium, Washington has the audience in his hand:

"Not because he so much surpassed the others in eloquence, but because of what he represented with so much earnestness and faith. It is this that all of that small but gallant band of coloured men who are publicly fighting the cause of their race have behind them. Even those who oppose them know that these men have the eternal principles of right on their side, and they will be victors even though they should go down in defeat. Beside them I feel small and selfish. I am an ordinarily successful white man who has made a little money. They are men who are making history and a race. I, too, might have taken part in a work so glorious.

". . . I cannot repress the thought that, after all, I have chosen the lesser part, that I have sold my birthright for a mess of pottage."

Is it true what those labels say, NO SALE IS EVER FINAL?

1990

four

genitalia and the paycheck

corporate boys

Deandra, my crazy friend the photographer, is scoffing down rice and beans at a Cuban restaurant on Flatbush Avenue and talking about Negroes. Most of my straight women friends in their late twenties are grumbling about the one-in-four problem (one out of every four black men in this city is in jail, to which we add: number two is on drugs, number three prefers gentlemen or blondes, and number four already has ten women), but not Miss One and a Half. She always has a Negro or two on hand. Girl, *let me tell you* (Deandra loves to milk it), I've got myself a corporate boy. I drop my fork.

In college, Miss Bohemia wouldn't have been

caught dead with a Negro in an alligator shirt and Levi's, and now she's dating corporate boys? I still believe in revolution, Deandra assures me, it's just, Che Guevara doesn't turn me on anymore. Revolution or no revolution, Deandra's attracted to power, so her taste in men changes with the political forecast: Today Huey Newton, tomorrow Ron Brown.

Deandra confesses that she's been watching corporate boys for a while. The ones who ride the iron horse into the city from buppie enclaves like Fort Greene, Prospect Heights, and Park Slope. They went to the right schools, and now they have the right jobs and the right cars (though between student loan payments and Amex bills, repossession is around the corner). And, of course, the right suits. (They work those suits, don't they? It's not about the suit making the man, it's about how the man is filling out the suit.) Something about their swagger and confidence started ringing my bells, Deandra says, Girl, forget about the dreadlocks and the dashikis, just give me a clean head and a Brooks Brothers charcoal gray (or even a Cricketeer, I'm not a purist).

Deandra goes on about corporate boys and how the suit is such a loaded symbol in their lives. It's their badge of honor (stamps their professional degrees on their sleeves), their passbook to the white-collar world (even gets them a cab sometimes), and immediately "neutralizes" their skin color in the company of what corporate boys call their "majority brethren."

And, Deandra tells me, they have such a way with language. In familiar company they speak a creole of King's English and blacker-than-thou neologisms. You know, girl, they have to prove they're down all the time (lest we think they're sellouts), so they come up with the most endearing homeboyisms. Check out hommie's wig, my corporate boy said to me the other day, why doesn't he comb it? Looks like Nipsey Russell got lost in the African rain forest. It's that fascinating mix of extreme self-love and seething self-hatred that middle-class blacks do so well. Enough already, I tell Deandra, fix me up with some of your corporate boy's friends.

Lunch with bachelor number one is in the corporate dining

room of a major commercial bank. Needless to say, he and I are the lone spots of color in the place. The only son of a large West Indian family from Bedford-Stuyvesant, Keith Browning (names changed to protect corporate identities), twenty-four, went to an Ivy League school to learn how to be a banker. Keith's staid blue and black suits are custom-made by his father, a tailor, and he is quite proud of how they fit him, unlike the "off-the-rack polyester jammies" worn by the lower level management types who work a couple of floors below him. Being a "custom man" is not so much a question of ego. Like many black men, he's a hard fit. "If you have a high behind," Keith says, "pants will ride up on you and ruin the line of the suit." As we nosh on our bow-tie pasta, I can't help staring at the knot of Keith's paisley tie, which is slightly askew. "You can't look too good," he tells me. "Then you're perceived as a threat. You already stand out as a minority. And I definitely do because I'm six-foot-four and most of the majorities I work for are Lilliputians."

Bachelor number two receives me in his Prospect Heights duplex: exposed brick, Levolor blinds, every electrical appliance known to mankind. The walk-in closet I pass on the way to the john is a virtual gallery: creamy leathers, mossy suedes, and a few dozen or so Cosby-style sweaters. And this is the *casual clothes* closet, mind you. Wonder where he keeps his suits. Damon Givens, twenty-eight, grew up in the South Bronx, went to college out of state on a basketball scholarship, and is now a second-year attorney at a Madison Avenue firm. He tells me that going to college with fifteen pairs of sneakers and checking out his wealthy white roommate's closet (loafers, snow boots, and a pair of track shoes held together with duct tape) taught him a lot about priorities. Instead of high tops, now he collects Italian suits. Damon says his Armanis ("Manies," he calls them) and Hugo Bosses ("Hugues") make him something of maverick at the firm, but they're a better fit. He can get a way with a lot more in terms of cut than color because in the corporate world "it's about avoiding anything threatening. And color is threatening psychologically."

In his Toyota Celica ("just lean back and pretend it's a 280 SL"), bachelor number three takes me on a tour of the Brownsville housing project where he spent the first thirteen years of his life, before winning a scholarship to a Massachusetts prep school. After B-school, Michael Geffens, twenty-eight, worked at an investment bank until last year when he was laid off in the crunch. This is how Michael bought his first suit: He took the annual report of a company he wanted to work for to Barney's and matched a suit in a photo with one on the rack. Today he wears custom jobs by a guy named Rock out of California. Rock comes to Manhattan several times a year to hold fittings at the Waldorf Astoria, then sends the measurements to Hong Kong. The suits come back with the label: "designed exclusively for Michael Geffens." Michael and his boys share this same tailor and they refer to their suits as "rocks."

Michael describes the cockiness he feels as a young black man in an expensive suit. He savors the reactions he gets. Older black women smile at him like he's their son; young guys in kente-cloth kufis size him up, he feels, like "Who's the wannabe in the suit? Doesn't he know that he's still a nigger?" At work once, Michael changed to sneakers and jeans in the bathroom. A co-worker, one of his majority brethren, was shocked to run into him in such an altered state: "Gosh," his co-worker marveled, "if I saw you in the street with that on, I'd never think you're as intelligent as you are."

Deandra calls later in the week to ask how I did with the corporate boys. They talk a good game, but girlfriend, how do you get past the elitism? One bachelor kept going on about "mutants" (any "homeboy in a Gumby fade who's not rolling nine to five") and "perpetrators" who hang out in buppie watering holes like Honeysuckle's and B. Smith's but have to go home first to change into a suit. Deandra wants me to meet her corporate boy because, naturally, he isn't like that. (Not only does Deandra get the Negroes, she gets the exceptions.) Dodd Hicks treats us to a Thai meal on the Upper East Side.

Rising close to six-foot-three with the beginnings of a paunch and back-set hairline, Dodd reeks power. He humors us by engaging in the type of mock self-deprecation that only the truly confident can afford. Dodd tells us about the "who's-that-other-nigger-in-a-suit look" he gives and gets from other young black men on Wall Street. "White people have done a good job of convincing us that opportunities extended to others limit our own," Dodd says, fingering the lapels of his Hugo Boss. Deandra looks up at him like he's the best thing since the Afro pick. What could be more attractive than nationalist rhetoric from a boy in a suit?

1991

open letter to a brother

I'm not gonna lie. I have an attitude right now. It has something to do with: witnessing a "domestic" tragi-comedy on Flatbush Avenue; an ad for Smirnoff vodka on a bus shelter; and thinking of you, and how you equate freedom and power with the ground you can cover with your johnson.

What I'm talking about, brother, is the Dog Syndrome. Gotta have more than one female, or "piece," as we're known in some circles. Take pride in declaring that no woman alive has shackles, rings, or papers on you. Don't mind profiting from the dire black male/female ratios out here (in this city, we outnumber you and are more likely to have a higher level of formal education, while one in four of you is in jail). And, so says the rap anthem of moment, you're "down with O.P.P.," that's "other people's pu . . . ," let's call it pudendum. (Nowadays, see, it's not even enough to have a couple *p*'s of your own, you have to be all up in somebody else's *p*.) It's not a class thing, or a regional thing, or necessarily an African-American thing, but it seems to be, the way you flaunt it, quite the in-style thing. "Who's down with O.P.P.?" is the call. And the chorus comes back: "Every last homie."

The latest contest over authenticity (who gets to market the race) is particularly ironic given the fracas between black men and women. You've seen the books: From Shahrazad Ali's *The Blackman's Guide to Understanding the Blackwoman* (a sister points the finger at sisters) to Nathan and Julia Hare's *Crisis in Black Sexual Politics* (a brother and sister point fingers at the white power structure). The battle is not just over who's to blame for what's being called the crisis in black male/female relationships. It's also over "oppressed within the oppressed" status—who suffers most from racism, whose issues will top the racial agenda. ("Babies making babies" has been eclipsed in the last year by the "endangered black male.")

So it's clear everyone's coveting the soapbox. Yet how many of us really have an investment in togetherness beyond the neat platform of race? I mean this in the largest sense, not just heterosexual coupling, but as a community of individuals with shared interests. A cultural communion based on right here, right now, not on some glorious polygamous past in a storybook Motherland. The brawls being so ugly and constant, lately I've been thinking *black people* is just a polite misnomer for a bunch of folks with guns to each other's heads.

Back to the bone I'm picking with you, brother. The reason I feel entitled to bring "us" up in public is because of that old mantra, "the personal is political." This is what I've found: Who we sleep with, how we dress, and the music we listen to define us politically in a more immediate way than who we vote for, what dogma we espouse, and which racial box we check on the census.

I have this theory, brother, that the Dog Syndrome is more than a rite of sexual passage for you; it's your very own liberation politics. Quiet as it's kept, I know very few of you who yearn to dismantle the Mandingo myth. (Hell no, party over here.) Truth be told, you're out here getting mo' and mo' p like your very being, and your very *blackness*, depended on it. Like AIDS is something that is happening to other people and not to us (in fact, more and more, it's happening primarily to us). Or like you can have little or no responsibility for what fucking can reap: babies. When over 60 percent of African-American children are being carried financially by women alone, one wonders where the men are at. Getting O.P.P.?

This comes at a time when black female life is assigned—in the infotainment industries, in popular language, and on the avenues—such little value, despite the gains of the civil rights movement and feminism. It's a time when Andre Young, Dr. Dre of N.W.A (who sells a zillion CDs preaching "One Less Bitch"), can assault—as in punch, kick, and body slam—television host Dee Barnes and get tapped on the wrist with a petty fine and probation. It's also a time when, to follow the example of the St. John's acquittal, the victim's race—black—may have made the rape less of a heinous crime, in the minds of those who tried the case and a largely indifferent media, than the Central Park rape.

You'll find the print ad I spoke of playing larger than life-size at your local bus shelter. Not a shot glass in sight, it shows a woman on the arm of an Armani-suited brother whose neck is wrenched back in an obvious and quite awkward manner so he can scan the anatomy of another woman. Poor urban districts have a disproportionate number of ads for liquor and tobacco, and now this, which hit me in my "positive image" weak spot. What's the sales pitch here for young black men? Disrespect a sister today, it's perfectly cool, and downright stylish?

But listen, brother, I'm looking to talk to you, not the ad industry. We black folks hide, like everyone else, from our demons. No historical guilt, no sense of personal accountability. Wrong. Brother beware, this Dog Syndrome is one mean, undercover demon. If your access to power in the real-world arena is limited, there's always the power of the johnson. And what a cheap fix it is. When I see a brother all caught up in the Dog Syndrome, I see the tragedy of black male impotence masquerading as power. Sad truth is, those who traffic in impotence/ignorance—like the harder-than-thou Dr. Dre, who takes on "nigger" as an honorific and favors a woman for a punching bag—are hightailing it to the bank.

Imagine an entire generation of young males coming of age and modeling themselves on men of means like Dr. Dre or finger-happy Mike Tyson. Will they live forever as adolescents, clutching their bozaks like teddy bears, hiding under their N.W.A caps, and being as hard as they wanna be, or they claim they have to be, O.P.P.'ing their demons away? Sorta like Prince, stroking his way through "Lady Cab Driver": This is for the Middle Passage, umhh, this is for chattel slavery, umhh, this is for Howard Beach, umhh, yeah, that's the one.

About that domestic scene on Flatbush: A man chases a woman down the street. He grabs for her pocketbook, she resists. "Give it to me, bitch," he yells. "That's why I dogged your ass with Tanya. You ain't worth shit, bitch." Finally he corners her, takes something from her pocketbook, and shoves the pocketbook back in her arms. He shuffles away with the object of all the fuss: a twenty-cent pack of Bon Ton corn chips.

Yours in love and trouble,
Lisa

1991

drop-dead fine

Bloodcurdling was a word without a case history before this scream. This scream traveled two rooms to lodge itself in the girl's aorta. She ran, half naked, half asleep, from her bedroom to the front window. A knife fight was happening down below in the street involving two men, one knife, and a woman in the middle, screaming to put all screams to shame.

Operator 911 took the address and asked for a description of the man with the weapon. The girl hesitated; it was dark, she couldn't make out details. True to routine, Operator 911 pressed ahead: "Is he a male black?" Then raising her voice, strangely insistent: *"Is he a male black?"* The girl was suddenly wide awake. She had been dreaming, before the scream, of frolicking with a "male black" in a celestial sea. Now she was standing barefoot in America, watching a knife fight on a Brooklyn street corner, and being force-fed racial stereotypes by a 911 operator.

No coincidence. Everywhere the girl looked, paper tigers like the endangered male black and the suspect male black stared back at her. She worried about who was labeled endangered, and therefore worthy of protection (young men), and who was not worthy (young women), and how anyone could make this distinction. In music and films, she saw the prey/predator role embraced, as shield perhaps, but also as badge, and saw it sold proudly, almost gleefully, to the masses, most of whom were eager to consume large quantities of male black without getting anywhere near where male blacks might live. Always statistic, always suspect, where did male black exist outside of this?

Is he a male black?

The night after the scream the girl went downtown to hear poetry and jazz. Poet Carl Hancock Rux came to the stage backed by gospel singers. Though a young man, Rux talked the talk, his voice, way deep, the voice of preachers and Last Poets past. He opened with a piece he called "Save the Animals": "I got a name/Call me nigger/Negro/negritude/black boy/ bastard child/African/Afro American/afrodisiac/young buck super stud . . ./So how do you make love to a Negro without getting tired?/You don't make love to him at all."

Is he a male black?

Always, but not by way of danger, by way of pleasure. The girl was looking to uncover the meaning of an ancient stricture known as "fineness." This was an important project. Only fineness, she reasoned, being as romantic and esoteric as she damn pleased, could help her break through the male black's sloganized endangerment. In fineness, there was wisdom. Fineness was no pseudoscientific black essence, it was critical inquiry. It was, as a fellow fine-watcher had schooled her, a "specifically, culturally black means of appreciating someone's black aesthetics in a way that no other word captures." Fine, to hear another fine-watcher tell it, was the motivating force behind most if not all activity. "That man was so fo-ine, he made my car run into a tree," and so on. And by virtue of being so lusciously onomatopoeic, it had to reveal something precious, hidden, and old.

The girl recalled her first intellectual encounter with fineness. She was maybe six years old, at her father's house in Newark, lucky to be hanging with some very grown teenagers who had a new portable record player and one 45, Marvin Gaye and Tammi Terrell's "Ain't No Mountain High Enough." They played the song for hours straight, and each time, these young women would fall to their knees and lament that Marvin was oh-so-fine. What was this fineness that it could possess the grown like hard liquor or religion?

Raised within earshot of sixties' Black Arts poetry, the girl would become even more intimate with fineness. Sonia Sanchez laid praise for all things lanky, fine, and committed to the struggle. A major text was Nikki Giovanni's "Beautiful Black Men (With compliments and apologies to all not mentioned by name)," which sung of brothers with "they afros" as "the same ol' danger/but a brand new pleasure." The girl came to think of fineness as an exalted state that would be realized after the Revolution. Later, to poets of the seventies' loft-jazz scene, the observance of fineness could produce a spiritual trance capable of healing sexism, racism, colorism, and any other 'ism that might be bothering folks. Here the girl was thinking of work such as Ntozake Shange's "lotsa body & cultural heritage" or Thulani Davis's "Zoom (the Commodores)," which engaged fineness as rhythm and blues: "Zoom you Commodores/maybe you are the best of us/that can love & believe."

Webster's take on "fine," the girl was surprised to find, matched fineness as a state of physical grace ("hardened close to the limit of efficiency . . . superior in conception"). An example, in the girl's mind, might be a clean head with a hairline shaped with diligent—almost painful—precision. To others, fine was a code that meant, precisely, big thighs, big butt, no exception.

Beyond the visuals, fine carried with it a sense of coolness, defiance, brilliance of gesture, a signature walk, a devastating smile, slyness, nobility, wit, uplift of the race, and, without question, a particularly African-American poetics with the English language. Fine was not *fly* (a material judgment that had something to do with the way one's clothes hung and how one's attitude tended to match). And fine was not necessarily handsome. Fine was handsome with a story. Like Deandra describing Michael Jordan as a "bird in the mythological sense. Like when you read about dinosaurs and wish you were there." Or Cheryl saying that when she was young, fine had meant "wavy-haired, bow-legged, and tall, but this was changing now." When asked if fine would one day become as mainstream and uniformly Caucasian as the high five, she sucked her teeth, "Honey, fine ain't going nowhere."

A sweetness of the girl's life had been to share in the ritual of naming fineness. It was among those stolen moments of communion that Cornel West might call black joy. The dissection of fineness was art obviously, specifically art that healed. The girl and her cohorts imagined Fine Studies to be, not some double standard of male objectification, but a way they recouped black men from the ugliness of their surroundings. Anointing male black with fineness put him in a magical world where he wasn't the hunter, the hunted, or the fossil. (Fineness was plentiful.) It redeemed and elevated, often beyond the fragility and hollowness of love relationships. Fineness was fantasy too.

The quintessential, nouveau-classical moment of fineness is still Denzel Washington in the Civil War drama *Glory*. Removing his shirt to take a whipping from the Yankee captain, Denzel bares scars that suggest he was a runaway before joining the Union army. The actor gives us real teardrops here, not born of pain, but in steadfast pride and remembrance: Pure race-man fine. A lost and now exhumed text of fineness that the girl is fixating on lately is a photo of Huey Newton in Elaine Brown's memoir of the Black Panther party. Brown paints Huey as a psychotic misogynist of genius stripe. (He punished and humiliated women, then named one to lead the party during his exile.) Of the drop-dead fine canon, Huey is photographed at home, shirtless and surrounded by books, pulling Bob Dylan's *Highway 61 Revisited* from its record sleeve. Was Huey's world a ghetto rebellion fantasy that hid boho aesthetics? Ah, fineness, ain't it deep?

Is he a male black?

The girl surrounded herself in this fineness, this aroma, much like Calvin Klein's Escape. Eau de Fine. No one would ever take male black from her and her sentimental self, ever again. Not all the 911 operators or the male blacks themselves, with their loves unrequited and deferred. This fineness belongs to her and to those who do the ritual. In her chest, split open like an Alison Saar sculpture to reveal trinkets and talismans, are all the fine ones. And there they stay, talking shit and playing ball, as Marvin sings "Ain't No Mountain High Enough" to Tammi, over and over, and over some more.

1993

brother jon

Jon Jon is this guy I met in Minneapolis. I stopped by Applause Records one Saturday and working the counter is this brother who could be the son of Valentino or Eddie Kendricks, but dressed up sixties mod, like Cosby circa "I Spy." He scans my choices and asks if I'm hip to Me Phi Me, Ephraim Lewis, and other young black musicians, post-Fishbone, who have deals with major labels and whose work resists industry race prisons. (Yes, most of the artists who hold this pass card are men.) Chitchat about apartheid marketing in music leads us to the blue-green swamps of race, class, and sex. Customers are waiting to buy Stravinsky and Tom Jones. Jon and I are having a town meeting about stagnant images of black masculinity and quadroon balls in nineteenth century New Orleans.

Like many young folks who work record-store plantations, Jon makes music himself. In the late eighties he sang with a band out of Chicago, Hot Sauce, which he describes as the "psychedelic side of Fishbone." Hot Sauce followed the Purple rainbow to Minneapolis in search of a deal with an indie record label. The group broke up soon after, though Jon stayed in the Twin Cities tinkering with various bands, including his latest, Dope Fiend, "a pretty noise thing with a big beat to keep the brothers interested." Jon lives in music, it's his political party, his religion, his family of choice, his take on blackness.

I tell Jon about this story I've been writing called "All the Boys were Hendrix," riffing on my days as a groupie to young black rock bands caught between King Jimi and the void. This was in the seventies, a few years before Prince and Living Colour. Hendrix's own image fused drag queen and pimp Mack Daddy, and the brothers I knew who worshiped at his throne had a male energy different than Funkateers and gangsta rappers; one that often acknowledged its woman self and had its own erotic cool. I wondered how a twenty-six-year-old like Jon, who flips through record bins that include (rainbow baby for peace) Lenny Kravitz and (hip-hop's hardest) the Geto Boys, chose what kind of man to be. Jon's model, it turns out, isn't a dead president like Hendrix or Sly, it's Fishbone's Angelo Moore—equal parts blues archivist, rock scientist, minstrel, race man, ambassador of integration. Heavy on rhythm and pictures, Jon has a songwriter's way with words that is savored best raw. So here I bring you Jon, and "his own self's thing," just about unadulterated:

"Jon Jon, the alternative Negro, is what my friends call me. That boy *al*-ternative, they always joking around, 'cause I like to debate black stereotypes, what people say black is. They say black folks don't be listening to that shit you be listening to, Jon. You better turn that Dinosaur Jr. off, motherfucker, you're with the brothers now, listen to some brother shit.

"I got this friend who's always boasting about being from the hood, from Brew City, where brothers get capped day and night. That I'm-from-the-ghetto attitude really gets me. Somehow we're not *real* unless we're ghetto enough. I went to live with my grandmother for a year in Chicago after high school. The lady's eighty-fucking years old, drinking every day. Some of my friends thought I was cool because my grandmother's place was so crazy; 'cause the house got roaches and kids going crazy; and the TV's up loud; and everybody's hollering at everybody, drinking and smoking; and somebody's shooting up in the back room; while my frub uncle's twirling around downstairs listening to his stereo. Ain't that some shit?

"Growing up in Chicago was "Good Times" and "The Cosby Show" at the same time, 'cause Grandma was up in the ghetto and my parents lived in some kind of good section, at least it stayed good for a while. I'm adopted. Wonderful home, great fucking family values, and then they got divorced. Dad hooked up again, this time to a woman he met on tour as road manager with the Delfonics. He came home one day and said he wasn't gonna work for the white man anymore. So I said, what man are you gonna work for? He told me he'd figure that out later. Dad joined the Nation of Islam, and from seventy-three to eighty-one we followed Islam from Elijah Muhammad's perspective. Me and my brothers and sisters went to Muslim schools and the whole bit.

"I was on a little free-base journey before I put a band together. Cam, my best friend, went to the air force for a year after high school. That's when I really fucked up, 'cause it's Cam that keeps me alive when I'm out there too foul. When Cam came back, me and him had an agreement that if he caught me basing he could knock the shit out of me. I could always hear his noisy ass car pull up in the driveway, so I could've thrown the shit under the bed and played like I was watching *Superfly* on TV, but I didn't. That's how I stayed straight.

"After Cam's adventure in the air force we started reading these cute *Id* and *Face* magazines and doing a London hipster trip. We had been to every house party on the Southside and had used that up. We hit gay discos for a while, which was cool, but it wasn't our scene, we were into guitars. That took us to the Northside and put us in this integrated environment. I got hip to politics on a global scale hanging with white kids who talked to me about the shit. I had white kids schooling me on Malcolm X, even though I grew up a Muslim. Trip.

"I used to make excuses for dating white girls; I went through that whole period. Sometimes I do still feel that by hanging out with girls who aren't black, I'm messing up on a responsibility. I was chilling with my friend Star the other night, and Star says, 'Hey man, we live in fuckin' Minnesota, everywhere we go there's fuckin' white girls. If we run into a black girl, that's cool, I'm sure we're gonna talk to her, but if we don't, we're not gonna just sit back and wait.' That's true. If you go to First Avenue on weekends when they play rock, there aren't that many black girls there. What you gonna do? Go on funk night or 'black night' just to meet the black girls? My friends in Chicago still give me shit, though. Jon Jon, you got a black girlfriend yet? When I do get with a black girl she has to be down with Tribe Called Quest *and* the Cocteau Twins, that's all I know. And when I make it to London or New York, I'm gonna scoop me one up. I know y'all out there.

"I don't refer to women as 'bitch' or 'ho' any more; my friend Iyanna told about myself, though growing up in the hood, you hear girls say 'bitch' all day; it's almost as natural now as 'nigger.' Lots of girl buddies of mine talk to me about their problems. Like, girl buddies call to ask if they should get an abortion. I tell them, it's on them. Basically I'm against abortion, being that I was adopted. If my mother had aborted me, I wouldn't be around to talk as much shit as I do, so I'm biased! But since I don't have a vagina and a womb and all that, it's not my right to tell a woman her business. So when it comes down to it, I believe in choice. My sister's twenty-one and she has a one year old. Sometimes she says shit like, 'Fuck this ugly-ass baby, I wish I never had the motherfucker.' Mama thinks she's talking out of her head, but no, no, sis means it. It's incredible that someone would feel that way about a child. Society looks at little black girls with babies and says, foul, so maybe my sister picked up that message. To me, though, it's birth, and birth is positive.

"In junior high school I started listening to rock accidentally 'cause my bedroom was in the attic and I could only get AM stations. I dug Led Zep and shit they call 'rock that will never die,' then metal, then shit that was cooler than that, like the Cure, your Smiths, Sonic Youth. Then Fishbone opened for the Beastie Boys in Chicago in eighty-five. I forget how my hair was looking at the time, but we said, Wow, here are some brothers that look just like us, brothers who didn't grow up listening to R&B radio. Brothers who probably grew up outside of the city, went to school with white kids, and spent a good amount of time listening to the Butthole Surfers. Cam had been writing music and he said, Jon come over and scream on some of these tunes, we can do this kind of punk thing. Three months later we were playing shows.

"When you see bands like Bad Brains or Fishbone, they're saying, I'm just as much man as you are even though I don't play basketball or wear gold chains. It's about being a man with another type of edge. There's rowdiness, but it's playful rowdiness, it's not a 'niggers killing niggers' rowdiness. You hear about police brutality, but in Fishbone and 24-7 Spyz songs you also hear about racial harmony, probably because some of the guys have interracial relationships and they need to let folks know that it's okay.

"Brothers who are coming up now, brothers younger than me, the first band they saw playing instruments, period, not rapping, was Living Colour. Seeing Living Colour changed their ideas about what black guys are supposed to be doing. But is it a sign of social change that brothers are allowed to express their complexity in music and get bankrolled? I dunno.

"To me, we need to stress individualism right now. We all make individual choices and these choices go beyond skin color. Brothers don't get a break from me just because they're brothers. Like, I can't buy the line that it's the white man's fault that we're doing crack. Sure the white man put crack in our communities, but the white man didn't put the pipe up to your mouth. That's your dirty work, my brother."

1992

the signifying monkees

FORT LAUDERDALE, FLORIDA—Though the state of Florida's case against hip-hop lewd boys 2 Live Crew has been front-page news here since June, the dailies can't print the charge itself—too many dirty words. When the Crew's leading *mensch,* Luther Campbell, hears Judge June Johnson read it aloud for the first time to the original jury pool of twenty-five—twenty-two whites (who turn pink) and three blacks (who turn gray)—he bolts from his seat in the small county courtroom and storms out. Campbell probably pictured himself doing a year of solitary confinement, and here's why:

. . . as live persons before an audience, [they] did knowingly conduct, perform, or participate in, by words and/or conduct, a show or performance which was obscene . . . [which] included . . . an apparent version of [2 Live Crew's song] "Me So Horny," consist[ing] of verbal depictions or descriptions of sexual conduct . . . deviate sexual intercourse, as defined in Florida Statue 847.0011, and actual physical contact with a person's unclothed buttocks, examples of which are: "Let me stick my dick in your behind," [and] "I'll be fucking you and you'll be sucking me, lick my ass up and down, lick it till your tongue turns doo-doo brown" . . . and in the course of said performance . . . did simulate an act of deviate sexual intercourse as defined in F.S. 847.0011 . . . examples of which are: placing the face of a woman into or in very close proximity to the groin of one of the performers, Luther Campbell, and through the acts of another performer, Mark Ross, uncovering and exposing the breast of another female.

In the court hallway, in front of a dozen television cameras, another dozen scribbling reporters, Campbell yells at his attorney, Bruce Rogow, "What the fuck is this shit? You told me the shit was gonna be played on tape!" Rogow explains that what he's just heard is called an "information," and though issued by the state, it's not evidence, just an accusation. The judge, who has long blonde hair, blushed herself as she struggled to get through the awkwardly worded statement. The overall effect: Heidi reading porno confessions to a classroom of retired grade-school principals.

condoms and microcassettes

In the Safeway supermarket parking lot on Las Olas Boulevard one car's bumper sticker reads BEAM ME UP, LORD, another's CENSORSHIP SUCKS. Both have Broward plates. That's Broward County. Home to the county seat, Fort Lauderdale, known as "Fort Liquordale," until media darling Sheriff Nick Navarro and the FLPD kicked out spring break a couple years back. Their goal: to attract a calmer breed of tourist and eventually remake Spuds-MacKenzie-by-the-Sea into the "retirement capital of the retirement capital" to compete with Miami next door in Dade County.

Broward has been better known lately as home to Hollywood, Florida. As part of an ongoing crusade for "family values," Hollywood mayor Sal Oliveri recently proclaimed "Pornography Awareness Week," corresponding with the final week of the 2 Live Crew trial. (Oliveri's crusade has included painting over a beach-side mural of the Coppertone Girl's nude buttocks.) 2 Live Crew made history here last June when they were arrested for performing songs from *As Nasty as They Wanna Be,* the group's third album, ruled obscene by a Florida federal judge earlier that month. Club Futura, where the bust took place, now sells T-shirts with the legend BROWARD COUNTY: CENSORSHIP CAPITAL OF THE WORLD. Birth of a tourist attraction?

But that bumper sticker isn't for sale at the Safeway in downtown Fort Lauderdale, a couple blocks away from the Broward County courthouse, where 2 Live Crew is standing trial. On the display rack closest to the cash register, instead of copies of *Family Circle,* you can choose from five types of condoms and microcassettes sold by the three-pack. Remember that: condoms and microcassettes.

two live jews

"'Two live Jews, kosher as they wanna to be." It's day one of the trial, and the first one-liner comes from a legal eagle in the spectator pews, one of many young attorneys and prosecutors who flock to the courtroom for a piece of the action. "I'm a Jew," he says, "so I can make fun of them all I want." The eagle is describing defense lawyers Bruce Rogow (representing Campbell) and Allen Jacobi (in for Mark Ross, a/k/a Brother Marquis), who have just arrived in court.

The two do cut an odd pair: Jacobi a rock-&-roll lawyer whose clients have included Eric Clapton, Peter Max, and the Church of Scientology, was raised kosher in Miami Beach, though with his deep tan and longish black hair, you might mistake him for Greek. Rogow, professor at Nova Law school in Fort Lauderdale and former president of Florida's ACLU, represented Mississippi civil rights workers in the sixties and has taken a half-dozen cases to the Supreme Court. If it weren't for the distinctive schnoz, Rogow's Ivy League suits and narrow bow ties could label him a WASP from Connecticut, where he grew up.

The prosecution, surprisingly enough, is also awash in the melting pot. Leslie Robson, born in Hong Kong and educated in England, finished her law degree at Nova and is now assistant state attorney in charge of Broward County's vice division. With her slight British accent and Eurasian features, Robson doesn't fit the stereotype of the Southern cracker fundamentalist after an improper acting colored boy like Luther Campbell. Neither does her coprosecutor, assistant state attorney Pedro Dijols, a supervisor in the misdemeanor division. Dijols, a black Puerto Rican from New York who went to law school in Florida, describes himself as a "fan of rap music." He tells female reporters about the tattoo on his left bicep: Underneath a Cheshire cat in a fedora is the inscription, in Latin, "Let the thing speak for itself." The motto turns out to be the prosecution's losing strategy in the case.

Then there's her honor June Johnson, who the press pool refers to affectionately as "Judge June," a Louisiana native with a dry wit, whose sideline remarks in court evidence a concern for matters affecting women and children. The judge, who usually tries DUI cases, even brings her mother to court one day.

"If you think of Miami as Los Angeles," Jacobi explains, then Broward is the Orange County of Florida." And though everyone from Florida, says a reporter, "is from somewhere else originally," it's amusing that it is this group of "outsiders" who will struggle over this case that represents, in the minds of some, the Wonderbread majority versus the "others."

It's these outsiders who will instruct, in the case of the judge, and interpret, in the case of the lawyers, Florida's obscenity law, modeled after the Supreme Court's 1973 *Miller v. California:* "The average person applying contemporary community standards, would find that the work, taken as a whole, appeals to prurient interests, . . . describes, in a patently offensive way, sexual conduct . . . [and] lacks serious literary, artistic, political, or scientific value."

These outsiders—and the fifty Broward County citizens who they sift through to pick a jury of six—will raise complicated questions: What constitutes a community, and is it acceptable that the standards of some people in the community are different from others? And just what, if anything, is obscene? As well as, what is art and who decides?

the signifying monkees
And what about the defendants? Multimillionaire Campbell, twenty-nine, president of Luke Records, from (as the media lathers it up) the "hard-core Miami ghetto of Liberty City," who can choose whether or not to wear a custom-made Italian suit to court. Ross, twenty-three, 2 Live's primary lyricist, originally from Rochester, New York, dresses in baggy clothes and beads and is fond of "cultural rap like De La Soul and Tribe Called Quest." (Says Ross, people probably think the group is a bunch of "backwards niggers and geechees who don't know how to do anything but cuss, but that's not the case.") And Wongwon, twenty-six, a Trinidadian of African and Chinese ancestry, who grew up in Brooklyn and founded the group five years ago on an air force base in California with David Hobbs (Mr. Mixx, the Crew's DJ). Mixx was not charged because detectives didn't consider his contributions to be an integral part of the performance. Another strike against the state.

In a case that is all about 2 Live Crew's words (or, as the defense points out, their "lyrics"—making us pause to consider if there is a difference), it's strangely symbolic that we never hear the three speak in the context of the proceedings (the law says they don't have to, it's the state who must prove its case to the jurors "beyond a reasonable doubt"). The jurors watch them like one-eyed hawks. Their body language: Ross often slumps in his seat and chews on a toothpick. When the state plays an audiotape of the group's infamous concert, Wongwon, who has a disabled left arm, taps out the beat on the table with his right hand. Their clothes: Campbell doesn't wear a suit during jury selection because he doesn't want the "white, blue-collar workers who may get on the jury to think I'm uppity." Their every gesture: Ross blows his nose often; Campbell hands his cellular phone to his bodyguard, who sits, every day, right behind him. It must be a strain for these guys who sell shock value to sit still for so long and be so silent. But they do—like See No Evil, Hear No Evil, Speak No Evil—they sit through the eleven-day trial while words are slung back and forth all around them.

At one point a detective who testifies for the prosecution translates "Marquis's babies"—a line from a song performed the night of the bust—into "monkey's baby." Ross (whose rapper's ID, Brother Marquis, comes from the Marquis de Sade) sits through the botch in the courtroom but complains bitterly during a break. After Henry Louis Gates, Jr. (whose works include *The Signifying Monkey*, a collection of postmodern criticism of black literature) testifies that the music of 2 Live Crew has artistic value, I tease Ross that the group should change its name to "The Signifying Monkees." The joke doesn't go over well; no room for sarcasm in a court of law.

After all, there is a trial going on. And even though Dennis Barrie and Cincinnati's Contemporary Art Center were acquitted the week before in an obscenity trial involving the exhibition of photographs by Robert Mapplethorpe, this is Broward County—a lot further away from New York than Ohio is. This isn't a collection of silver-print photographs exhibited in museums; this is rap music performed in a nightclub. In fact, Campbell never once refers to his music as art, though he often calls it "entertainment" and is quick to tell you it has "artistic value." ("Rap music is not on trial" is a constant refrain—initiated by the prosecution and carried by the defense. Repeated so often, as an argument for and against the artistic content of 2 Live Crew's music, it becomes a hollow slogan.)

This isn't work with a large critical following; this is music that received scant critical attention until it ended up as a free-speech mantra. And these aren't "righteous rappers" like Boogie Down

Productions's KRS One (quoted in the *New York Times* as spokes-man of a new black youth culture), but the Miami-based nasty boys of rap, whose rude snipes on record about other rappers have lost them friends in the hip-hop community. (Kid N' Play and Salt-N-Pepa are called "faggots" and "dykes" on *Banned in the USA.*) The creator of this work is not a dead white man but three living black men; "young and virile," as they're often referred to in the press, perhaps perceived by those who wish to see them prose-cuted, as capable of violence, rape, or miscegenation.

The pipes squeak so loudly in courtroom 354, where the trial takes place, they often interrupt the proceedings. In this small, aging county courthouse, which is connected to a brand-new, very large county jail, prisoners are handcuffed together in twos and led back and forth by deputies. Most of these deputies are white, and most of the men in handcuffs are young and black. On their way to lunch during the trial's first week, the Campbell entourage runs into a group of prisoners and their keeper on the staircase. The men call out "Luke, Luke, Luke Skyywalker" (a name George Lucas sued Campbell to drop), hailing the rapper as a hero. He looks a bit embarrassed, but gives them a "Hey, what's up," and continues down the stairs.

Symbolism aside, this is a trial. A real trial, say Brother Mar-quis's eyes. If convicted the three could be charged with a misde-meanor, fined one thousand dollars, and slapped with a year in jail. When the state asks a detective on the witness stand to confirm that Campbell, Ross, and Wongwon did indeed perform songs ruled obscene, and that they did so that night in Hollywood as "live persons," Judge June adds, "that's their problem. They're too live."

motion sickness

The first day of the trial is all motions—each side attempting to get evidence admitted and procedural questions answered in a manner that will advance their case. Rogow, the trendsetting constitutional-ist, argues that selecting a jury pool from voter registrations lists, the method in Florida and most states, is unconstitutional in ob-scenity cases. Obscenity is the only charge, he holds, that requires jurors to bring their knowledge of "community standards" to bear on the decision.

In a county where 13 percent of the population is black and only 5 percent is registered to vote, black people are automatically underrepresented in the jury pools, as are young people. This, Rogow contends, gives the court a narrower frame of reference with which to judge community opinion.

Rogow's motion is a sweeping gesture that feels at first too grand a consideration for a county court. The judge rules against it, but it turns out to be an effective framing device for the trial: establishing the importance of a diverse jury and of looking at "community standards" as more than just the dominion of middle-class whites from Broward suburbs like Plantation. Rogow's challenge even makes it to page 16A of the *New York Times* with the amusing pullquote, "Middle-aged whites aren't representative, the court is told." Campbell schools reporters during a break that the only way he can foresee a fair trial is if "the judge lets us have black people on the jury." And "young people," Jacobi pipes in. "And young people," Campbell repeats.

Later in the day Campbell signs autographs for three white teenagers—hillbillies in high-waters who sport fresh hickeys on their necks. The teens shout in court, "2 Live Crew, doing the right thing!" Campbell tells them to watch out, "Y'all might wind up here with us."

suicide mission

Assistant State Attorney Dijols, whose usual beat is DUI cases, eventually admits toward the end of the trial that when he first heard the state's only piece of evidence—a barely audible microcassette recording of the performance in Hollywood that night—he knew the case was a "suicide mission." This is an odd admission from a prosecutor who made it very clear that he had volunteered for the case, and was not, as Campbell had charged early on, a "token" brought in by the state attorney to lend "ethnic credibility" to the prosecution.

The state makes every possible move to postpone the case and bolster its scanty evidence. They ask that a "transcript" of the performance prepared by the Broward County sheriff's office be admitted as evidence, to "assist" the jurors in judging whether the performance is obscene. This amuses Rogow at first, who says "no one gets a transcript of the performance when they go to see *My Fair Lady*."

The prosecution does manage to get four songs from *As Nasty As They Wanna Be* admitted as evidence, despite high-pitched objections from the defense ("This record is not on trial!"). Judge Johnson is given the opportunity to review the songs before potential jurors arrive. "Are they talking or singing?" The judge wants to know. Rogow beats out the prosecutors to answer her: "They're rapping, your honor." "DO YOU BELIEVE IN HAVING SEX?" blares from the speakers set up in the middle of the courtroom. "HELL YES," the speakers call back. "Is this like an act you see in Las Vegas?" Judge June asks. "No," Rogow assures her, "rapping is music that engages in call and response with its audience."

twenty questions

Time for jury selection. First, the prosecution and defense take potential jurors through voir dire (from the French phrase, "to speak the truth"), the question and answer session attorneys use to determine which jurors will best advance their case. Jurors are quizzed about explicit language, oral and anal sex, their tastes in music, and what they know about 2 Live Crew.

Dijols questions jurors if they can stomach "offensive language" like "anal sex, oral sex, and ejaculation" that will be dredged up in this case. One woman replies that, as a teacher, she hears worse every day. "What grade do you teach?" Dijols asks. "Kindergarten" (the evening news's soundbite of choice). A middle-aged man with thick red glasses says he heard the group's music was "promiscuous." When Rogow grills the would-be jurors if they consider oral or anal sex to be morbid or shameful, they all shake their heads "no." No one bothers to remind them that oral and anal sex are illegal under Florida's sodomy law.

Rogow is approached during a break by a French television

crew who inquire if all sex is obscene in America. Rogow chuckles, "No, but in America good sex is illegal." Later that afternoon, two fifteen-year-old white girls in Catholic school uniforms scurry over to the defense table to get Campbell's autograph.

race is not on trial

Assistant State Attorney Dijols is shaking his head. (There's a silent style war being waged in the courtroom between Dijols's loosely curled hair, cut into a seventies-style shag, and Campbell's closely cropped fade.) "Race has reared its ugly head again in this trial," Dijols rants. You get the feeling that Dijols is the kind of person who would like to leave race out of it. He's referring to the case of Bernard Kinnel, one of three black people in the original twenty-five-person jury pool.

Kinnel, a truck driver, wears a gold earring and a beeper. (Campbell has two beepers.) In voir dire Kinnel admits to liking rap music, and even to hearing the clean version of 2 Live Crew's "Me So Horny" on the radio once. "What did you think?" the judge asks, genuinely interested. "I didn't give it a rating," he shrugs, and the courtroom snickers. Later, when Dijols presses Kinnel on whether he considers himself a fan of 2 Live Crew, he hesitates a bit, says yes, but adds that he is also fan of other rap groups. Rogow asks Kinnel later if he could be a fair juror despite his interest in rap. He can, he says, because his real love is "slow music," not rap. (Might Kinnel have been using the word "fan" differently than Dijols? Which speaks to yet another subtext of the trial: How words and their meanings are so speaker- and context-specific in this age of cultural relativism.)

Dijols moves to eliminate Kinnel as a juror based on the fact that he referred to himself a fan of 2 Live Crew. Rogow then charges that Dijols is striking Kinnel because Kinnel's black. Follow the twists: Here you have a white defense attorney (a progressive, free-speech advocate) calling a black prosecutor (a registered Republican) a racist. (Campbell is with Rogow all the way on this one; he nods his head up and down furiously.) Dijols is livid. He jumps from his seat and yells at the judge: "I want the record to state this prosecutor is a black prosecutor, a member of Mr. Kinnel's same race!" The judge strikes down Rogow's challenge; Kinnel doesn't make the jury.

When the trial ends for the day, reporters rush over not to Campbell, but to Dijols: "The basic premise behind this is that blacks can somehow relate to this music more, and therefore have lower moral standards. This music is obscene. It would be obscene if it was country western, reggae, or rock & roll. If they were so concerned about the black and white issue, why isn't Campbell using black defense attorneys?" On his way out, Mark Ross, in a pair of exaggerated "field-hand" overalls that belong in a high school production of *Huck Finn*, walks by Dijols chewing a toothpick.

translating from the crew

"Cultural translators" are a crucial part of this trial.

Exhibit A: The witnesses for the prosecution, Detective Eugene McCloud, a heavyset black man with glasses, fourteen years with the Broward Sheriff's Office (BSO), and Detective Debra Werder, a heavyset white woman with frosted blond hair, married to Sheriff Navarro's chief of personnel.

The BSO had the detectives prepare "transcripts," which are their interpretations of the garbled microcassette recording of 2 Live Crew's concert that night at Club Futura. According to Campbell and defense attorneys, these transcripts are quite inaccurate—rife with misnomers and editorial comments. But the state wants to introduce the transcripts as evidence; it could be the only opportunity for jurors to read 2 Live Crew's dirty words and finally be shocked. (After hearing the judge's first reading of the "charge," the jury has been largely unruffled by 2 Live Crew's language arts.)

Robson's numerous attempts to get these transcripts admitted as evidence, as reading material for the jury, are denied by Judge Johnson. What the state manages to do in lieu of this is have the detectives translate the "remixed" performance tape line by line. So the tape plays a bit, then is stopped by Assistant State Attorney Dijols, who works a mixing board from a corner of the courtroom. Detective McCloud then "translates" what he's heard (refreshing his memory with his "transcript"). This goes on for two-and-a-half days.

The effect of McCloud's translations is pure pathos. Here's a thirty-eight-year-old man in a suit repeating lines like a trained parrot—some he flubs intentionally. It's as if he's translating from the Jive (remember that long-lost lingo?). The tape blares: ALL HOS SUCK DICK. McCloud translates: ALL WHORES SUCK DICK. Or sometimes McCloud narrates action in the club: "Ross [Brother Marquis] approached the girl from the back and embraced her. The girl's breasts came out."

Assistant State Attorney Robson: "The breasts that came out, were they the breasts nearest to you or away from you?"

McCloud: "Away from me."

At one point Robson has McCloud in the middle of the courtroom demonstrating how the dancers moved on stage. Campell bitches loud during a break: "People are supposed to be judging our concert in its entirety—as a whole, like the law says. But the state keeps stopping the tape and they got a man up there narrating! Worse part about it is you got to listen. You can't say nothing. That lying motherfucker!"

At a coffee shop across the street from the courtroom, the Campbell entourage eats lunch. Debbie Bennett, Luke Record's publicity director, brings Campbell a plate of soul food from a Liberty City greasy spoon. Campbell is so mad about the McCloud performance that he blows up at lawyer Allen Jacobi in the middle of the luncheonette. Why aren't the lawyers butting into McCloud's testimony if it's so inaccurate? We've got strategies, the lawyers say. "This is some nigger shit, isn't it?" charges Campbell, not used to delegating authority. "I may be a nigger," he belts at the top of his lungs, "but I ain't a dumb nigger." He storms out. Word comes back to Debbie, forget about the soul food, order him a turkey sandwich.

After lunch there's a breakthrough. The jury has sent a note to Judge Johnson asking if they are allowed to laugh. It's a deciding moment in the case. Campbell calls it as soon as he can speak, which at the advice of his lawyers is only outside of the courtroom: "That's your verdict, right there." He grins like the Cheshire cat tattooed on Dijols's arm.

Like I said, cultural translators are a crucial part of this trial.

Exhibit B: Witnesses for the defense, Duke University professor and literary critic Henry Louis Gates, Jr., and *Newsday* music critic John Leland.

I have an amusing encounter with Gates and Leland in the lobby of the Riverside Hotel, down the street from the courthouse, the night before they testify. This is my first time meeting Leland, and when he arrives at the front desk, Gates announces him: "Ladies and gentlemen, this is Luther Campbell." Certainly one could say, for the day they spend in Broward, Leland and Gates are Luther Campbell. They explain his music, his "entertainment," his "artistic value," whatever it is he does, better than he ever could. But then, says Gates, Campbell's an artist, so that's not his job.

Leland's an old hand, having testified on the Crew's behalf on three occasions, the first in February 1990, at an obscenity trial in Alexander City, Alabama. He gives an entertaining, annotated history of hip-hop, which includes a stop in Miami for the birth of ghetto bass, as originated by the Ghetto Style DJs, of which Luther Campbell is a founding father. Jurors' eyes widen.

Gates defends the artistic value of 2 Live Crew's music to the jury by establishing it as part and parcel of a black oral and literary tradition that is twice as old, and then some, as the courtroom they sit in. He breaks down big words, for these parts, like "signifying," "hyperbole," and "parody," and explains why works of art are rarely to be taken literally. 2 Live Crew's music, he argues, takes one of the worst stereotypes about black men—that they're oversexed animals—and blows it up until it explodes. The jurors study him carefully: the suit, glasses, cane. When Gates compares 2 Live Crew to Archie Bunker, buzzers go off in the jurors' heads. The two black women in the jury, Gertrude McLamore, a retired cook, and alternate Wilma Williams, a retired school principal, beam at him, as if to say, finally someone to vindicate these ignorant colored boys.

Dijols spends most of his cross-examination attempting to put literary criticism on trial, a losing battle to fight against Gates, the dean of the signifying monkees. Dijols asks, "Does this work advance black culture?" "Yes," Gates answers with a straight face. Dijols continues: "Are you saying that this is part of fighting for civil rights and fighting for equality? Are you equating 2 Live Crew to black leaders like Martin Luther King?" Gates hesitates; not even he can go that far. "I never equated the two. There is a difference between a civil rights march and exploding a stereotype."

Something Gates tells the court sticks to my head like Velcro: "There is no cult of violence. There is no danger at all that these words are being sung." I wonder if he's seen 2 Live Crew in concert and watched them push women to the stage floor, pour water on them, and chant, "Summer's Eve, Massengill, bitch wash your stinky pussy!" I've been watching Brother Marquis around the courtroom. With his signifying, double-entendre way of dressing and speaking, I wonder if he can answer some of the questions I have about 2 Live Crew's "entertainment":

"We recorded 'Throw the D' in Eighty-Seven. It was kinda X-rated and it was a hit. Common sense told us to follow up on our hit. We put our minds to work and came up with this whole thing here: being the nasty boys of rap. We knew we had to talk about something. At the time, L.L. Cool J was talking about how bad he was, and the Fat Boys were talking about how fat they were. Since Miami is up on sex—anything nasty these cats go for around here—we said, let's talk about sex.

"The bottom line is getting dollars and having your own. It's really a black thing with us. Even though people might say we're not positive role models to the black community, that if you ask us about our culture, we talk about sex, it's not really like that. I'm well aware of where I come from. I know myself as a black man. I think I'm with the program, very much so. You feel I'm doing nothing to enhance my culture, but I could be destroying my culture. I could be out here selling kids drugs.

"The women come on stage on their own. Sometimes we do grab a girl. The water-fighting thing, that's not for me, but that's our job. We go out there and do it to the best of our abilities, then we go offstage and carry on like regular men. I'm not really like the way I talk on records and act onstage.

"I'm not gonna try to disrespect you and call you all those names like I do on those records. I would never do that to a young lady, especially a sister. I'm degrading you to try to get me some money. Richard Pryor was degrading you on record. And besides, just let me do that. You got pimps out here who are making you sell your body. Just let me talk about you for a little while, you know what I'm saying? And make me a little money."

campbell's souped

I'm in a black BMW convertible heading towards Miami from Fort Lauderdale on Interstate 95. This is not my car. I couldn't even rent this car. This is Luther Campbell's car. Luther Campbell is talking on one of his two car phones. The audio outfit where the state attorney's office had the infamous concert tape remixed is a place where Luke Records *used* to do business. Campbell's pulling the plug at this very moment. First he's got to yell in the owner's ear for a while.

I notice a copy of *Fortune* magazine on the backseat. We're speeding fast now. Campbell thinks he spots a cop car in the rear-view mirror. This is all I need: To get busted in Broward County with Luther Campbell, I'll never live this down. My friends think his music is nothing but "misogynistic smut." They compare it to "farting" and say it "defiles an entire culture." They'll disown me and I'll have to move to Miami and work for Luke Records. Okay, no cop car, relax.

Campbell is bitching about how many people are serving him with lawsuits these days. ("They see a nigger making money and they want to jump on the bandwagon.") He has a child on the way from his current lady, Tina, and an eight-year-old daughter, Shane-tris. (Campbell just arrived at a child-support settlement with her mother, Terry Brinberry.) Another woman from Miami is filing a paternity suit against him.

I share my theory with Campbell that he probably grew up

middle class and, through his music, lives out some rough-riding homeboy fantasy. He doesn't appreciate this theory at all. 2 Live Crew is just a gig, he says tiredly. Luther Campbell is the business-man, the president of Luke Records, the scrupulous investor, the property owner, the little-league team sponsor, the man whose net worth, rumor has it, is over five million dollars. The man whose office is dominated by framed portraits of Martin Luther King and Malcolm X.

Campbell talks about his childhood in Liberty City, growing up in a two-bedroom house with five brothers. The Campbell brothers are all superachievers: one's a physicist, another's an executive chef. Luther is the youngest, the spoiled one, the only one who didn't go to college. Now he makes more money than all of them. And no, he was not in a gang. And yes, he did get started selling records out of his car.

"Two bedrooms, you know what that means?!," he says. "All of us were in one room, and *they* were in the other." Campbell's father, Charles Sr., born in Jamaica, is a custodian. His mother, Yvonne, who is under five feet tall, was a hairdresser until her arthritis got bad. The Campbells have been in court with their son for the last four days. They say they're "extremely proud" of their son's accomplishments. A reporter in court tells this story: Appar-ently Campbell would prefer that his parents not see his adults-only act. Once they did slip in. He spotted them in the crowd and refused to do any more dirty songs. The audience wanted their money back. Another story: When asked if he planned on getting married anytime soon, Campbell said, no, because the only woman he had ever thought of marrying was already taken. His mother.

mr. america

"What's happening?" Brother Marquis asks Mary the bailiff, the court's unofficial court jester, whose tiepin is pair of miniature handcuffs. "Nothing yet, you just keep smiling. You want some water?" she offers in a thick Southern drawl. "Here's your last glass."

Gates and Leland had helped, but Rogow's thorough cross-examination of the detectives put the case to rest. The odds for acquittal are at three to one; reporters take bets in the court hallway. Campbell's family and most of the twenty-five staffers of Luke Records pack the court. The court clerk is a young black woman with extensions who cracks a big smile when she reads the verdict, "Luther Campbell, *not guilty.*"

Campbell kisses his mother first.

Outside of the Broward County Courthouse palm trees are blowing in the wind. TV cameramen are jogging backward to get a frontal shot of Campbell as he jaywalks across the boulevard. Campbell is the tallest man in the crowd, he is the brownest man in the crowd. His girlfriend, Tina, very pregnant, is two steps behind him. Campbell's parents, on the sidewalk, watch him disappear in the distance. This is a Norman Rockwell painting.

One consensus in the 2 Live Crew trial is that the only thing obscene in America is spending money the wrong way. Another constant refrain was "it's a job." Lots of people seem to do work that requires that they separate what they do from themselves. It suddenly hits what an American phenomenon Luther Campbell is. He's sold us soft porn as music, he's sold us the First Amendment as entertainment *(Banned in the USA)*. And he goes out of his way to let you know that he is not what he sells.

As much as we think he doesn't speak for us (me, you, your grandmother), he speaks for our country. As American as Pete Rose, McDonald's fried apple pie, and Luther Campbell.

1990

pussy ain't free

Remember the Roxanne wars of '85? U.T.F.O. cut "Roxanne Roxanne," cold dissing yet another "stuck-up, devious, and sinister" homegirl. Along comes fourteen-year-old Roxanne Shanté from the Queens Bridge projects, Long Island City, the unauthorized rapper behind "Roxanne's Revenge." Shanté (real first name: Lolita) tells the U.T.F.O. crew to "suck my bush." Requests for "Roxanne's Revenge" pour into black music stations before Pop Art Records even presses it. U.T.F.O., after threatening to sue, answer with "The Real Roxanne," sung by the Roxanne of their choosing. Shanté takes it to the stage, namely the Roxy–Red Parrot club scene in New York, and wins the battle with fierce freestyling. In 1986 she drops out of sight.

After having a kid (Kareem), Shanté surfaced last summer when producer Marley Marl convinced her to record "Have a Nice Day" (Cold Chillin'). She came back Ali-style, proclaiming in her trademark squeak that she's "the mike's grandmistress . . . the queen of the crew with the juice"—laurels that, in her absence, MC Lyte, Salt-N-Pepa, Queen Latifah, and others have dibs on. (These contenders are so young, the title in question should be princess; if there's a queen in the house of rap, it's Millie Jackson.)

Shanté's three singles to date deliver their share of quick draws, but improvising live is where Shanté has most rappers beat; given an inch, she'll read any man in the audience faster than a snap queen can raise his right arm. On the subject of male rappers and their female problem, Shanté, who's seventeen now, has no use for any oppressed-other politics. She accepts what rap boys have to say about girls, for the most part, with a shrug and a smile. Yet her freestyle "The Pussy Ain't Free, You Gotta Give Up Money" isn't about acceptance. It's much closer to Janet Jackson's idea of control, and seems more sound advice to Shanté's young female audience than Madonna's promo for teen pregnancy "Papa Don't Preach." Just who owns the means of reproduction? I'd like to hear someone answer Shanté on that.

Tell me about your live show.

ROXANNE SHANTÉ: They turn off the lights. My MC says, "Are you ready for Roxanne Shanté? Well, here's the queen!" I go out there and say, TELL 'EM WHO I AM! My DJ cuts in Heavy D and The Boyz's "The Overweight Lover's in the House." Again I say, WHO AM I? Then the DJ cuts in "Payback." I rap freestyle to that, do my new single "Have a Nice Day," and end with another freestyle.

How do you work a freestyle?

Usually I start with, "The Pussy Ain't Free." And more [ad-libs] about guys. My language is very vulgar, and that's bad, because I have little kids who come see my show and they go home quoting me. I had somebody's mother call me up. Her kid is four and she took her to see me at a stadium in New Jersey. For the past two weeks this kid's been going around the house saying, "The pussy ain't free, you got to give up money." Some people tell me, "Listen, don't you think you oughta cut it down?" If I did cut it down, what would I do—"One-two, one-two, what we gonna do?"? My audience is used to hearing me say things like, "See that guy right there? He makes me sick. Always wanting the blank, but ain't got no blank." You can imagine what goes in there. [Whispering] "Always wanting the pussy, but ain't got no dick."

You can say that in this paper.

Really? I must sound like I'm terribly nasty. I'm not.

If you use explicit language, there must be a reason for it.

Some people say I use it just to be known, 'cause I had to work so much harder than men did. L.L. [Cool J] can go out there and say, "Rock the bells," and the crowd yells.

And when you use explicit language . . .

They love it. If they didn't love it, I wouldn't use it. When I pick a guy from the audience and start dogging him 'cause he said something smart, the crowd goes wild.

You bring him up on stage?

No, he stays right there in the audience, behind the guards, 'cause he might get mad and try to punch me. If he yells something like, "Yo, fuck her," I'll be like, "What? Fuck your mother," and such and such. I'm a little nicer now. I don't get that many hecklers 'cause don't nobody wanna get cursed out and be embarrassed the next day in school. "Ahh, I seen Roxanne curse you out." Though some guys like it 'cause they think it makes them popular. They be like, "Talk about me, talk about me!"

So you get out there and you really dog 'em, but these guys get off on it?

Guys like me; it's the girls who don't. The guys be looking forward to getting the drawers. [In a sexy male voice] "Yo baby, you need such and such." They be giving me all that coon-neckedee-neckeedee talk. They be looking forward to gettin' some so they can say, "I got Roxanne!" Now, girls, they roll their eyes, act like they don't like me. Some girls I meet are nice, they'll say, "Yeah, I like your records." But most will be like, "I coulda done better." Well, bitch, if ya coulda done better, why am I up here and you're down there? Why you waste your fifteen country dollars to come see me, if all you gonna do is stand there and stick your lips out? Me and girls never got along.

Is that why you started rappin', because you hung out with guys?

I hung with guys. Never with girls. Girls cause problems. I'd say guys encouraged me to rhyme. Guys like Hakim, MC Shan, and them. You know, beating on tables and stuff like that. They inspired me a lot.

When "Roxanne's Revenge" came out, you were fifteen, right?

Fourteen. Tasting success. I would go to the park with my friend Sherron and the fellows wouldn't want to give me the mike. How dare they? When I got it, I'd start with, "You right there in your mock neck and Lees/Scratching your ass like you got fleas." The crowd would go crazy 'cause I was so little, with a high-pitched voice.

In songs by male rap artists it seems all women are hoes or bitches out to steal their seed or, in the case of Dana Dane, run with all their Gucci stuff. What's up with this?

See, there's no such thing as an "in-between girl." Even the homeliest girl wants. She wants gold earrings, chains, et cetera. Anyway, guys pamper girls and make them want these things. So what makes a girl a ho? Because she won't give you none? I walk down the street and guys say, "Yo baby, yo baby, I'm talking to you, yo Trooper." (I wear a Troop jacket.) And when I don't speak, they say, "Yo, fuck you 'cause you ain't fly anyway." I'm the type to turn around and say, "Then why the fuck was you chasing me?"

Guys dis girls for the stupidest reasons. They want the kind of girl they can just slap up. No nigger slap me. I haven't been slapped yet. Let somebody slap me . . . Wait a minute, I have. So I lied.

You told me you don't like "Dumb Girls" [Run-D.M.C.], but "Dear Yvette" [L.L. Cool J] you like. Don't they both dog women?

To me, "Dumb Girls" had no meaning. What's the sense in

making a record called "Dumb Girls"? Girls aren't dumb. If you think about it, a dumb girl can get more out of a guy that a really smart girl can. 'Cause the dumb girl could be playing dumb. It was a stupid, dumb record. I started to make a record called "Dumb Guys," but I didn't want to do anymore answer records.

I didn't find anything wrong with "Dear Yvette." L.L. was talking about one girl. Her name was Yvette. I know a lot of girls like Yvette. He wasn't downing her, he was trying to get her to better herself. So he wrote her a letter telling her what she should do—get a GED and stuff like that.

Are you saying you don't mind the records male artists are making about women?

Rap is about using fighting words, instead of fighting. Instead of saying "Let's fight," people say, "Let's battle." I bet rap shows have saved a lot of lives. Even though there were shootouts afterwards!

Half of it is about people getting so dressed up for the shows. Not in regular suits, but in stuff that cost more that: leather, Gucci suits, Fila suits and sneakers. We're talking expensive shit here. So if somebody steps on homeboy's sneakers, of course he's gonna break and wanna fight. Especially if the other guy got on Pro-Keds, flair-leg jeans, and a mock neck. There used to be this guy going around called the Slasher. He'd slash leather jackets at parties and concerts. Do you know how ugly a leather looks after it's been cut?

As long as you're able to defend yourself with words, you don't care what they say?

Exactly. But sometimes I do feel hurt about records made about me. I have had records made about me that have gotten deep-down dark and dirty. I've been called "project ho" by niggers who never got a bit o' pussy. One guy was talking about "Roxanne Shanté is only good for steady fuckin'." How long he been knowing me? Turns out he never even met me. I could've bugged out, ran up to him and killed him, and he wouldn't have known what I looked like.

Regardless of how hard I play on the outside, I'm still a woman. I'm still sensitive. I don't like to see dogs get hit by cars. I don't like to see children get beatings.

What do you think of the other women rappers?

There's enough room for everybody. I'm not against no female rappers, just as long as they don't get in my way.

How about a battle between women rappers?

That would have to be a Don King promotion, because it would be a strict fight afterwards! That's something you'd want to put on before a Tyson fight! Let everybody get in the ring, let all the mikes come down, and let everybody go for theirs! I think girl rappers are more fierce than guys. I can't rate myself. I might not be the last one standing, 'cause girls can get down and start writing, and I'm the kind of person to do mine off the top of my head. I'd be so nervous, I'd be downright vulgar. I'd say the kind of stuff that makes people's mothers climb into the ring.

What do you wear when you go on?

Anything I have on. I walk out there, get a seat. I look like a female Bill Cosby. I have my legs crossed and I just talk. I don't get dressed up, 'cause I find it fake. A hip-hopper is a regular street person, so I wear my regular clothes. If I was doing a show tonight, I wouldn't wear this hat, but I'd wear these jeans, these sneakers, this shirt, and put curls in my hair or throw on a Gucci hat. I'm not a dressy person. That's why when I go out, people see me and say, "That ain't her, look what she got on."

1988

reckless igging

A peculiar little crime called "reckless eyeballing" cost Emmett Till his life one hot summer night in Money, Mississippi, back in 1955. The fourteen-year-old boy visiting from up North allegedly ran his eyes over a white woman and let out a whistle. Till turned up in the Tallahatchie River with a bullet in his head and the motor of a cotton gin tied to his neck with barbed wire. No one ever found his testicles.

Fast forward twenty-seven years and several hundred miles to Minneapolis, Minnesota. Folks whose only reference to interracial relationships is the Spike Lee film like to call Minneapolis "the *Jungle Fever* capital of middle

America." This liberal oasis in the Republican Midwest has, estimates say, the highest number of mixed-race unions per capita. Yet wander the Minne-Apple and you won't strike color-blind nirvana (the economic divide between the races, as elsewhere, is glaring). You will find something closer to *Purple Rain*'s Romper Room of black male–white female desire, especially on the nightlife scene. In clubs like Prince's new digs, Glam Slam, you'd think black women were prehistoric mammals that didn't make it through the Stone Age. Just us fossils holding up the wall.

A local musician tells me that he can accept institutional racism, but what bothers him most—really, really bothers him—is still not feeling safe walking the streets with a white woman. Is the pinnacle of personal freedom and power for him, I wonder, unfettered access to what the lynchers saw to it Emmett Till would never have?

If I don't sound my jolly, multiculti self, it's that seven months here and the Rodney King verdict have replaced my New York–melting-pot/interracial-family-of-origin questions with what you might call a simple dose of black women's rage. Miss Columnist has been touched by a common phenomenon for sisters in these parts: She's been recklessly igged, which is to say, in the vernacular, ignored, disrespected, tossed off.

In the week after the L.A. uprising there were three hits in a row. At a cocktail party, a woman, white, came on to the man I was with, in my very presence, like I was the rug on the floor. A few days later, at a restaurant, my quick trip to the john provided enough time for the waitress, also white, to proposition my dinner date. Then, the finale. On the street, a close friend, with an X cap on his head and a blonde on his arm, would have passed me by without a hello if I hadn't flagged him down like a traffic cop. Mr. X had guilt plastered all over his face. He's a buddy of mine and I could give two ideological shits about the race of his partner. I *did* mind being disposed of so cavalierly as a thinking person, as a friend, as a *real* sister. But hey, maybe fossils just aren't visible in broad daylight.

These events sent me to get the tea on *Fever* issues in Minneapolis. For young African-American women here the stylishness of black male–white female coupling is a thorn in their side deeper than what one woman called "the polygamy issue." The women I spoke to consider themselves multiculturalists. They are not opposed to interracial relationships. A couple even have white parents. What vexes them is how little value they're assigned in a sexual marketplace where white femininity still has tremendous currency. Walk around town some days, they say, and you'd think Afrocentricity and rhapsodies to the Nubian Princess never made it past Cleveland.

An actress who's lived in Minneapolis and Chicago, Tina, who's twenty-seven, tells me that her black male friends say they're attracted to white women for their sexual bravado. Yet these same men are turned off by hers: "A white woman's aggressive, but I'm a slut, a skeezer, or a ho." Nandi, twenty-three, from a mixed-race family in Canada, is a senior at the University of Minnesota. Her parents are happily married, she assures me, though looking at interracial couples at the U, she thinks, "these relationships have no integrity. The brothers lower their eyes when they see me. Sometimes, in all my anger, I have to remind myself that my own mother is white."

Then there's Lynn, a singer who grew up in Minnesota and returned after graduation from Spelman. Lynn spent her young adulthood in social situations where it was all the rage for men to date exclusively white. Spelman helped her disengage this fact from her sense of self-esteem and belief in black political community. Lynn has "stopped walking into Glam Slam wanting to kill every white woman with a brother," yet sometimes she asks herself why the black men she knows "don't see what is beautiful as me? If you have a problem with my hair, don't you have a problem with yours too? Isn't us being together what binds our culture and community? By favoring white women, aren't you saying that your idea of our community is not dependent on me? How can you not want me and still want my politics?"

"The Debbies are bold in Minnesota," is a mantra that Sasha, twenty-six, a publicist and Minneapolis native, teaches me. "Brothers give them big juice," she reports. "They know the advantage is theirs and they milk it." We work out as much frustration as we can with Debbie Lingo ("Debbie-free zones," "invasion of the Debbies") without choking on our own bigotry. After hanging out with Sasha, I'm left with the old questions of where white women have stood in America's coiled legacy of racism and race mixing.

In Minneapolis's feminist circles one hears the party line of white women as racial innocents. Sasha et al. are quick to disagree. Tina tells of a white coworker who thought she was humoring Tina with lusty details of her black-male conquests. It was hard for Tina to imagine that the woman could be so blisteringly ignorant of black-relationship politics that she would carry on so thoughtlessly. Tina's convinced the coworker was flexing her muscles. What stake would she have in dismantling a pecking order of femininity that puts her at the top?

New York–based playwrights Laurie Carlos and Aishah Rahman were in the Twin Cities recently to talk about their work. There they sat in high-art diva wear: a mix of African- and Japanese-inspired prints, kitsch scarves, basic black, and the odd bolero hat thrown in for drama. A young woman in the audience asked Rahman why she'd "said good-bye to naturalism" as an artist. There was a lot bubbling behind the question. She seemed to be saying, how do you blossom when the guns are against you, how do you speak your stories when everyone calls you a liar, how do you stay beautiful to yourself when every mirror tells you otherwise? "Well, my dear," said Rahman, batting her eyes, "I didn't have to say good-bye to naturalism, because I never said hello to it."

1992

it's racier
in the bahamas

We found out a long time ago that everyone masturbates and that everyone wants to be rich. The new truth is that everyone is consumed with the same racial mythologies that made this country so great:

Blondes have more fun if they're sleeping with black men; black women of all complexions prefer dark-skinned black men; white men love themselves exclusively, they invented masturbation; Puerto Rican women in Hartford have the hots for black men; women who love women want to make it with women of color; white men in leather want black men, also in leather; Asians of both sexes adore whites of both sexes; Jewish women from all countries want it bad with everyone; light-skinned black American women with money think they invented pussy; light-skinned Latin men, especially Colombians, love and marry dark-skinned women from all Latin countries; progressive black American men with money say color isn't an issue, yet are only seen in public with women with "good hair"; progressive, dark-skinned black American women who get no play from color-struck brothers are experimenting with white men; the finest men in the world are all black and are usually from Zimbabwe, Atlanta, or Brooklyn; the finest women in the world are from Brazil, come in all colors, but usually have hair like Troy Beyer, Diahann Carroll's daughter on *Dynasty*. And if you think you don't fit into all this, you're lying.

Two things happened recently that convinced me these allegories are held to be self-evident:

One: Last year before it got too cold, two friends and I were drinking beer one Sunday at an outdoor café on Bleecker Street. Sucker for heated discussion, I suggested that instead of sexual fantasies, we trade race fantasies (which would lead us to class and sex anyway).

First on the chopping block was Idris, a Latina from the Bronx, who confessed that her race fantasy was to be rich, like Donald Trump, and to marry a man who was even richer, like Howard Hughes. Though it was not crucial that her husband be Howard Hughes—after all, he was dead—it was most important that he be white, and for all practical purposes, impotent. She would jet around the world giving her husband's money away to people of color fighting wars of national liberation. She would take lovers at every port. These lovers could be of either sex, but would always be of color.

Up second was Patrick, black and gay from East New York. Pat said his race fantasies involved that idea of uplift as well. He wanted to be very rich, like Rockefeller, and run a home for young black and Latino homosexuals. He would be an idol of desire, father figure, and priest to these young men, but take none as his lover, preferring to date rich white men exclusively.

I am a child of leftist bohemians, so my fantasy involved the American dream. I'd bury my racial impurities forever by marrying into an old black family of race men, mother five heirs to the mantle, live in a huge house in the suburbs of a thriving black metropolis, vacation in Sag Harbor, and solely by virtue of my virtue as a black woman, be involved in changing the world every moment of my life. Some who know me well say this scenario is not true, and others say it's true without a doubt; which I guess gives it credence as a fantasy.

Even funnier than our three-hour conversation was that during the course of it we each witnessed an ex-flame of ours actually pass by strutting his fantasy. (Pat's, an intense middle-aged black man in a beret, was strolling close to a young blueblood.) Was Bleecker Street really the crossroads of the fantasy world or had we been in New York too long?

Two: I went to the Bahamas.

You know about the blue waters, as in gems, and the white sands, as in powdered platinum, and the trees that tower like dinosaurs and bear fruit. You know about the bright drinks with too much rum, and the Isles of Perpetual June, where you spend petite eternities on the beach, toasting your body and reaping your soul. You know about the music. "Hot, Hot, Hot." You know peas and rice go with conch fritters, and that crawfish walk backward and taste best with lemon and butter. And that "Purple Haze" is not about an acid trip, but the way the sun sets in the Caribbean, clinging to the sky like a scorned lover. These things you know.

But consider this ad for a film released through United Artists in 1958: " 'Island Women.' The Whole Ripped-Bare Story of the Beach Babes of the Caribbean! White-hot off the blazing beaches of the Carib sin-ports. . . . The story of excitement-mad 'nice' girls looking for 'kicks' in the luxury isles. Everything you've heard about them is TRUE!"

So it's been going on for a long time. And thirty years later, on the sin-port of Eleuthera—the Bahamas's Beauty Queen, as it's called; one hundred miles of exquisite scenery and beaches, rolling hills and farmlands, white cliffs and seventeenth-century villages, once home to the world's premiere pineapple plantations—it's in full swing.

I'm here for a wedding. My oldest friend, a white woman, gave up painting a couple of years back and went to live in the Bahamas. She is now to marry a local gentleman of reputable family who was educated in North America. They will tend bar together, he will build her a house on a majestic cliff overlooking the aquamarine abyss, and she will find reason to paint again.

The wedding party arriving from stateside includes my friend (I'll call her Sarah) and her three college chums: a Jewish woman from California, a black man from Massachusetts (accompanied by his fiancée, a white woman), a brown-skinned Cuban woman with "good hair" (accompanied by her fiancé, a light-skinned brother with an M.B.A.); along with, Sarah's sister (married to a black man), her mother (once married to a black man), and me (looking for a black man). We will spend a week together, including Thanksgiving Day, and share many things, race fantasies not among them.

Traveling in foreign countries is the only time I truly feel like an American. I'm middle class, more or less, and Ivy League–educated, though I'm still ranked as a perpetual minority (read: underclass) by belonging to a caste of people who, worldwide, even in their own countries, are disenfranchised. What this means in my own country is that I am never quite a citizen; or I don't feel like one; or more often than not, I'm not treated like one. One reason I do feel like an American when I travel is that I carry a verification of my citizenship. Even so, I usually spend my entire trip lugging my American baggage—the Howard Beach "accident," the ghost of Eleanor Bumpurs. And just when I've set all this down—it's time to go home.

But this is not home. Here I am in the islands. The sky is blue. The sun is shining. And everyone who is an American—minority, majority, whatever—belongs to one class, the foreigner class. And it is through this identity that I happen upon the curious sensation of being under the skin of a white girl, or at least, under the skin of the stereotype; the one who voyages to Carib sin-ports, meets handsome men who look something like Calvin Lockhart or the young Belafonte, and is wined and dined (though she may often pick up the tab) and made to feel like the most desired woman on the face of this earth.

This is an experience you are not often privy to as a black American woman, even if you are light-skinned and heterosexual like me and have a certain amount of privilege in your own culture. There is always a woman who is lighter, brighter than you are, has longer hair, and lighter eyes than you do, and is willing to give up more to get to that brother in the suit. Yes, despite *Elle* magazine–style affirmative action and rap nationalists talking good-brother talk on your radio, the most desired woman on the face of this earth is still a Breck Girl.

And for most of my trip to Eleuthera, I am reminded of this. Perhaps even more so because my beach-side reading material is the copy of *Invisible Man* that I bought at the LaGuardia Airport bookshop before the flight down. (They had an impressive selection of books by black authors. Though I have a copy at home, I chose *Invisible Man* to send a message to the buyers that sacred black texts sell at airports.) *Invisible Man,* even on the beach, even on this beach, which is silver and littered with weeping palms, puts me in a mood: dark, brooding, and very colored (or, should I say, very judgmental?).

Over and over I read the passage in which two crazy men, on a bus bound up North, discuss the fate of our young hero: "Most of the time he'll be working, and so, much of his freedom will have to be symbolic. And what will be his or any man's most easily accessible symbol of freedom? Why, a woman of course." Then I instant replay a couple of scenes in my head:

One: Drinking at a local bar plastered with photos of the foreigner class in various states of debauchery, I encounter a young Bahamian who greets me with lust in his eyes. When I don't respond, he moves immediately to the woman on my left, a full-bodied brunette with blonde ambition. She arranges herself, with a deep breath, to receive his look, her cup size expanding by two letters. The fantasy I assigned the scene: a queen lapping up the sweat of a slave. The way they saw themselves may have been a different story.

Two: Sarah's father, who owns a furniture business in Latin America, tells me at the bar one night that, not only is he giving his daughter to her husband, he is giving her to the entire island. It's an offering the white man's burden requires him to make.

The well-to-do ladies of Eleuthera—the most dizzying array of light-skinned black women in polyester ever assembled under a thatch roof—throw Sarah a bridal shower. The women of the American wedding party, myself included, arrive late and are ushered to a table in the middle of the room where we sit by ourselves surrounded by red and pink streamers. As we file by the local women shoot us with looks that could raise the dead. I know these looks well because I am usually not on the receiving end, but dishing them out.

I realize that this is the first time in the five days that I've been here that I have spent more than five minutes in the company of black women. On the beaches and in the bars, it's women of the foreigner class and island gigolos. Here I am relieved to be setting eyes on them finally, and they're looking at me like I've got honorary white status. And I'd get more scorn for that than the other Americans would get for being white. And what about the white Americans? How do they see me down here? While Sarah is opening her gifts, the Jewish woman from California whispers to me, "I'm so glad they did this for her. Sarah's busted her ass for *these* people," as if Sarah had spent ten years doing missionary work on the island.

One day we drive out to Savannah Sound, the poor Eleuthera. Goats and chickens cross the roads casually. The sun seems brighter on this part of the island, as in no rest for the weary. Here the trees really weep, the wind makes their branches bow to the ground. Sarah has taken some of the American wedding party to visit her husband's poor relatives. They live in a little rectangle of a house that looks like a train car, worn at the edges, yet tended with love.

In the back room sits a pretty young woman in glasses, brown-skinned and petite, surrounded by ten children, two of them infants. She tells me that with two kids of her own, she is too poor to work outside of the home, so she minds neighborhood kids instead. The white women rush to the children, who are mostly boys, all pretty and brown with holes in their clothes, and pet and coo over them as if they were small animals. These are children who in the States would be passed up for adoption, who as young men would be seen as angry and without options—and by routine feared. I turn away to avoid shooting looks at anyone I have to share a hotel room with later.

In bed that night I read about the other Bahamian islands in a guidebook called *Welcome Bahamas.* "San Salvador: This island is preening for its Big Moment, October 12, 1992, the 500th anniversary of the arrival of Christopher Columbus in the New World. . . . Cat Cay: Posh, Yachts, millionaires, and fishing tournaments . . . the Prime Minister has announced plans to increase per capita income to $10,000 annually. This is the primary criterion for entering the First World, a goal sought for the Bahamas by the twenty-first century." I write in my journal: "The way Sarah walked through the shack her new relatives live in; how grand she must feel living among such humble, appreciative people who treat her like royalty, make much of her otherness, gladly step and fetch. What security that yields, what accomplishment, what an affirmation of her femininity, of her class position, of her self worth."

What about Sarah? In grade school we took modern dance from a vampire on the Bowery; at fourteen, we were groupies to a black rock band; at eighteen, we did Europe by backpack. What could a nice bohemian girl like her want with a Cinderella fantasy like this? And why did she have to travel to the Caribbean to find it? For one thing, she didn't have to dress up like an investment banker and work overtime; or beg, borrow, and steal, like Sherrie Levine, for a loft in Tribeca. In America, these days, even a white woman has to work hard to get to that brother in the suit. Down here, all Sarah had to do was be. The natives took care of the rest. I am reminded of the woman at the bar with the expanding cleavage: Who can affirm a queen, but a slave?

The wedding is a grand opera of color. The road, jet black from last night's rain; the trees, fragrant and moss green. As our car approaches the church, wedding guests overtake the road, and we must drive behind them forming a slow, almost lazy procession. The healthy brown of their skin sparkles red in the noon light. And the clothes: pink satins, every imaginable blue, from busy royal to powder pure, hot orange coupled with lace, reds that scream (as in hibiscus), and reds that moan (as in burgundy). The church, pastel green trimmed with vanilla, sits on a hill, earth green, and spread out below are fifty perfectly whitewashed steps. The groomsmen, magnificent in a white even brighter than the steps, their bow ties and cummerbunds scorching aqua; the groom himself, all in white, could be off to his first communion. The gold piping on the bibles, the purple stained-glass windows, the little chestnut-skinned flower girl whose hair glistens as orange as flying fish eggs. The bride, like a pearl, her dress shimmering under the sun, tells me later that she was completely naked underneath. When the reverend reads the objection clause, the packed church holds its breath. The groom's legs shake violently. I expect an old girlfriend of his to come running into the church and lay a baby at the altar. No one is safe in paradise, I think. Not even a white girl.

The reception is held at a country club facing the Atlantic Coast of the island. It was built in the fifties and hasn't been used for years; its white-painted verandas and gazebos blistering under the rays, its paths and gardens in need of grooming, all adding to the old-world elegance of the place. (Oh colonialism, such a style war.) After the toasts, the reception turns into an island jump up. At the bar, men in tuxedos place colored potions before me: Bahama

Mama, Torpedo Sunsplash, Lone Wolf (crème de menthe, vodka, amaretto, with a garnish of rhubarb), Castro Libre (a Cuba Libre with 150 proof Bacardi). A drug kingpin, who now owns hotels, a regal black man in a navy blue jacket and white colonial kickers, asks to ride me back to New York in his six-seater. A customs officer I met at the Nassau airport offers me a job as his mistress. To my right and left, I hear lines like: "God bless America, she lookin' fine,"; "This package wrapped nice, mon,"; and "Gimme a beautiful sister like you, I'll cut the white girls loose tomorrow."

For the first time in the seven days I've been here I realize how black women of the foreigner class fit in. It seems we have an even higher currency in these parts. The experience we offer is like traveling to China and buying a Coca Cola T-shirt. And what does the experience offer us? If you had no ambition other than to feel like an heiress on the run from Mommy and Daddy, being ogled over by brown-skinned men with wide white smiles and large hands (playing Shirley Temple to his Bill Robinson or Fredi Washington to his Paul Robeson, however you see yourself, ladies, this is the islands, no one is judging), you could have stopped the clock, stood right there, with one eye on the ocean, the other on the subject at hand.

But me, I'm sightseeing. Just want to look. Yes, I'm just here for the sights. The breeze off the ocean, ninety degrees in the shade. Just a little look see. "Nice girl travels to sin-port meets carefree island hunk. Everything you heard is true" is not my fantasy. My fantasy, the consummate race man, is only a reality. In fact, that's his problem. He's back in America giving it to some undeserving babe and giving it to her good: He calls it freedom. Oh the horrors. The tide has turned; I'm indignant. Someone has the nerve to request "Hot, Hot, Hot" for the third time. Two beach blondes, burned golden and flaunting it in white minis, walk into the country club and are carried aloft, like figureheads on a ship's bow, by five Bahamians gyrating to an R&B ode to Casanovas. This is a freaking minstrel show. I'm calling Delta tomorrow, change my flight god-dammit. No, I don't want another drink. Don't even think about putting your hand on my thigh. I'm a black American, goddammit, and I'm not impressed.

The only person who could get a rise out of me at this moment is Denzel Washington—the closet thing Hollywood has to offer to a young race man. And, sure enough, he walks in. Not really, but there's enough of a resemblance to prompt a full-body rush. He appears under a gazebo, materializing from thin air, like Denzel did when he played Steve Biko in *Cry Freedom*. When you see a man like this, you realize why white men had to convince themselves colonialism was a God-given right. Michelangelo's David ain't got a thing on this. This is God's idea of Development. If blue collar is your fantasy, you've got the wrong number. This is the lost Nubian prince hotline. Never mind the class wars, give us a king, but make him dark skinned. The sculpture of the head and always the dialectic: blackness of hair against brownness of skin. Every gesture, done as if to music, and the eyes, the brown eyes. Later for Cupid's bow, this boy is throwing javelins from across the ballroom, and they're aimed straight at the groin.

I went back for Christmas.

1989

genitalia and the paycheck

Remind me that Deandra is in love again and therefore not to be trusted. Before euphoria arrived, this time wrapped in dreadlocks and mud cloth, old girl and I would kick womanist ballistics any time, be it four in the morning, whenever. Lately, all I get is an answering machine with Aaron Neville wailing, "Love came out of nowhere/ baby/just like a hurricane." You do realize, I tell Deandra when I finally catch her, that you've committed a cardinal sin in the girlfriend canon. When I say, girl, we need to talk, you don't say next week. The appropriate response is, *Jump?,* sister, how high? The womanist-guilt card still works; Deandra grants me an audience.

It's about that Terry McMillan book again, and the Mike Tyson case again, and a sitcom called "Martin," and something some guy said to you on the street, am I right? Deandra can guess me a mile away. Sister, she offers with the heavy sigh of a Baptist missionary, you have Deandra's permission to unload.

MISS COLUMNIST: I see this guy reading *Waiting To Exhale* on the D train, so I ask him what he thinks. Now we all owe Miss McMillan a million pounds of gratitude for upping the stakes for black women in publishing. But wasn't the book a Harlequin romance minus the blonde woman on the horse? Turns out this guy loves the book because, I quote, it tells *the* black woman's perspective on relationships. I happen to be a black woman, as you know, and I am *not* spending my life waiting to exhale until brother in the Prince Charming suit pulls up in the Range Rover, okay? (Not this week at least.) Why does every last character suffer from the same brand of BMW materialism? And must *Exhale* regurgitate the fable of black woman as insatiable hyena of the boudoir? Between rappers turning "ho" into a national chant and *Exhale* telling African Americans that our real problem is the shortage of brothers who are both well hung and well paid, I'm getting to think that all we can offer each other as black women and men is genitalia and the paycheck. Assuming it is, we might as well move into separate armed camps surrounded by those bulletproof partitions you see in candy stores in Washington Heights. Then we can exchange the goods in generic Pathmark baggies. Pussy: weight fifteen pounds. Though contents may shift in packaging.

DEANDRA: Who needs stodgy white men when we can look forward to folks like you as the high-art police? You just wish two books of yours were being made into major motion pictures starring a matinee Negro like Wesley Snipes so you could play Queen to his Chicken George out back in the trailers. And let me get this straight: Are you recommending that black artists be limited to presenting sociological position papers? *Exhale* doesn't pretend to be a floor plan of the psyche of every black woman in America. This is a novel about four middle-class women in the suburbs near Phoenix who buy teddies from Victoria's Secret and are waiting for that brother in the Prince Charming suit. This is not about you, me, or the homicide rate in Detroit. And as I know quite a few details about your personal life, perhaps I don't need to remind you that waiting to exhale in Phoenix (as it is in Brooklyn, last time I checked) is also an S.B.E. (Significant Black Experience). I myself was not above learning from *Exhale.* It helped me identify very clearly the kind of woman I don't want to be, and for this I'm grateful. It also made me realize that this longing I have for black men is far deeper than dime-store romance. It's how I gather lost family, love brothers I never had, make peace with the father I barely knew, make a home out of ashes. The ceasefire begins with you, sis. So, how's Mike Tyson bothering you today?

MISS C.: Groupies like Pamela Des Barres who ride the axes of the white guitar gods and live to write memoirs about it are celebrated as cultural heroes. Their bed jumping and their peekaboo minidresses are called creative expression and rarefied performance art. When a black woman goes to some famous guy's hotel room and tells the world what happened there, she's called a two-dollar ho looking to get paid. Meanwhile, brothers have elevated pimping into not-too-rarefied performance art. Rappers like Big Daddy Kane compose songs such as "Pimpin' Ain't Easy" and Negroes with Ph.D.s chuckle and add the line to their repertoires. Black girls don't go into hotel rooms looking for heroes or black men to tell them they're beautiful. Pimps, on the other hand, are just misunderstood father figures from dysfunctional families who become the inspiration for great soundtracks.

DEANDRA: Your point again?

MISS C.: Tyson will walk on appeal, a nouveau riche brother who could afford to buy himself some William Kennedy Smith–style justice. Sad thing is that no one (black folks, the media, Baptist ministers, feminists) is really interested in justice for Tyson the man or Desiree Washington the woman. This is all about the boxer and the beauty queen, windup toys for Nielsen families. Would anybody have commissioned a documentary on any old black man who raped any old black woman? If you noticed, Barbara Kopple's film did little to question the image of Tyson as brute minus brain cells, as Cus D'Amato's nigra Frankenstein. There was no attempt to show Tyson as a man who acted intelligently on any front. This is a champion, mind you, one who apparently knows boxing history inside out. To be great at anything requires a mind. Don't tell me Tyson doesn't have one. Listen to this: One woman interviewed in the documentary actually recommended clemency for Tyson because he's from the hood; that his anger is ultimately created by the white power factory, and therefore he can't be held responsible for it. That there's nothing any man from Brownsville or Compton can do to hurt us that we shouldn't excuse him for. Including rape. Well, sorry, that's just not in my program. I cannot accept rape as one of the occupational hazards of being a black woman. And tell me, what maxim says Tyson's crime is endemic to the ghetto? Certainly not statistics on rape and domestic abuse, which run the gamut of class. There are plenty of men from mean streets who don't make a habit of pummeling and raping women. I say keep Tyson on ice.

DEANDRA: It amazes me that you can call for another black man to rot in prison when something like one quarter of the population, more in some cities, is doing just that. Do you think prison qualifies as reform? Do you think a black man—or any man—learns gentleness and respect for women in prison? And where is it written in the womanist rule book that we must exonerate every woman, including Desiree the beauty queen, because we share genitals? Why should the media dictate my call to arms when I could be writing screenplays about Ida B. Wells? So, where does poor Martin and his sitcom fit into this?

MISS C.: Poor Martin, my rump shaker. I loved that show. Martin Lawrence is a funny Negro. I adore the way his ears stick out and how humor occupies every part of his body. So why does "Martin" go break my womanist heart? Last week, Martin's girl Gina, played by Tisha Campbell, leaves work in the middle of an important presentation that could win her a promotion. Why? To take care of Martin, who has the sniffles. The episode ends without us finding out what happened to Gina's promotion or indeed to girlfriend's job. Here we have this adorable sitcom in which the O.P.P. generation gets cozy with monogamy. Then we are shown that for women, monogamy probably equals poor job ratings and/or indentured servitude. A seductive payoff if there ever was one. For a break, I turn to talk TV, where the hottest act in the big ring is the face-off between black men and women. Watch Bubba and Bertha strut and slobber like Dobermans. They're so colorful when they're mad at each other, we could laugh at them forever. Gag me with the remote! Finally, yesterday I nearly lost it when on Houston Street in broad daylight I hear a young man say, and verbatim I quote, "I wouldn't even rape that skank ho." He wasn't reciting Ice Cube, he was asking for my number. Rewind?

DEANDRA: Don't tell me you're still waiting for commercial TV and angry man hip-hop to affirm you? Broadcast your own fairy tales. Why aren't you writing about me? Nubian American Princess meets Nubian American Prince. He cooks her omelettes. His Valentine's cards have charming nationalistic soundbites, like, "Black-love, struggle love, reciprocity love. Our ancestors quake with our power." Once he left a message on her answering machine with these four words: "I love you, sis." To be his sister, to be his lover! Revolutionary petunias were blooming everywhere and it was only March. Write about *that*, girlfriend.

MISS C.: Not enough genitalia, and not enough paycheck.

1993

five

the hair trade

planet hair

I haven't read J. A. Rogers's *100 Amazing Facts About the Negro* yet, so I wonder if it tells of any amazing triumphs over Bad Hair. Like our patron saint of Good Hair, Madame C. J. Walker, who made a small fortune off the scalps of Negro women who had so little time to "Fix that Mess" (says a recent ad for Le Kair's Black Satin Cream Relaxer). Or of the incredible balancing acts of Tamara Dobson ("Run your fingers thru my nine-inch 'fro if you want to, daddy, I got a gun to your jugular") and Miss Ross ("I need twelve inches or more")?

Is there mention of Harlem's Hair Station on 125th Street (owned by Koreans, Rogers would have pointed out)? Or of its manager, Alexis Smith, a black man, who for the past nine years has made his living putting that heifer Mother Nature in her place?

It's a just-got-paid Friday, just after five. You can see the sign from Lenox Avenue:

HAIR STATION

MANUFACTURE

100% HUMAN HAIR

BRAIDING & WEAVING.

Near the IRT entrance on Lenox and 125th, Rastas selling bootleg shearling are blasting Marley's "Could You Be Loved" ("Don't let them change you/Or even rearrange you/Oh no"). The sound trails down the block to Hair Station's small storefront, where hair, real human hair, hangs in neatly coiffed horsetails from every inch of wall space. Some is displayed, like scalps, in glass cases.

The after-work crowd works the counters. A half dozen young women in black shearling (real) and leather (real) hover over one counter petting a length of "Bone Straight." (Which may take its name from the new relaxer by TCB. "Not just straight," the ads promise. "Bone Straight.") They compare it to "French Refined" (European stock: bouncy, silky, with a hint of curl), which Alexis says is tied with "Bone Straight" for best-seller: " 'Bone Straight' is hot right now, but the most versatile hair out is 'French Refined.' It doesn't condemn you to one style."

CAUCASIAN STRAIGHT, KINKY STRAIGHT, KINKY AFRO. Whose hair was this before? Hair Station imports it in bulk, mostly from Asia, where poor women sell their long, straight locks for money. The hair is "retextured" in a secret heating process ("bogus places use chemicals," says Alexis) to match black hair types, permed, Jheri curled, or untreated.

"There's Chinese hair and hair from Italy," adds the Korean owner, a stocky man who asks not to be identified. "The European hair is more expensive because it's rare. One or two people a year come to us off the street to sell their hair, some Spanish girls, but we can't do that. That little amount doesn't help us."

You choose from unlimited blends of brown, black, and blonde, or novelty colors like neon yellow (Phyllis Diller), deep purple (circa George Clinton's Brides of Funkenstein), and siren red (Chaka Khan). "We don't dye like everyone else," Alexis confides. "We have a secret way of dyeing."

PRICES ARE SUBJECT TO CHANGE WITHOUT NOTICE. "Price depends on texture and color," Alexis will tell you. "I got hair, twenty-two bucks, good hair. Places try to sell you the lower quality stuff for more money. Buy bad hair, after a couple days, it tangles, it itches. If you sweat, the chemicals go to your scalp.

"Big-time salons, downtown and Fifth Avenue, buy our hair. They condition it before they do the weaves or the braids and charge their clients two and three grand. Places in California make it four or five."

WEAVING THREADS AND NEEDLES SOLD. Alexis holds up to my temple the most expensive item in the store, a thirty-inch auburn length of "Kinky-Straight." It passes my knees. The owner nudges Alexis in the ribs. "Tell her about the bald ladies with the bald hair. That's funny. They don't want to show it to you."

Alexis explains: "Women come in, you know what they need, everybody knows what they need. But you have to find a way to tell them, without saying your hair is bald, whatever. Without offending them. Because people are very offended. Their hair is thin."

What would you say to a woman who doesn't have a lot of hair? That she needs a wig?

"*No!*"

The faux pas is mine. Wigs, you see, to a midwife of manes like Alexis, are a last resort, a lazy way out. "There are many different methods of weaving or braiding hair in." Alexis counts off on his fingers as if addressing a group of preschoolers. "You can glue it in, you can sew it in, do box braids. There's a new system called interlocks. It's so good, a guy could run his fingers through your hair and nothing could happen."

HEADS WITH HUMAN HAIR AVAILABLE FOR BEAUTY SCHOOL USE. Let me ask you this, I say to Alexis. Some people say, uhm, some people think, that it's not right for black women to wear hair, you know, weaves, and maybe they should just wear their own hair and be natural. What do you think about that? Uh, the politics of that?

Alexis rolls his eyes. "Most women who buy hair for weaving actually don't have short hair. It's the convenience of it. If the weave enhances them in the process, so be it. By all means use the hair. But if the black man really likes you, he's gonna like you for you, not because of your weave."

SUPER WAVEY, EUROPEAN WAVEY, KINKY AFRO. A mature woman in Blackglama mink slaps Alexis's cheek when he tries to have a look under her matching hat. He can only smile.

"Me dealing with women, I really understand. When you wake up every morning and you gotta hot curl, press, comb everything, *and* go to work? It's not gonna happen.

"My customers see guys walking past the door and they go 'AAAAyyyye!' " Alexis hides his face in his hands. "But me, they don't care. When I first started working here I was like a male looking in. You're coming to a whole new world. I can't say I'm a woman now, but I got a pass card."

DEEP WAVEY, BODY WAVEY, JHERI CURL. This is a blood bank. Hair types A, AA, B. Bad hair, warns Alexis, the kind that Hair Station doesn't sell, the kind tainted with chemicals that irritate the scalp, is a bad transfusion.

"They sell low-quality hair all over the city," Alexis tells me. "Places have even started carrying the yak hair, which is animal hair."

You mean they try to pass it off as human hair?

"Yeah, yeah, this is New York," says Alexis. "I won't get egotistical and say we sell the best hair in the city, but we're the leaders. When we deal with hair, it's a personal thing. Our customers trust us like they trust their doctors."

It's almost seven now. With fifteen minutes to closing, women pack the store so there's scarce breathing room. They push between counters in search of the perfect weekend piece. A young woman in purple shearling pounds on a display case, her sights on a length of "Bone Straight" protected behind glass.

They forbid me from coming back Saturday. Alexis keeps shaking his head: "It's a madhouse." I want to stay behind the counter some more with Alexis. Watch him watch us get close to the mirror, real close, painful close. Like this: You hold a length of hair up to your face and you squint. Give us profile, straight on, squint some more. Picture your man's hands in your hair or "hair that moves" (says an ad for TCB No Lye Relaxer) or fifteen minutes of extra time in the morning. Then Alexis saunters over, hand on your shoulder. That'll work. Remember, he cares, he's not here to play you. And when the time is right, when you've decided, *really* decided, he sends you home, with the real you, wrapped up neatly in a brown paper bag.

1990

the hair trade

In my personal stash of obsessions, hair rules (though Elvis as the Antichrist and chicken wings with Alaga syrup run close seconds). So when I say cracking the hair trade was on par with making that hajj to Mecca, you'll understand where I'm coming from. No offense meant, just my jones talking. Besides, the hair trade had all the Mecca prerequisites: mystery, an obstacle course, the sacred inner core. It was a pilgrimage bound to uncover a solidly American hash of race, kitsch, and commerce. But to 'fess up, I had no theoretical master plan, I was just plain nosey. Who were these alchemists, and how did they turn bushels of straight hair nappy?

So I set out to find *that* factory. Such a factory, or so I imagined, was in Brooklyn, perhaps tucked away on a Flatbush side street, near the bustling Afro-Caribbean stretch of Church Avenue, and most certainly above a fruit stand that sells okra and salt beef. In this factory, "raw" hair would be magically, or not so magically, transformed from "Bone Straight" (straight out of the Liaoning province) to "French Refined Wavy" (a/k/a African-American hair under the influence of a perm). Korean supervisors would keep watch over poor Haitian and Salvadoran women as they tended boiling vats of hair with long wooden sticks. Mecca would be a place that mocks nature and makes a pretty penny at it. Mecca would be a hair factory.

Of course, this took a minute because, so it goes, Mecca ain't about to find you, you go in search of it. My odyssey carried me first to shops that sell the finished product, 100 percent human hair for braiding and weaving, textured to match black hair types, untreated and permed. For looking too long and hard at labels, I was chased away, or shopkeepers would murmur things that made perfect sense like, "We don't know where it comes from, we just sell it," and nudge me to the door. When the dependable creatures who work in hair salons were asked to direct me to . . . (having no name for it, I made one up) a *hair factory,* they ditched the subject quick. "Trust us," they said. "*We* provide the hair," which I translated as: Something bad will happen if you step foot in such a place or, child, don't go stirring up no dirt, especially if it's gonna affect my personal livelihood, thank you.

The official information machine was of little help. The health departments, trade commissions, barbershop licensing offices, and regional customs bureaus of the world passed me back and forth. No one had clue one, and I became a quack for asking. Was this . . . (the name problem again) *hair product* a vegetable, mineral, or human appendage? Like a single strand of hair, it floated through the cracks.

———

The use of human hair extensions for weaving and braiding boomed in the seventies, yet it's a practice no doubt as ancient as Jerusalem. Herbert Feinberg's *All About Hair*, a short history of hair replacement, reports unequivocally, though without supporting detail, that hair weaving—the attachment of hairpieces to beget length and volume—was invented by black people a century ago. (I'd take it back another two.) The contemporary American trend seems to have piggybacked from the Motherland-inspired braid styles exhumed in the sixties. Ancient cornrow braids—often adorned with beads and cowrie shells—had their renaissance. By the next decade, braids were being elongated to Gidget-glam lengths with synthetic and human hair extensions. With the advent of buppiedom and *The Cosby Show*'s blow 'n' curl vision of America, permed tresses came back strong in the eighties. Weaving was an obvious next wave. Weaves are best done with human-hair extensions called "wefts," so human stock, as opposed to the synthetics that flooded the market in the seventies, returned en masse to corner wig shops.

The importing and processing of human hair is a tiny, tight-lipped business. In this country, very few companies actually process hair—convert it from straight to curly/kinky textures. Most "raw hair," as the trade calls it, is processed abroad, in Korea primarily, and sold prepackaged here at Asian retail shops like Folipa International Imports on Fulton Street in downtown Brooklyn, a stretch known as "weave row." The smattering of American companies in the processing business, most in New York and California, have showrooms where they retail by the pound, though the bulk of their work is in supplying salons and shipping mail order around the globe.

A small hair world, it is. The processing companies—call them hair factories—are a closely tied, though intensely competitive, pack. These are family outfits, Jewish and Italian, that have intermarried employees and managers over the years. Old names in the business are the De Meo Brothers, the Tucciarones, the Rubins. (AlKinco Hair Company, run by the Rubins, has been in what the industry tags the "Afro side" of the business for ages. Trade gossip has it that the name "AlKinco" is a polite version of "El Kinko," code for, he who processes kinky hair.) Several of these companies have been up and running for close to eighty-five years. Processing techniques have remained the same over time and are treated as family heirlooms. Employees outside the family take vows of silence. When asked about her processing methods, one company president would volunteer only this: "Does Sylvia tell you how she cooks her collard greens?" Case closed.

Even harder to track down than the hair factories are the import firms. Only a handful of companies do this end of the business full-time. No import license is needed to transport human hair Stateside, and more and more, storefront businesses are shipping in their own product. (These days hair arrives primarily by UPS and Federal Express.) Older hair factories express concern about a budding cottage industry where shady retail operations process hair out of bathtubs and have the public convinced they're selling the same fussed-over hair goods.

Just as Korea came to dominate wig production worldwide in the late sixties, it has moved on the braiding and weaving market. Americans once bought most of their raw product from China, Korea, and India; now Koreans buy from the same sources, process it themselves, and ship to their own retail networks in the States. The Jewish and Italian hair factories say Korean-made goods are mass produced and of cruder quality. (Quality is a big word in the hair business and is used in ways arcane and racially demeaning, but more on that soon.)

"Foreign" hair is imported to the States for two main uses: human hair for wigs and hairpieces; animal hair—goat, pig, and horse—for paintbrushes and hairbrushes. The hair trade buys raw stock in bulk by the kilo. In most cases it's treated abroad first in an acid bath to kill bacteria. Processing companies "refine" the raw hair, a process that involves, among other things, removing the roots, as they mangle easily. Refined hair is then chemically or steamed processed to hold curl. The end product is called "commercial hair." After all these conversions, commercial hair maintains a top and bottom and must be braided or attached accordingly. Treated and processed hair lives forever, making it congruous perhaps to an embalmed corpse. (Though if given the chance, silverfish and moths could devour an entire warehouse.)

The Census Bureau assigns every imported product a fixed description and commodity number, and you might be yearning to know that "human hair, dressed, thinned, bleached, or otherwise worked," is commodity number 6703.00.3000. Last year hair came from eleven countries, all in Asia and Europe. Top on the list were Korea and China; Indonesia, which hair traders consider be an "up and coming hair market," ranked third. Through the seventies, stock imported from Europe was the only hair product sold to what the industry calls the "Caucasian trade." Now that the European market is drying up, Asian hair goes to all races, in most cases, unless specially ordered. When you buy human hair in lengths for weaving and braiding, in wigs, and as male hair-replacement product, what you buy nine times out of ten is Asian hair.

The trade also peddles animal hair, used mostly for braiding, as it can stand in for very tightly curled, "wooly" hair. (Often dreadlock extensions are made from animal hair. Animal stock is bleached and sold as human gray hair as well.) The animal of choice is yak, a long-haired wild or domesticated ox found in Tibet and central Asia. Yak hair is sometimes mixed with angora (from angora goats) to soften it. There are those who balk at mixing animal with human (animal), yet it happens to be an old practice. In the sixteenth and seventeenth centuries, hairpieces were commonly made from animal and human hair. And until synthetic wigs became so common and cheap, the theatrical market always relied on animal hair, particularly yak wigs.

Many in the trade are worried that the seemingly abundant supply of raw hair from Asia could be on the wane. Most raw stock comes from China, though it's processed in Korea, and the concern is that the supply will dry up as China is gripped ever tighter by the long arm of the West. (Apparently beauty shops are sprouting up in

China that promote ye ole magic Western elixir—the perm.) Adorable Hair-Do, in Manhattan's design district, has been importing Chinese hair since 1910 and isn't worried too much about the China supply. Despite westernization, Adorable believes population growth will zoom on, and the manes will be there to cut, especially in the rural provinces.

But what of the Italian story? Italian hair, once thought to be an ever plentiful source, has diminished to nearly a custom-order operation. Says one importer, every month he used to bring in twelve cases of Italian hair at 110 pounds each. He can't even get a fifth of a case today, and the costs are out of bounds. (Adorable bills an item they advertise as "Italian First Quality Human Hair" for ninety-five dollars an ounce.) Another importer is convinced that the product known as Italian hair is no longer. A good percentage of the hair processed in Italy, he says, is "cut" with raw hair from Spain and India.

Asking industry types where raw hair comes from, and how the business is organized abroad, is to knock up against a covenant of silence. From a dozen conversations you might end up with this: In China, hair is much like a crop. There are hair farms, where hair is collected and packaged for shipment abroad. In India, women cut their hair and offer it to the church as a sacrifice. Allegedly the church supplies exporters, who then ship raw goods to Korea or directly to the States. Factories in Italy that collect and process hair have been in business since the nineteenth century. Before the war, peddlers supplied these factories by crisscrossing the Italian countryside to buy hair from poor women. Ponytails were bartered along with "combings," from combs and brushes, which women stored in glass jars. With Italian hair now scarce, and white American buyers ever in search of Cortez's fountain—pure European stock—Russian hair has been flown in as a substitute. The fall of the communist bloc has paved the way for a busy black market in Russian hair.

An old rating system operates in the hair trade. Italian stock is the number one European hair import, despite how much the supply has declined. It's still referred to as "first quality" hair and is gobbled up by custom-wig makers and the men's toupee market. Labeled as "second quality" hair, Asian and Indian hair costs less and at one time was sold only to what old-timers in the business call the "colored trade." Among salons that specialize in weaving and cater to a black clientele, there's another rating system: "Good hair" is human hair, period; "bad hair" is prepackaged hair that's been cut, or mixed, with synthetic or animal hair.

Asian retailers are adamant about not rating hair. They insist that all the hair they sell is "best quality," which of course is as much a feel-good strategy aimed at consumers as it is a reversal of the rating system's racial hierarchy. Still, the old rating system predominates. A throwback to nineteenth-century racial codes, the system is augmented symbolically by the industry's overall race schema. In this country, white and Asian-American men sell commercial hair for braiding and weaving, which is bought and worn primarily by black women. The one black company in the processing business in the New York area might very well be the only one in the country. A black salon owner who buys hair wholesale in Brooklyn sizes up the race dynamic like this: Tensions between those who buy and those who sell aren't expressed overtly, yet resentments are bubbling near the surface. The owners of an established hair factory made sure to note several times during my visit that they sell to the Afro trade "by default, not by design," as over time the more lucrative side of the business has shifted from white to black. Meaning, one assumes, if they could pitch Ferraris to nouveau riche whites in Ramsey, New Jersey, they might feel better about their line of work.

After hiking much pavement and nosing my way into shops, I found two hair factories in the most obvious place, the Yellow Pages, under the banner of "hair replacement, goods and supplies," and, small wonder, they invited me down. It didn't matter that ten others slammed the phone in my ear, convinced I was out to steal their processing secrets. Mecca was near.

A hair factory might often attempt to camouflage itself behind the more respectable label of "designer of hairpieces" or "supplier of hair." Their sales pitch, on the other hand, is a dead giveaway: "Manufacturers of 100% Human Hair," they boast, in phone book ads and on street signs. Lugo Hair Center in Brooklyn is of the boastful. (Lugo, it turns out, *is* in East Flatbush, though it's run by Hispanics, not Koreans.) The company claims to manufacture "First Quality Caucasian Hair in All Colors & Textures." This might translate as: We process straight hair to curly textures, but all our raw product is imported from Europe. Prepare: Even before you step foot into a hair factory, you are required suspend reality. They *make* human hair. This is not a grammatical error; this is a way of life.

Welcome to Harlem. Where 125th Street meets Fifth Avenue, look for the McDonald's billboard framed in a kente-cloth design, as it's a stone's throw from W.A.J. Wigs. In the hair business for thirty-one years, W.A.J. predates the nouveau-kente generation by a couple of decades. W.A.J.'s second-floor factory/showroom/salon shares space with a business called "The Miracles of Rev. James," which offers the services of a spiritualist who guarantees results in twenty-four hours. Jean Church, niece to company president Verlie Wyche, runs the showroom desk, where traffic never lets up. Women in search of the perfect match pull wefts of hair out of shoulder bags like dead rabbits, or juggle adjectives to describe the hair of their dreams. ("It's like black dirty blonde that's a little nappier than French.")

The seventy-year-old Verlie B. Wyche and other Harlem salon owners will tell you that W.A.J. invented the Afro toupee and was the first hair company to process raw Asian hair into permanent kink. Other hair factories hotly dispute this, claiming they've made straight to kinky conversions since the forties. As a maker of custom-fitted Afro toupees, W.A.J. is well known nationally on the black salon circuit. And Mrs. Wyche did originate in the early seventies a widely used method of weaving. But the title of inventor of straight-to-kinky-weave stock remains up for grabs.

Adorable Hair-Do ("Human Hair Manufacturers Since 1910") inhabits a floor of an upscale office building in Chelsea. Like

W.A.J., based on word of mouth rather than advertising, Adorable ships their texturized hair product worldwide. Adorable's showroom is a shrine to celebrity clients, with posters and signed publicity shots plastered like wallpaper. En Vogue thanks Herbert generously, profusely, lavishly. Company president Herbert Teitelbaum, ensconced in his office, reaches his son Gary, the V.P., by intercom in the showroom. Mr. Herbert (so he's called in the company brochure) reports that Patti Labelle's stylist just called from the tour bus to say how pleased she was, really, absolutely, better-than-before pleased, with the hair Adorable sent overnight rush. Gary blushes. On the way to the factory itself we pass a fashion spread with the models Cindy Crawford and Naomi Campbell. Campbell wears a pout and an ankle-length weave. Adorable has taped its own legend on the photo: "Both women are beautiful, but only one is Adorable."

It's at Adorable that I first enter Mecca. Rhyme, reason, and order seem clear only to the initiated. After a month of searching the city, there are boxes of raw hair wide open before me. This hair, in lengths of roughly eighteen inches, is wrapped at the top in twine and fans out below like a whisk broom. It's as still as a movie prop, a scalped ponytail from a spaghetti western. And it's bone, as they say in the hair world, straight. (When I asked Mrs. Wyche of W.A.J. if "Bone Straight" was shorthand for "born with straight hair," she said quite earnestly, no, "straight as a bone.") In another area of the factory, women, Salvadoran perhaps, uncoil hair product from dowels. It then joins a large pile of stiff coils for transfer to the next stage. Men, Dominican perhaps, pull the coils back and forth through upright stationary combs called "hackles." The hair comes out in a bushy mound, soft like a six-year-old's Afro puff before a lifetime of relaxers. Several more women, Honduran perhaps, take this crinkly hair and run it through a sewing machine, which attaches a thick seam on one edge. This seam, as you can learn in W.A.J.'s how-to-weave video, is used to anchor, with thread or glue, your living hair to the commercial hair.

I am led into the Kaaba, the sacred shrine, the inner sanctum, where straight is brewed kinky. I see dye buckets, shampooing machines, vats of bleach labeled DANGER POISON. I leave the room dizzy with fumes, as if I had spent the night at the old Paradise Garage riding the moon on poppers. Mecca at last, yet the mystery, like the smell, lingers.

Touring W.A.J. fills in gaps. Raw hair is washed, then wrapped on dowels. Dowel width determines kink. (In W.A.J.'s closet-size "wrap room," two West African women wrap hair as methodically as metronomes while they chew gum and listen to Afro-pop on the radio.) This hair on dowels is dyed and processed chemically (smells like an industrial-strength version of a home perm). Processed hair goes through hackles to loosen curl and blend colors. Weft seams are made on a special machine that creates a stitch as intricate as an eyelash. Finally, lengths of commercial hair are sealed in small, clear plastic packs (dead ringers for bagged narcotics), then shipped in white gift boxes. During my tour, a Hasidic man delivers a large rectangular box. I ask President Wyche if there's raw hair in the box, and if so, if it's from China or India. She gives me one of those looks: Girl, you're far too grown for your age. Mrs. Wyche has quite deliberately evoked the archetypical black godmama with the eyebrows-raised legend spirit. Quite a power move. Mecca was only letting me in so far.

Hair factories are a storehouse of kitsch beauty culture, but they can also hip us to that unwritten chapter of American social history, the hair trade.

In the 1970s, its prime, W.A.J. was a prominent Harlem institution. (The company sponsored two Miss Black Teenage America pageants. Actress Sheryl Lee Ralph, in an elegant short Afro, was a runner-up one year.) Wyche tells stories about traveling to hair shows in the South to demonstrate W.A.J. hair goods, and of the informal networks of salons run by black women, which, in the tradition of Madame C. J. Walker's beauty colleges, also functioned as community centers and counseling offices. As a memento of my tour, Mrs. Wyche and her sister, Ella "Terri" Dufau, the factory manager, present me with a copy of a W.A.J. flyer from the early sixties advertising "kinky wigs and toupees for the Negro woman and man." The flyer was autographed by Mrs. Martin Luther King, Sr., on a visit to W.A.J.'s showroom.

With a name as suffocatingly cute as its product line, Adorable Hair-Do was founded in 1910 by owner Herbert Teitelbaum's great-uncle, a Jew who emigrated from England. Until the seventies, the company maintained its original showroom above the Baby Grand Nightclub on 125th Street. (The Teitelbaums say "race riots" pushed them downtown.) Adorable claims to have done the original research on the machine-wefting process and has papers to prove it. (Before machines became standard in the late forties, hair was sewn into wefts by hand, strands at a time.) Gary the V.P. will also show you the company's 1942 catalog, where yellowed newsprint illustrates hair for weaving. "Crimpy hair transformations," as they were called, fit around the head with an elastic band, the whole apparatus resembling a theatrical beard. By Mr. Herbert's account, Adorable, called Howard Tresses at the time, began processing straight to nappy in the early forties, stewing hair in crocks on the roof of its Harlem showroom.

The Tucciarones are the most picturesque historians of the hair trade, no contest. That's Biagio ("Bill") Tucciarone of B.T. Hair Goods, established in 1969 (taking the name of his grandfather's company, founded in 1910), and his father, Joseph, now retired, of Accu-Hair International Consultants, opened in 1949. Joseph Tucciarone sold his business in the eighties to a woman who crafts *sheitels*, religious hairpieces, for the Hasidim. These days B.T. Hair Goods is a small custom-order sample-matching operation run out of Bill's mother's cellar in the Bronx, though at one time five generations of Tucciarones worked the Manhattan factory. Being a Tucciarone means you can name different "grades," really nationalities, of hair in the dark (i.e., Russian: "dead straight, but also tends to be lumpy"; Belgian: "more durable, better food"). The family has always sold "first quality" hair to the Caucasian market—and still upholds the old rating system. But Bill Tucciarone will assure you "taking care of the colored trade" is not beneath him. "Don't get me wrong," he says, "if they want good hair, they can come to me. They just got to want it first." (Alas, if us coloreds would only aspire to "good hair," it would be within reach.)

The annotated and subjective chronicle of hair trade to the Americas as told by the Tucciarones goes something like this: Outside of medical and theatrical uses, early markets for commercial hair in this country were married Hasidic women and Chinese women (who, following ancient practice, embellished styles with add-on hair). During the Second World War the Italian connection dried up for a spell, sending American hair factories scurrying, like they are today, after black-market Russian hair. Supply from Italy has never returned to its original volume, as after the war Italian hair donors discovered two American imports: the beauty parlor and the haircut. "Second quality" hair goods have always been steered to Negro consumers. (Hair traders consider Asian hair to be a coarser stock that lends itself to curly conversions.) The only change is, by the seventies boom in black-hair extensions, Asians got rid of their middlemen.

It's clear that the manufacture of wigs and hairpieces for black women has been an active industry since at least the turn of the century. The business picked up steam during the war, an event that corresponds with the second great migration of African Americans to the urban North. Gary the V.P. from Adorable puts it this way: "More black people came to the cities to work in the forties, and therefore they needed hair for style." "Style" or social necessity, the manipulation of black hair has been key to the assimilation equation since square one.

And so ends the Tucciarones's saga, and so we peck at the surface of the hair trade as American social text.

Humanitarian spirit manifests itself in the oddest places: hair factories. Factories are often approached by people whose need for hair has little to do with lipstick vanity: burn victims, victims of leukemia and alopecia (sudden, in some cases unexplained, loss of hair).

Hairsmiths treasure these cases, especially when children are involved. It lends a certain largesse to what they do; not only do they manufacture human hair, they're in league with the tooth fairy. The elder Tucciarone has his story about the little leukemia victim who was able to go to school without shame wearing a wig he made from her own hair. She died nine months later. Mrs. Wyche has hers about the dog-bite victim so grateful for his Afro toupee he showed up at the factory with a Christmas present every year for twenty years straight.

In W.A.J.'s case the hair doctor–medical rescue worker role is supplemented by an even greater mission: race work. When Verlie Wyche talks about why she "invented" the Afro toupee it's with the righteous tone of one who has undertaken to uplift the race, despite how the world and the race may resist the effort. (Mrs. Wyche found it "ridiculous and demeaning" to see the black and hairless walking around with "Caucasian toupees.") Early photographs of Mrs. Wyche show a remarkable resemblance to the young Diana Ross. Not just looks; the aura of self-invention floats around both women like expensive perfume. Mrs. Wyche made kinky hair, those raised eyebrows are quick to remind you. What did you do for the race today?

With Mecca and my tour of the Kaaba behind me, I am feeling less wooed by the kitsch mystique of hair factories. I have my concerns. Given the hush-hush nature of the trade, do we know what we're getting? Commercial hair undergoes so many chemical processes, could it be caustic? And what of a particular rumor that dogs the trade like the smell of rotting flesh? If this rumor is true, should we pull the commercial hair from our heads right this moment and beg the higher power for quick forgiveness? *Is* cosmetic hair kosher product? You decide:

Poor labeling is rife. A common problem users encounter at the smaller retail outfits is that human hair is cut with synthetic. (Kanekalon, the synthetic that's made into wig and braiding stock, is the same fiber used for Barbie doll hair. Apparently Barbies exhaust more of it than the sum total of human wig wearers.) Though in some cases hairpiece makers combine human and synthetic for durability rather than for rip-off purposes, consumers feel that labeling should be required and monitored. Another typical complaint: Yak is cut with human, which is something to watch for, being that allergic reactions to yak are not uncommon.

False advertising is business as usual. Retailers and hair factories routinely trump up an item they call "French Refined" hair. This is no special feature. All commercial hair has been refined—it is by definition. ("Refined" merely refers to the chemical process that de-roots hair.) The French component is also meaningless, along with being inaccurate. Very little hair is actually imported from France; that which is, according to several importers, is probably Spanish or Indian hair that was processed within French borders. The French angle is so widely exploited, though, that most hair factories and retailers carry "French Refined" as a standard hair texture. Adorable, for instance, advertises five standard textures, including "French Refined Wavy," "European Straight Look," and "Spanish Wavy" (a "texture style" that they claim to have originated). All are made from Asian hair.

Human hair, the import, isn't governed by special regulations from any government agency, including customs. It's classified as a cosmetic (a product applied to the body to promote attractiveness), so it falls under the jurisdiction of the Food and Drug Administration. Customs and the FDA took my queries about the bacterial or health risks that might be associated with commercial hair with amused patience. "Not a high enforcement priority," customs compliance officers and FDA cosmetic specialists offered with a chuckle. (Did this response fall into the category of "We are sorry, your problem is not male enough or white enough to rate serious discussion"?) *If* customs opens boxes of raw hair they'd be looking for lice, but there's only a slim chance they would, because hair, I repeat, is not a PRIORITY.

The open-door policy on human hair is curious at first glance. Hair is human tissue—but dead cells. Of the body, bodylike, and, to quote shampoo ads, "full of body," yet not a body part, at least so says Western science. This doesn't stop hair from being an intimate and certainly sexual "personal object" that calls out for cleansing, grooming, vigilance. Hair product (embalmed hair), since it no longer grows, is classified as an inanimate object. It's sold as "human" in the same way leather is sold as animal hide. What all this amounts to is that no one worries. Certainly customs and the FDA aren't losing any sleep.

The health concerns I have about cosmetic hair don't rate an international crisis, mind you. Nevertheless, mostly women make use of it—particularly women of color, particularly women who aren't heard from as consumers—so it's worth raising the questions. Hair factory queen bees told about the mysterious acid baths hair receives abroad to kill bacteria. Okay, so what kind of acid? Does this acid go away when the hair is washed? Or does a wearer continually absorb it into her skin when she perspires? Raw hair is by routine bleached and dyed. Is the cosmetic-hair wearer also absorbing bleach? Dyes, too? Allergic reactions to hair bleach are common. Certain coal-based dyes are toxic and no longer allowed in over-the-counter hair dye products. Could a storefront industry out to cut costs be using cheap, unapproved dyes?

Tucciarone Jr. of B.T. Hair Goods, who's worked with hair since he was thirteen, believes the acid treatment performed on raw hair could be harmful to wearers if not washed out properly. He questions if most hair factories bother to do a thorough job. Dr. Deborah Simmons, an attending dermatologist at Harlem Hospital, frequently sees patients with skin problems brought on by extensions. Most of these involve braids that are too tight (which can lead to alopecia) or scalp conditions from not washing braided hair adequately. Simmons hasn't come across an allergic reaction to processing chemicals, though she believes the potential is certainly there.

Which brings us to, what if? What if cosmetic hair was recognized one day as a bad-boy product? An unlikely event, but let's consider it. Would consumers rush to kick the habit? There's an expression in the salon world, relayed to me by stylist Brenda Davis: "I'll wear extensions until they cause cancer, or a bit longer." Like the breast implant ban—some users would go kicking and screaming, if they went at all. The most common anxieties clients have about commercial hair, according to stylists, don't involve health risks at all. They worry about the cost of hair and what will happen to it in the rain.

Fables of the hair trade could make a flamboyantly stereotypical, international spy thriller set in Milan, New Delhi, and "the Orient," starring Mata Hari's great-granddaughter as a British-raised, black Eurasian agent in the employ of Her Majesty's Secret Service. A black belt in Goju-Ryu Karate, Kenya Hari sets out to crack the hair trade, then is lovingly derailed by American hair-care scion Wesley Snipes. Legend has it, as passed down by the hair trade's more colorful historians, that in China before communism, hair was cut as an offering to the gods. This hair was then stored in caves for hundreds of years. At one time, caves in China were brimming with perfectly preserved hair, and for a good part of this century, hair traders made do on this back stock.

Another myth conjures up an underground market in *American* hair. During the war period, from 1941 to 1949, B.T. Hair Goods actually did process American hair. Founder Biagio Tucciarone solicited the hair by putting ads in newspapers across the grain belt. Tucciarone couldn't turn much of a profit on the slim pickings here (a length of hair must be at least eight inches long to process, and Americans weren't producing the length), so he went back to the import business.

Finally, there's that smelly rumor the hair trade can't shake: Some in the salon world are convinced that raw hair comes primarily from cadavers. Factories and retailers deny this with great passion. How could it? they object. Raw hair must be in excellent shape to undergo processing. The Tucciarones, however, will tell you otherwise. When Bill Tucciarone was a teenager working at his grandfather's hair factory, he regularly saw pieces of scalp mixed in with the hair. His father Joseph will swear to you that at one time at least 85 percent of the hair was cut from dead folks.

Interestingly enough, from the FDA's point of view, the sale of cadaver hair, if it is taking place, isn't illegal. There are no medical warnings against it and no agency regulations currently forbid it. In the 1980s, anti-abortion groups were riled up about collagen-placenta beauty care products, which they thought were being concocted from aborted fetuses. These objections were never substantiated, yet there was no law on the books at the time that prohibited the use of "fetus-derived products." So fetuses or no fetuses, these products could have remained on the market.

All my gallows-humor illusions about the hair trade and the warehousing of "dead" hair were shattered by a very brief conversation with dermatologist Claudette Troyer of Harlem Hospital. Hair by definition is not exactly a bundle of life. "The thing is dead, medically speaking," says Troyer, "when it comes out of your head." Hair, like nails, is made from keratin. The growth activity happens below the skin. So, dead or alive, hair donors are created equal. Consumers can object to the sale of cadaver hair on spiritual grounds, but that's about it.

Enter a voice of lucidity: Braid designer Ruth Sinclair. Sinclair tells me I've been crawling up the wrong tree. The hazard of cosmetic hair, she says, doesn't strike the body, it eats at the soul. Sinclair is of the new school of Afrocentric cosmetologists who surfaced in the mid-eighties at salons such as Tulani's Regal Movement in Brooklyn and Cornrows & Company in Washington, D.C. With partner Annu Prestonia, Sinclair owns the braiding salon chain Khamit Kinks, which has shops in Atlanta and Brooklyn. ("Khamit," an early name for Egypt, means "land of the blacks." By adding "Kinks," Sinclair explains, "we've taken a word perceived as bad and made it good.") Sinclair has been braiding hair for eighteen years, and to her, the real concern isn't the possibility of chemical emissions from commercial hair (no more a risk, she says, than perming one's own hair). It's a beauty industry especially oppressive to black women. Sinclair's rap is a familiar one. Although it neglects two vital points, women's personal agency and hair as a creative turf, it still has currency:

"Black women are told that in order to be attractive and successful, we must emulate a European image of beauty. The damage this does to us subconsciously has never been studied. Just the daily pressure. Caucasian women will never have to live with the stress of taking their hair from straight to kinky on a daily basis just to be visually accepted in society.

"We are told as black women to assume an image that goes against what most of us are born with. Basically, the industry is saying that there's something wrong with us. And that this something must be controlled with artificial means—with their help. The industry will continue feeding us this line because it makes money off of us. Of course, the industry is not about to give up the revenue that comes from [commercial] hair, chemicals, and rider products. If they could find a way to make more money off of natural hair, believe me, they'd be selling that."

Hair extensions were the black-hair coup of the eighties, even more than the short-lived, vilified Jheri curl. They are more "yours" than a wig, if only by virtue of being more securely attached. They sell convenience and cultural versatility. In April you can wear a weave, invent an entire mane of processed curls, and carry forth like Diana Ross. By May you can put in braids and make a statement of racial pride—or not make one. Hair is still corporeal, except now it isn't necessarily biologically determined. But the real social innovation is that, unlike costly wigs with few styling options, extensions have made hair affordably disposable. *Disposable hair*—the postmod answer to racial difference. Disposable skin can't be too far behind.

Which is not to suggest that the racial allegories of the hair trade are so cut-and-dried. If anything the trade throws a curve ball at assumptions of racial difference. First look at the trade route. Hair is dispatched from Asia, processed in the States, and sent to points in the diaspora. (Take Paris, where hair for weaving and braiding is sold from kiosks in the Metro.) You have companies like W.A.J. Wigs, which buys hair from New Delhi, refines it in Harlem, and ships to, among other places, West Africa—a journey that suggests a gumbo of transcontinental influences.

In West Africa, braided extensions and weaves are "huge," to quote a frequent traveler to the region. Older women even wear them—in elaborate, braided styles that resemble hats. For little girls in Nigeria, it's the rage to have your braided extensions curled in Shirley Temple ringlets, a style called "the darling." So while African Americans are looking to Africa for cultural affirmation, Africans are hopping on the bandwagon of a "Europeanized" standard of beauty symbolized by wavy, loosely curled extensions. Or let's be more critically expansive, to advance the ideas of critic Kobena Mercer, and call it "New World": a syncretic beauty culture born in the diaspora.

If hair is the key racial signifier after skin, then the trade makes a fine mockery of it. Processed Asian hair passes as black hair. Italians allegedly blend hair from the Third World and it passes as European. The hair of yaks (the "black sheep" of the ox family) passes as nappy hair. As well it's worth remembering that most of what the hair trade sells is not dead straight hair—it's "texturized" hair; hair that is quite particularly African-American/African-diaspora hair, hair that is emulated in perms by European women worldwide. So toward the close of the twentieth century, what we have is a whole industry devoted to selling black hair (or, let's not get too excited, a particular type of black hair). Though black hair nonetheless: hair that was once demonized. Hair that was downcast. Hair that was "no good."

The Afrocentric braiders are on to something. They avoid the political swamp of extensions as European imitation by using synthetic stock. The likes of Khamit Kinks and Cornrows & Company design styles that are not simply hairdos; these are elaborate constructions, with hair piled high, woven with ornaments and shaped like fans, wedding cakes, hourglasses, and halos. Maybe they're crowns, maybe they're altars. Extensions here are used not to showcase length or "naturalness." This is hair as textile, fiber art, as nothing less than sculpture. What links the African-American/Africa-diaspora cultural practice with African traditional cultures is not the naturalness of the braids, it's the idea of construction. Hair in both traditions suggests spectacle and pageantry. It's always handled and adorned; hair is never left "as is." Hair exists to be *worked*.

Those wise ones, the ancient Egyptians, played their own game with hair: They cut it all off. They thought it barbaric, scholars say, or maybe just too damn hot. Egyptian-designed hairpieces used materials like palm leaves and wool that suggested hair, yet didn't try to duplicate it, allowing much room for creative play. (By the sixteenth and seventeenth centuries, Europe was hip to headpieces, and they were being worn there as tokens of class privilege.) Perhaps there's a cave full of Egyptian hair, perfectly preserved, waiting for us in the Nile Valley. Given the war of historical interpretation, it could be Nappy by Nature (to borrow the name of a hair salon just opened in downtown Brooklyn). Then again, it could be "Bone Straight." But ask Verlie Wyche. I bet she'd know.

1993

Hair grease has revealed itself to be the cesspool of racial politics that those of us who take hair seriously always suspected it was.

This is why: A profitable, white-owned company, in the business of selling what the industry calls "ethnic hair-care products" to the African-American consumer, is waging a legal battle with a smaller black-owned company over the trademark and product likeness of grooming aids that use an Afrocentric theme. The white-owned company is also claiming title to "African" as the first word in a hair product's trade name. A federal court in Atlanta will soon decide whether to lay a preliminary injunction against the black company. This injunction could prevent the black company from distributing its current product line, and possibly from using the opener "African" on any new merchandise until the case comes to trial.

On one side is the white-owned Shark Products of Brooklyn, New York, which makes hair-grooming potions and lotions under the trademark African Pride; on the other, B & J Sales of Fayetteville, Georgia, with its product African Natural. Both lines are aimed at the X-appareled, braided, and faded crowd of young and recently Afrocentric consumers. And both offer the same types of hair goo: leave-in conditioners, braid sheen spray, and so on. The two-year-old African Pride came out of the gate strong; this year selling nearly $2.5 million in the first quarter. African Natural, on the other hand, had been distributing for only three months when this controversy hit. Though to Shark, African Natural was enough of a financial threat and a "colorable imitation" of their line to hire a lawyer.

It's akin to grand larceny to some folks that African Pride is a white-owned product given its name, but also its Afro-chic packaging—red, black, and green—and high profile in the black press—full-page ads in *Ebony* and *Essence*. And what did Shark choose as the signature fragrance for African Pride? Watermelon.

Until a court rules otherwise, both Shark and B & J Sales have legal trademarks on their products. Still, Shark believes that B & J Sales is trying to capitalize on what it considers to be its unique success story. With African Pride, Shark is convinced it invented a whole new segment of the black hair-care industry, one defined by an African heritage concept. Plainly, Shark thinks it owns the Afrocentric sell and wants competitors to have no part of the booty.

Shark has had one scrimmage so far. It sued the California-based Walbert Laboratories, a company that makes the hair grooming aid Mother Africa, for copying its "trade dress," which included the use of the word "African" in the same color that it appears on Shark products. Walbert insists it chose red, black, and green, the colors of the African nationalist flag, independent of the African

Pride label. The case was settled out of court, with the smaller company abandoning the nationalist color scheme. Shark plans to sue Bronner Brothers of Atlanta, a black-owned company forty-seven years in the business, for marketing its new line, African Royale. Several black manufacturers and distributors are so outraged by Shark's bum rush they're weighing a boycott. "How the heck can he [president Brian Marks], a white man, try to patent the word 'African'?" one company manager snapped. "What's next? We'll have to ask his permission to call ourselves African Americans?" Marks refuses to comment on any of the court cases. All phone calls concerning Shark's legal disputes are referred to the company's public relations rep, who happens to be black.

Do a federal trademark search and you'll find scores of products that use "African" as a prefix (like African Queen cologne) or a derivative (Afroshave shaving products or Afro Sheen, hair dress, circa 1971). These include nearly a dozen hair tonics, some registered long before African Pride. African Formula, a line well known to health-food store patrons, has been on the market since 1983.

Put aside for a moment this bit of lunacy: that one person or company—white or black—could declare ownership of "African," just as one might own Subaru or Pepsi or any number of brand names. Or the idea that a white-owned company could have legal sanction to prevent black-owned companies from using their continent of heritage as a means of drawing black consumers. But just think of Shark claiming that it masterminded the Afrocentric sell when, long before African Pride's debut in 1991, or even African Formula's in 1983, Black Muslims hawked African-inspired hair concoctions on city streets. And decades before that black hair entrepreneur Madame C. J. Walker's products were sold using buy-black themes and Madame's own mahogany-skinned, broad-nosed image. From any angle, Shark positioning itself as the grandfather of Afrocentric hair grooming is a caper lifted from a blaxploitation flick.

Expect more of the same. With women of color recognized as the beauty industry's new frontier, mainstream companies are scurrying after their share. In the case of the $1.5 billion black hair-care industry, now dominated by white-owned companies, the challenge is not to enter the market but to rule. And Afrocentricity has become the sales ticket de rigueur. Revlon cashed in this spring with Kente Kreations—grooming aids named for African tribes. Try Masai℠ Polishing Mist or Fanti℠ Moisturizing Hairdress.

The kente pitch is in such high gear, in fact, that black companies are being forced to "out-Afrocentricize" the white competition, says Geri Duncan Jones, president of the American Health and Beauty Aids Institute (AHBAI), which represents the leading black manufacturers. Kemi Laboratories makes Kemi-Oyl, one of the many hair-skin multiuse oils you'll find at your local drugstore chain (where hair products are still segregated by ethnic category). To cut through the kente glut, Kemi and other companies are now advertising that they're black owned. But is this enough, with companies like Kenya Products in the mix? Kenya, a white-owned manufacturer based in New Jersey, sells an Organic Hair Skin & Scalp Oil that promises on the bottle to be a "remedy" of "exotic oils" drawn from the "darkest region of Africa."

If a black hair-care product is popular with consumers, does it matter, as Michael Jackson might chide us, if the company that makes it is black or white? AHBAI calls white companies' use of Afrocentric marketing "deceptive" to black consumers, who often assume these companies are owned by blacks and that their revenue goes back to African Americans in the form of jobs or community programs. (Often white-owned black-hair-care companies, which make 98 percent of their profit from black folks, don't employ equally high numbers.) Viewpoint of Chicago recently published a brand-awareness survey that showed black consumers were unpleasantly surprised and downright disturbed to find that major black hair-care products such as African Pride, All Ways, TCB, Dark & Lovely, Right-On Curl, and Let's Jam are not made by black businesses. Most customers surveyed said now that they know which brands are black made they'd show a preference for these in the future.

One ebony shopaholic wondered what all the ruckus was about.

Black folks, she said, were gonna buy heavily advertised products like African Pride and Cream of Nature's Kente Oil anyway, no matter who owned the plant. Wasn't it good tidings to see, at the very least, a healthy reflection of black culture in the packaging of these products, rather than a bunch of golliwogs pulling the wool off their scalps and talking about "Fix this Mess!" (to quote an ad for LeKair Styling Gel)? Elayne McClaire, marketing director of Creme of Nature and a black woman, spoke of the letters that have poured in from black patrons commending the company for "embracing African culture," as they believe Revlon did when it swaddled its product in kente and trademarked the names of African tribes. Perhaps to some folks, how many African Americans aren't getting the sales and manufacturing gigs in these mainstream corporations, or how many smaller black-owned companies are being edged out of business, or even the politics of a white enterprise trademarking the term "African Pride," aren't issues of concern; kente *is* enough.

The African Pride case shows how detached words and symbols like Africa (just a hair practice), black pride (a marketing pitch), and kente (a *Good Housekeeping* seal) have become from their cultural beginnings. Ethnicity, as the postmod watchers warned us long ago, is emerging as nothing more than a market niche, a field of products ripe for anyone to sell or consume, and the hair trade is leading the way to the mountaintop. What is Africa to me? Countee Cullen might have waxed in 1993. Just a hair grease.

1993

This article appeared in the *Village Voice* in August 1993. Shark dropped its case against B & J Sales three months later. The court, however, denied B & J's request that Shark reimburse the company for the considerable amount of money spent in attorney fees. Both companies have maintained their trade names and both continue to manufacture hair grease.

hair again

Hair issues are among us. We must tease them out, hold them up to the light, and coax them into art.

The girl thought she had figured it all out. Hair was just hair, not a badge of correctness. And thanks once again to modern technology, which brought us no-lye relaxers and such, chemically altering your tresses was now a process somewhat removed from antiquated notions like self-mutilation and disfigurement, and was just as innocent as a five-dollar nail job. Jewish women iron, Asian women perm, WASPs highlight. So what if black women burn and fry? After all, isn't it impossible to tell where society's force-feeding leaves off and we begin?

Notice black women are dyeing blonde in droves? This is probably because it warms our souls and brings out the chestnut in our eyes. Be assured, it has nothing at all to do with Christie Brinkley.

Besides, we were at a magical interlude in black hair history. Lord have mercy, hair seemed practically depoliticized! At least in the New York City subway, where you could see every possible configuration, from curly permed shags to dreadlocks ablaze with purple henna. Revisionist hair theory was surfacing too. Kobena Mercer's essay "Black Hair/Style Politics" in *Out There: Marginalization and Contemporary Cultures* (MIT Press) puts the hair police out of a job. Mercer reads curly perm and relaxed styles not as white imitation, but "New World creolization," in the same vein as a diasporan miracle like jazz. Then the moment we'd all been waiting for: *Essence* invited men to comment on women's hair practice. Men gave thumbs-down to weaves and drippy curls. Women wrote back telling the men to mind their business. As if to say, this ain't about y'all and this ain't about The Man, this is our creative space, best you stay out.

So, yes, it was a wonderful time. Then, out of nowhere, massive hair drama took hold. The girl's hair was getting gray, prematurely mind you, but gray. This was a fact, and she planned to deal with it like a womanist with a capital W, by telling everyone she was practicing to be old, fine, and silver-haired like Camille Cosby. She had not planned, however, on such strange occurrences as having men she barely knew run across the street and exclaim, no, EXCLAIM, over her gray hair like it was a national tragedy on par with the Clarence Thomas confirmation.

Or, on the response she'd get from a good friend upon revealing plans to have her hair cropped short in pursuit of life as Camille. The friend recommended, without a dime of irony, that she reconsider because "girls like us need hair to balance hips." The girl had been under the impression that girls like us with college degrees and trips to Africa and Europe only need brains. She realized now she'd been gravely wrong.

What ensued was a tailspin of epic proportions. The girl plain lost her mind. Not only did she *not* cut her hair, she went and got more. Taiwan hair that is, lots of it down her back, the ends seared with a Bic lighter to keep them from unraveling. This produces a smell that can only compare to fumes from a crack pipe. When the girl looked in the mirror, she saw Milli Vanilli. She didn't scream, she just calmly found a scissors and started cutting. The hairlike substance landed on the floor in a decorous mound, looking not unlike conceptual art by David Hammons. Just add a chicken wing, some Gucci bags, and a snowball.

How the girl managed to spend a third of her paycheck on synthetic hair, then cut it off five hours later, is still a mystery. But the torture didn't stop there. Minutes after the scissors ordeal, she was on the phone with another hairstylist. It was late afternoon Saturday, the worst time to be up in anybody's salon, yet she had to get her hair streaked "brick brown, not red" or she'd die by morning. The stylist heard the edge in girlfriend's voice and had mercy. In the salon, with the "dye cap" on, having her scalp gorged with knitting needles, the girl freaked again. She pleaded with her stylist to rinse out the bleach. The stylist cursed her out in Spanish. The girl went home with half a head of streaks.

The girl's best friend told her to get to the couch on her hair issues. This is a woman who recently traded in her short natural to become a John Atchison Salon gal. She goes around saying things like "I love the respect I get because my hair moves," in jest, but you know she means every word of it. Why listen to her?

Suddenly everything was symbolic. Audre Lorde passed. The girl remembered a line from one of Lorde's poems: "Is your hair still political/tell me/when it starts to burn." This was surely a message from God that hair was the true battleground. The girl thought of how much was still done to placate polite white, black, and Hispanic society by keeping kinks in the closet. She thought of the girls in D.C. who sued to wear braids to the office. Of the girl rap stars who preach nouveau nationalism, but favor "bone-straight" tresses. Of the rainbow babies who fear loss of their pedigree ringlets more than loss of life. She thought of her friends with short naturals who work corporate gigs and are constantly being asked if they are chemotherapy patients, as if no one living or dead should parade around with so little hair. She thought of children's formula relaxer kits for girls age six to twelve. And of her great aunt the hairdresser who took a five-month-old grandbaby on her knee and declared, "I need to get to this head right away."

She remembered the horrors. Of hot combs dropped on necks. Of sisters almost going out like Van Gogh. Of scalps lined with keloids from countless no-lye, no-lie perms. Of entire heads of hair lost. And of a friend, Inez, whose father decided to relax her hair himself. He left her, at age nine, naked and shrieking, almost blinded by lye, while he went out for a beer.

The men she thought of most. Their fetishes always got the better of their politics. Like the boyfriend who spoke of how proud he was of his girlfriend's short natural, though he called her a "bald-headed black bitch" in private. Or the boyfriend who slapped her for cutting her hair, then apologized in tears. She imagined that heterosexuality was the source of all her hair issues. Yet she knew better, or did she?

Just as suddenly, the hair drama passed. The girl was at peace with her silver strands again. Bless Camille Cosby, bless Susan Sontag. It became clear that she had "racialized." Racialize is a cute new word that means "make everything about race" (which of course it is, even if some folks like to pretend it's not). In the end, though, she came to see that what had happened to her was not race-hair drama at all. It was PMS, overtwentysomething, holiday-hair drama, which, as her mother reminded her, happens to women of all races, colors, and cultures.

Damn, and the girl thought she had an angle.

1992